As We Knew Adlai

As We Knew Adlai

THE STEVENSON STORY

BY TWENTY-TWO FRIENDS

EDITED AND WITH PREFACE BY Edward P. Doyle

FOREWORD BY Adlai E. Stevenson III

HARPER & ROW, PUBLISHERS

NEW YORK

Contents

Editor's Preface

This book was born on a July afternoon in the Assembly Hall of the United Nations; I think no one present that day at the memorial ceremony for Adlai Stevenson will ever forget the simple words with which Secretary of State Rusk closed his eulogy. We "sent you our best," he told the assembled representatives of the world.

As I sat in the UN Assembly Hall that day I thought of the many books that would be written about Adlai Stevenson. No predictable book by any writer, it occurred to me, could ever present the many facets of the man as they were known to his friends.

When I was a newspaper editor in Chicago this was one of the first things I learned about the Governor: that he had a tremendous number of friends; not the political hangers-on one expects around a politician, but devoted, undemanding, unselfish, intelligent men and women. Here, it was evident, was a rich mine of material for a book about this distinguished American.

In Chicago a few weeks later Adlai III welcomed the idea of such a book. Accordingly a letter was sent to a number of friends and colleagues of Governor Stevenson asking them to contribute to it. The project, they were told, envisioned a "number of friendly reminiscences. It would in effect be a memorial but its tone would be informal, anecdotal, and while friendly, not predominantly eulogistic."

The letter drew immediate and enthusiastic response; very busy people somehow found the time to express their feelings and their various differing recollections about the friend they so greatly admired. Moreover, the contributors showed their devotion to Adlai Stevenson by donating their articles to the Stevenson Memorial Fund.

As the editor, I am pleased with the result. It seems to me that this collection is a happy combination of biography, political history and personal reminiscence and that it contains a surprising amount of information that will be new to most readers.

EDWARD P. DOYLE

January, 1966

Foreword

The pages that follow are filled with reminiscences about my father by his friends. In the few months that have passed since his death many splendid, moving things have been written about him. Biographies have been published which record the major events of his life. Eulogies have sung his praise and lamented our loss. Other publications have dealt with his views on international problems. This book adds a new dimension to these many writings.

The truth about the man himself, not merely about his life and accomplishments, is the object of the book. It has certainly been the object of my collaboration, for I am convinced that nothing can be so kind to my father as the truth about him. I believe that the diverse views expressed here add up to a realistic portrait.

The contributors to this book make no claim to complete detachment—for after all, they were his friends. And all my father's friends were in differing ways close to him. This is one quality of his about which I do not hesitate to express an opinion. No matter what he was engaged in at the time, no vanity, none of the pomposity or self-consciousness which so often afflicts holders of high public office, nothing ever intruded between him and his friends. His guileless ways and keen concern kept them close. In part it was because he needed friends. In a hard and lonely life they kept him going.

Here some of these friends have told their stories, dwelling upon everyday occurrences in my father's life—the events, big and little, which shaped and colored his life. From these events, from his daily comments and activities, his peculiarities and his orthodoxies, the reader can take the measure of the man.

In a way, this is a homely book; it is also poignant—the words of thoughtful, sensitive men and women about a lost friend.

My family is grateful to these friends of Adlai Stevenson—for the strength and happiness they gave him in his lifetime, for the comfort they have given us since, and now for this book. And among these friends is Walter Johnson, the eminent teacher and historian, who while not contributing an article, did contribute invaluable editorial assistance. We owe our thanks also to Edward Doyle, who conceived the idea of this book and then carefully guided its course.

ADLAI E. STEVENSON III

January, 1966

As We Knew Adlai

JOSEPH F. BOHRER

Boys in Bloomington

I KNEW Adlai Stevenson well from 1905, when his family moved to Bloomington from California, where he was born. His parents built a house on East Washington Street a little more than a mile from where I lived with my parents and grandparents.

My grandfather, Joseph W. Fifer, had been a Republican governor of Illinois (defeated for re-election by John P. Altgeld in 1892). My grandfather's home was a large red-brick house at the north end of the block on the east side of Franklin Park. Three houses away, at the south end of the block, lived Adlai E. Stevenson I, lawyer, Vice President under Grover Cleveland, and Ad's grandfather.

Franklin Park had a Civil War monument in the center, with cement sidewalks running out like the spokes of a wheel and also concentric walk circles. It was ideal for kids roller skating, and Ad used to join us in our game of "Fox and Geese" and "Tag" on roller skates. He would ride his bike over from his house and could always get parental permission on the grounds he wanted to go to "visit" with grandfather.

Joe Bohrer of Bloomington, Illinois, is a lawyer and a life-long friend of Adlai Stevenson.

Grandmother Stevenson's cook made the most perfect beaten biscuits I ever tasted. You could hear her from our house as she slapped and beat the dough with a flat board for hours—it seemed to me. Grandfather Stevenson's Jack-of-all-trades was George, whom at the time I considered a very old Negro (I've

Wide World

Adlai E. Stevenson on his grandfather's lap, and (right) with his father, Lewis G. Stevenson, and his sister Elizabeth (Buffie).

since learned he was only thirty-two when I made this estimate). George cared for the yard and the horses in the barn in the backyard, drove the carriage and served dinner in a beautiful white starched coat. Every few months my family would be invited to Grandfather Stevenson's for dinner. Young Ad, his sister Buffie and his parents were often present at these occasions, and we youngsters enjoyed the beaten biscuits and seeing white-coated George perform. Grandfather Stevenson and my grandfather were both marvelous storytellers, and how we kids loved it.

I remember when the Vice President died in 1914. A long line of carriages, each drawn by black horses, stretched halfway around Franklin Park as the cortege formed to go from the house to the Second Presbyterian church for the funeral services.

Ad's Grandfather Stevenson was a Democrat and a Presbyterian, while his maternal grandfather, W. O. Davis, was a Republican and a Unitarian. I've often heard Ad jokingly say he was a born politician; he had taken his politics from the Stevenson and his religion from the Davis side of the family.

Ad and I regularly attended Sunday school in the old Unitarian church. I remember when the superintendent, Mr. Pearce, sponsored a new attendance-boosting gimmick. He would give each child an attendance ticket or coupon, and then when a pupil turned in twenty tickets he could claim a shiny new Bible as a reward. I well recall, after the first *six* Sundays following

The Bloomington, Illinois, home of grandfather Adlai Ewing Stevenson, Vice President under President Cleveland.

the initiation of the contest, Ad, his cousin Davis Merwin and I each walked up to Mr. Pearce with twenty tickets apiece, and claimed and got our Bibles. Bless his soul, he did not lecture us publicly on the morality of the whole thing, but he did announce that the Bible-winning contest offer was over and should be forgotten by everyone.

It was a long time ago—in the spring of 1915. Ad and I were quite interested in Josephine Sanders, our high school classmate, who was also the star performer of Miss Coleman's dancing class. Josephine had no crystal ball, which probably explains why she let me, rather than Ad, take her to the Sophomore Prom in the old gymnasium. I had a wonderful evening, as Ad pouted on the sidelines. After the dance I cranked up my old Model T to drive Josephine home. I noticed the engine was sputtering badly, but we did make it to the middle of the hill on Fell Avenue, when it conked out completely. Raising the hood to investigate the trouble, I saw there, on the hot motor block, frying and sizzling away, the ugliest dead yellow cat ever. While Ad never did fully admit his hand in that dastardly deed, I do know that he always detested yellow cats, and I had seen the green envy in his eyes all evening. Many years later, after law school and after he had learned the meaning of the term, Ad did agree that the "circumstantial evidence" was mighty strong.

Ad was away at school for a long time. He left our high school to attend Choate for two years and then went to Princeton. After graduation he went on to Harvard Law School.

After two years at Harvard, however, he returned to Bloomington to take a job on the *Daily Pantagraph*. This was at the beginning of summer, 1924. The paper had been owned by his Grandfather Davis, and at this time control was involved in litigation over the construction of Mr. Davis' will. Adlai and his cousins, the Merwins, represented their families, so to speak, and control eventually was divided between the two families.

On March 18, 1925, the country's most destructive tornado swept out of Missouri, crossing southern Illinois, and on into

Indiana. About seven hundred persons were killed, and Murphysboro, Illinois, was most severely hit. Ad was going to the area to report the destruction for the paper, and I too wanted to see the ravages caused by the terrible storm, so Ad got me credentials as a *Pantagraph* reporter and we took off the following day by train from Champaign to Carbondale, Illinois.

Murphysboro, about ten miles from Carbondale, was barred to the curious, but our credentials even got us special transportation. The devastation was horrible; the storm's path through the town leveled everything, even the brick foundations of the houses, and autos were literally wrapped around tree stumps. One schoolhouse we saw had been flattened and twenty-seven children killed. It was awful, and Adlai wrote several very moving stories for the paper. It was really the first time I knew Ad had such talent and power in expressing himself.

Reference to the files of the *Pantagraph* reveals passages by "Staff Correspondent" (no "by-line" in those days) that ranged from emotional to objective, from perceptive to ironic.

One story, date-lined Carbondale, Ill., March 20, began:

"Hello Tom, how's your folks?"
"Folks is all going to live, but the old hut is gone."
That is what one hears on every side in Murphysboro, except that frequently the folks are not all going to live.
The stoicism and heroic spirit of the citizens of Murphysboro will never be forgotten by the myriads of relief workers that have poured here through the last two days. . . .
There are now more than 180 dead and 250 seriously injured in Murphysboro alone and it will always remain a miracle that there was not ten times that many. More than 75 square blocks present a more completely devastated area than the Chemin des Dames did after five years of constant bombardment, and in Murphysboro it all happened in less than five minutes. Fire swept over a large area. The wreckage still smokes and in some places burns brightly. Many and strange are the freaks of the tornado. One sees mattresses and clothing in trees. Automobiles are on front porches, pianos and clocks standing quite unharmed and unconcerned amidst wreckage that no longer even faintly resembles a dwelling.

A few more passages reflect the emotional effect this experience of reporting a catastrophe had on twenty-five-year-old Adlai as well as his sympathetic and penetrating observations. From Murphysboro he wrote on March 22:

Four days have elapsed now since the Four Horsemen of the Apocalypse disappeared over the Indiana line on their mad, devastating race, leaving behind them a wake of horror and destruction that beggars description. . . .

Viewing this broad expanse of scattered, twisted, smouldering wreckage one cannot but reflect on the futility of life and the insignificance of man. Truly our destinies are cradled in the laps of the Gods. . . .

It will be a generation before the crippled, the disfigured, the bedridden, the blind, the insane have ceased to bear constant and touching witness in their life-long suffering to the horrors of that fatal March Wednesday. . . .

I saw a farmer dressed in his best blue suit, pale but dry-eyed and composed, push his way through a crowd in front of a morgue and emerge a moment later carrying a tiny white casket not three feet long. The crowd gave way in reverent awe and closed behind him intent on its own business. He placed the casket tenderly beside him in his Ford and drove away. That was Mary, aged 2. Baby Jane is still inside; he will come back for her. . . .

In a field not far from town stands a cow; she has been standing there four days. The wind deposited her with such force that all four legs are sunk in the mud above the knees and were she alive she could not move. The animals suffered too! . . .

A doctor in Murphysboro thought it more important to patch up his house than to help with the injured and dying. He has irrevocably lost his practice. Slacking, next to looting, is the greatest sin throughout the stricken area. . . .

The brick walls of a wholesale house fell on all four sides but the charred cans have remained standing piled up a story high in regular rows. Such are the vagaries that one sees on all sides.

Rereading these words, as I did in preparing this article, reminds me that Adlai's writing ability greatly impressed me at the time.

I suppose that reporting of this disaster was a high point in his journalistic career. I know I've never forgotten the experience.

Adlai remained on the paper for more than a year, and then decided to resume his law school career. Just before he did so he and I, and two other young men, took a vacation I'll never forget.

In August, 1925, four of us took off for the Quetico Provincial Park of Canada, lying just north of Minnesota, for a twelve-day, 110-mile canoe trip. Adlai, his cousin Scott Bromwell, Charlie Agle and I left Bloomington by day coach for Chicago, then Duluth, and finally on north from Duluth another seventy-five miles to Ely, Minnesota.

Scott Bromwell later became a Chicago financier, and Charlie Agle is now an architect living in Princeton, New Jersey.

Charlie was eight or ten years younger than the rest of us, his mother was a natural "worrier," and these factors had counted against his selection. However, Charlie had just graduated from Choate and was to enter Princeton the following month. Both of those points weighed heavily in influencing Ad's vote in Charlie's favor. Scott and I were unimpressed by the Choate-Princeton argument, but we could recognize a strong and healthy kid when we saw one, and Charlie thus became the fourth "paddle."

We three older adventurers felt fully competent to tackle the rigors of the north woods. We had all been at Charlevoix in the summers. Adlai also had vacationed at camps in Maine and in the western cattle country. Experiences like these made good campers. We didn't hold against Adlai the fact that he also had spent several summers in Europe and had gone to school in Switzerland for a while.

But we were truly "greenhorns," with no paddling experience, starting on a map-and-compass trip, without a guide. We did not see a road, a fence or a house for the entire twelve days. The only building was a vacant ranger's cabin and the only other person was a lone Indian fishing near one of the falls. We took nothing with us except an extra shirt and underwear (never used) and $65 each. The train ride from Duluth to Ely was taken up with planning our division of labor.

One team (No. 1) of two would pitch the tent, chop the firewood and cut the balsam boughs for our bedsprings. The other team (No. 2) would do all cooking and dishwashing. At Charlevoix, on the east side of Lake Michigan, lakes always meant "sand" on every beach, and sand is excellent for scouring pots and plans. The Quetico, on the other hand, has no sand, only huge boulders. This made the job of team No. 2 pretty rough after meals, as detergents were then unknown and we had only one bar of bathing soap. Scott and I decided Charlie, being only seventeen years old, rated only one-half vote. A ballot was taken, and Scott and I were "amazed" that we were chosen the No. 1 team by the margin of two votes to one and one-half. This meant that Ad and Charlie would do the cooking and dishwashing. The race for "Chief Cook" between Ad and Charlie was spirited, but the tally gave Ad two and a half votes and Charlie only one.

Here was a case of a "reluctant candidate" getting 71 percent of the popular vote. Ad often noted in later years that this Chief Cook Election marked his very peak of support—strictly from a "percentage of those voting" point of view.

We discovered how wisely we had chosen our chef, when midway on our trip we ran completely out of syrup—without which pancakes are worse than nothing. Ad reported his inventory showed ten pounds of pancake flour and about four pounds of plain white sugar. Every cooked meal had been mainly pancakes and syrup with an occasional slice of ham.

We were far from elated when Ad started the next meal in his old routine, by mixing batter from lake water and pancake flour, cooking the cakes a golden brown and stacking them on a hot dish beside the campfire. He then dried the hot skillet, poured in about a cup of plain white sugar and tossed it around tenderly until it was scalded a beautiful brown color. At his command, Charlie came running from the lake with two cups of water, which Ad slowly poured and stirred into the scalded sugar. The result would have made Aunt Jemima green with envy, and our lives were saved for the rest of the trip.

I have jumped ahead in this story, but we arrived in Ely and proceeded to the Ely Outfitters to buy our supplies and rent our gear. As I recall, we bought or rented two canoes, four paddles, one tent, two large packsacks of food, cooking utensils and blankets, one hand ax, a waterproof container with about twenty-five kitchen matches. This safety reserve of matches was vital in case our regular matches became soaked and useless.

Our chef, Ad, naturally handled the commissary purchases, while Scott and I had the storekeeper mark on our map, with red pencil, a circle trip through a chain of lakes and portages that would take not over twelve days. The rental price on canoes varied considerably, but our $65-per-man budget dictated the lower price. We were too far out on the trip to change when we realized we had taken old waterlogged canoes weighing about 130 pounds each as against only 80 pounds for the others.

Not knowing how our travel speed would compare with that of the native who had marked our twelve-day trip, and having to be back on time, we decided not to stop for any noon meals, but to parcel out one Hershey bar and two handfuls of dried raisins to be eaten for each lunch as we went along. The day before the trip ended we ran out of Hershey bars—or at least three of us thought we had—when Ad quietly and calmly pulled out his final five-cent candy bar. It was too much for the sweets-loving youngster to stand, and Charlie started his bidding. He and Ad were in the same canoe that day, and as our canoes pulled apart I heard Charlie's offer reach five dollars, when Ad slowly peeled off the paper and put it into his own mouth.

It was the only trace of sadism in Ad that I ever noticed in a friendship of over sixty years.

After outfitting at Ely, a short ride on a truck put us down at the west end of Basswood Lake and we were now on our own.

For the first three days our route took us through a chain of little lakes and portages forming the boundary between Canada and Minnesota, until we headed north into Canada. The first night out we had pitched camp when Ad noticed a boundary marker post about thirty feet back of our tent in the shrubbery. Ad

AES (left) and Joseph F. Bohrer during a canoe trip in 1925.

thought it would be fun to repitch the tent exactly straddling the International Boundary Line so we could sleep with our heads in one country and our feet in the other.

We moved the tent as Ad had suggested, and did the same thing the following two nights, reversing our head and feet direction each night. I am sure the rest of us did not recognize this simple sign as forecasting Ad's later distinguished career in the field of international relations, but it did show that he knew that international boundaries did exist.

We rotated our canoe assignments each day, so Ad and I were in the same canoe every three days. Frankly we were the slowest paddlers. We both smoked Bull Durham and the others didn't. Charlie was only seventeen, and Scott was even then a physical culture faddist and an ardent follower of some diet propagandist of carrot and celery juice. Scott was starting to lose his hair and someone had suggested the vegetable juice treatment. Scott did keep his hair, and Ad and I did not.

We had a glorious twelve days paddling, fishing in the evening after making camp, and portaging from the end of one lake over a hill (always) to the next one. No matter what our direction was by compass, we always seemed to paddle against the wind and frequently were buffeted by the quick squalls for which the Quetico area is noted. We caught our share of walleyes and northern pike; many spots below a waterfall would yield literally a fish for every cast. We went through Basswood, Birch, Knife, Kawnipi, Saganaga and Agnes lakes and many others whose names I cannot now remember, but, above all, we had the great good fortune to spend twelve wonderful days with one of the greatest guys I have ever known.

This was Ad's last Bloomington summer. The following fall he re-entered law school, this time at Northwestern University, and he never permanently resided in Bloomington after 1925. After graduation and passing the bar examination, Ad went with the law firm of Cutting, Moore and Sidley of Chicago. Judge Cutting was an old friend of my grandfather, and whenever I could drop in for a visit with Ad, we would go in for a chat with the Judge.

I well remember a day in the early 1930's when large oil portraits of Vice President Adlai E. Stevenson and my grandfather were unveiled in the Circuit Court room in Bloomington. The

Adlai Stevenson at the age of 23.

portraits were done by the Rev. Martin D. Hardin, a superb preacher and a talented artist. Ad was to accept the Vice President's portrait on behalf of his family. My grandfather, then over ninety years old but still very active, was to speak for himself. Ad spoke first and, completely switching the speaking assignments, spent his entire twenty minutes eulogizing my grandfather, and the latter was then introduced and gave a moving tribute to his old friend and neighbor. The portraits of these old friends now hang in the courtroom where they had often battled, and the two men, seated, look as though they are still chatting on the front porch of one or the other about the days long past.

I had known that Ad could write well from his earlier story on the Murphysboro tornado, but this was the first time I realized his superior talent with the spoken word.

In 1948, when Ad first ran for public office, it was my understanding that he preferred to try for the U.S. Senate and that Paul Douglas wanted to run for Governor of Illinois. Douglas had served as alderman in the City of Chicago and had quite a reputation as an independent liberal. The story was current that the "powers" in the Democratic party feared that they could not influence Paul Douglas in the rich field of patronage appointments which went with the governorship. The "powers" apparently felt they would have no trouble with patronage with the naïve and inexperienced Stevenson as Governor. So Stevenson became the candidate for Governor and Douglas ran for the Senate.

"Volunteers for Stevenson" groups were organized throughout the state, and I became co-chairman of the McLean County group. My grandfather and my mother had received high office as Republicans, and a few of my friends probably still consider me an ingrate and a traitor. I well remember on election night that Tuesday in November, 1948, we were in the Volunteers for Stevenson office in Bloomington, tabulating the returns from the precincts of McLean County, usually Republican by about three to two. The trend was clear that Ad would win the county by about 2,500 votes, when the phone rang. It was Ad calling from Chicago asking, "Are there any returns in showing how McLean County is going?" When I told him he would surely carry the county, he said, "I think that is better news than if you had told me I'd been elected Governor."

After his election Ad kept asking me if I would accept some appointment. I did not want a paying position—perhaps I was a coward and didn't want to hear my Republican friends saying that was why I had been working for a Democrat. I finally settled for a nonpaying position on the Teachers College Board, where I served the next four years. My main interest on the board was to obtain some method of assuring a degree of faculty participation in the making of administrative decisions at the five universities under the board. At that time the opinion of the faculties was seldom sought on matters of deep concern to them and their universities. Adlai always supported our efforts in this field.

Since his death I have frequently been asked, "In his youth did Adlai show any signs of his future stature?" A 1922 classmate at Princeton with Ad reminded me that the Class of 1922 at graduation had voted twenty-four categories, such as "Most likely to succeed," "Most popular," "Best politician," etc., and that Ad was not really in the running.

I must agree that nothing in his youth pointed out the role he was to play, but I also do know that he alone of all those fine friends I have had seemed to grow and learn every day of his life, constantly pushing outward the horizon of his knowledge of and concern for human beings and the world they occupy.

Two Stevensons of Princeton

Woodrow Wilson once asked these questions: "Men's hearts wait upon us; men's lives hang in the balance; men's hopes call upon us to say what we do. Who shall live up to the great trust? Who dares fail to try?"

Certainly no graduate of Princeton, where Wilson had taught and served as president for twenty years, sought more wholeheartedly and successfully to "live up to the great trust" than did Adlai Ewing Stevenson of the Class of 1922. In his career, which developed in such a fascinating way through his sixty-five years, he surely met the standard for a university graduate which Wilson had defined many years earlier, i.e., that he "should be a man of his nation, as well as a man of his time."

We shall never be sure how much credit redounds to his alma mater for Stevenson's rise to greatness nor how much the career and political philosophy of Woodrow Wilson may have inspired him. Obviously, factors of heredity and a family predilection for distinguished public service cannot be ignored.

William E. Stevenson was a Princeton classmate of Adlai Stevenson. He has been a New York lawyer, director of the Red Cross in the Mediterranean theater in World War II, President of Oberlin College, 1946-1959, and Ambassador to the Philippines, 1961-1964.

Looking back I cannot recall exactly when I first met my class-mate Adlai Stevenson, but it probably wasn't until midway in our first year at college. When we entered Princeton in the fall of 1918, a wartime atmosphere prevailed. Everyone was in the uniform of one of the services and much time was spent march-ing, drilling, counting off, cleaning under "bunks," etc. Unaware that even then he was preparing himself for World War II service as Special Assistant and Counsel to Secretary of the Navy Frank Knox, Adlai entered the Naval Training Unit, while I, after a short time in the Army ROTC, went off to Parris Island as a Marine enlistee.

Thus our freshman year didn't begin, in a full-fledged civilian sense, until early 1919. Making up for lost time, the members of the Class of 1922 then became rapidly acquainted with each other, duly stimulated by such orientation procedures as obliga-tory black freshman skullcaps, combating the sophomores in the Cane Rush, and sitting for the "Flour Picture." On the latter oc-casion (long since abandoned as a special Princeton feature) the whole freshman class posed for its first group picture, but only after the sophomores had basted us with highly decorative white flour. The fact that Adlai and I are seated near each other in the first row of that historic picture would indicate resignation or foolhardiness rather than that bravery customarily associated with front line combat.

As a friend of Adlai I can't look back on our undergraduate years and identify definite omens of his career of greatness to follow. As an author, yes—because he was prominent on the campus newspaper. That occupation was in the family tradition of journalism. I rather suspect that was a career Adlai Stevenson then felt he might pursue after graduation.

But in the realm of campus politics, Ad—as he was addressed by most classmates—didn't play an especially significant role. This may have been partly because his family moved to live in Princeton during his earlier years there. (At the time he reportedly observed that making their residence so near the campus was the "cruelest thing a parent could do.") With an attractive sister of marriageable age in that home, it was natural that he, with friends and associates, should have been drawn away from campus life, at least to some extent.

Nevertheless Ad did acquire a reputation as a politician. I think this was principally because he took an active interest in Democratic party goings-on. For example, he was among those who brought Presidential Candidate Cox to speak at Princeton during the 1920 campaign. Party clubs were formed on the campus and the *Daily Princetonian*, doubtless under the influence of editors like Adlai, strongly supported the Democratic side. Of Candidate Cox's visit to the Princeton campus, the Class History stresses the fervent cheerleading of the usually dignified and restrained Professor Henry van Dyke. The account adds that by election day several prominent classmates had become "staunch Republicans because of the treatment they received at the hands of the Jersey City Democrats." Apparently Adlai either fared better or was more dedicated or determined.

In the class voting toward the end of our senior year (not to be taken too seriously) Ad stood third in the estimation of his classmates as "Biggest politician," but his eight votes were in considerable contrast to the 124 votes of the winner, who, after such a promising start, eschewed political matters after graduation and devoted his life to the stock and bond business. Actually, of the eight classmates voted for as "Biggest politician" Adlai alone ever entered political life.

Adlai attained second, with twenty-eight votes, in the category "Thinks he is the biggest politician." Certainly future years proved that Adlai was the "biggest politician" the Class of 1922 ever mustered and that he had every right to think so.

In our class poll only two were prophetic enough to designate Adlai as "Most likely to succeed." Even at that, he was in exclusive company because he outranked 350 others, including myself, who received no votes at all in that category. Of those singled out by their classmates for success in life, nearly all met the class's expectations: Charles Denby in law; George La Branche on the New York Stock Exchange; Archibald (Archie) Jackson as head of several large insurance companies; James Russell (Russ) Forgan in investment banking; I. Ridgeway (Ridge) Trimble as a surgeon; and George (Cupe) Love as head of two of our largest industrial corporations—to mention only some of them. Tom McEachin, a close friend of Adlai, was voted the second "Most likely to succeed." Shortly after his return from three years as a Rhodes Scholar at Oxford his untimely death cut off what would undoubtedly have been a brilliant career in his chosen field of law.

Even Ad's keen wit had not become widely appreciated during college. Twenty classmates received votes for "Wittiest," but he wasn't one of them. The chances are that our undergraduate concept of "wit"—back in those days of Prohibition and F. Scott Fitzgerald—didn't coincide with that of our later years. As seniors our notion of wit might be illustrated by these attempts at humor which found their way into the class voting: a prominent economics professor was included among such "favorite fiction writers" as Tarkington, Dumas and Mark Twain; a certain histrionically inclined professor of English was mentioned among "favorite stage actors" along with John Barrymore, George Arliss and Ed Wynn; "women" and "timetables" were listed under "favorite study."

At college, as in later years, Adlai was known for his good nature. His sense of humor and friendly interest in people made him a delightful companion. He also was well able to hold his own among what we called "kidders," of which 1922 had a bountiful supply. Ad and I took many of the same courses and, for alphabetical reasons, we usually sat next to one another in lectures. I always looked forward to cheery and interesting talks with him. In later years I was surprised that his wit was criticized by political opponents, because his humor was in no way an affectation but rather an inherent part of his very nature. It was not the wit of a cynic or critic; rather it was that of a man who was friendly and human, and one who reacted to situations rapidly and with discernment. Adlai was pleasant to be with because he was not complacent, pompous or self-righteous. He had genuine humility and was motivated by that deep humanity which made him interested in and considerate of the viewpoints and problems of others.

By our senior year Ad had achieved recognition as a campus leader, not only because he was managing editor of the *Daily Princetonian*, but also by virtue of his election to one of the fifteen places on the Senior Council. I happened to be chairman of that august body, and I recall that Adlai's comments or observations frequently were helpful in our weekly deliberations about matters like the Intercollegiate Disarmament Conference held in Princeton early in 1922, or less serious items such as campus conduct and regulations, student peccadilloes or that hardy Princeton perennial: how to make elections to the upper-class eating clubs simultaneously democratic, all-inclusive and yet exclusive. At our commencement Adlai was a member of the Class Day Committee.

Adlai was a member of Quadrangle Club, as were all his roommates of different times during the four years: Bill Hale from California, Louis Jones from Baltimore and Doug Ward from New Jersey. Bill was the son of the renowned astronomer, Dr. George Hale, Director of Mount Wilson Observatory. Intending to become an architect, Bill followed a banking and business career until his death in 1962. Although he planned to be an investment banker, Louis Jones became a professor of English and Dean at Cal Tech. Doug Ward has spent most of his life in real estate just as he planned to do in his senior year. Both Tom McEachin and Charles Denby, already mentioned, were members of Quadrangle Club with Adlai. Like him they also held top positions on the *Daily Princetonian,* as chairman and editorial chairman respectively.

Although five members of our class at Princeton subsequently took degrees at Oxford as Rhodes Scholars (establishing a new record for any one college class anywhere), it was our classmate Adlai who received that highest distinction: an Honorary Doctor of Laws from Oxford in 1957. Princeton had given him an honorary degree in 1954, and many other institutions have done likewise.

After graduation Adlai's and my paths separated. He attended Harvard Law School for two years and then returned to Illinois. I studied law at Oxford and subsequently took up legal practice in New York City.

In no better way did Adlai Stevenson demonstrate the value of a Princeton education than through his constantly increasing intellectual curiosity and growth through the years after his graduation. This came to my attention in Naples in 1943 when we were both there on war service. He came to Italy as chief of an economic mission. As the official in charge of Red Cross operations in the Mediterranean I had been in the area for more than a year. I was impressed with how Adlai, in only a few weeks, put his finger on the principal economic and political problems and needs of that war-torn country. He took back to Washington a report that was comprehensive and astute. My respect for his thoughtful consideration and clear comprehension of the great human problems was increasingly confirmed in talks we had together during the years after the war.

Because of my admiration and regard for Ad, what he was trying to do for public life and also because of the alternative offered the voters, I became restless as a Republican in 1952. But before reaching a decision regarding a switch I wanted a chance to talk with Adlai, whom I hadn't seen for some time. At his invitation, in September, 1952, we flew together from Chicago to a friend's camp in Wisconsin where he sought a few days' rest before the more strenuous phase of the presidential campaign began. His philosophic calm on the plane that morning, as we read together the extreme, even nasty, things which the Chicago papers were printing about him, impressed me tremendously. It was a demonstration of maturity, restraint and character I shall never forget.

As a result of that trip I decided to support Adlai and do whatever I could to help his candidacy. As active in "Volunteers for Stevenson" as the presidency of Oberlin College would permit, I was surprised and disappointed to discover how few classmates would support Adlai, much as many admired him. However, I found the same thing was true among my fellow college presidents. Several confessed to me that while they favored Adlai personally, they dared not jeopardize their status with their boards of trustees or certain donors by taking a pro-Democratic public position!

In February, 1956, Adlai was the principal speaker at the Annual 1922 Class Dinner in New York City. I was the toastmaster, and, after introducing Ev Case, our classmate who was then president of Colgate University and who was also a supporter of Adlai, I took occasion to chide those classmates present who hadn't voted for Adlai in 1952 along these lines:

"Speaking of Presidents I often wonder why a certain one of us is seeking to achieve that particular appellation. I've been a Stevenson for fifty-five years and a president [at Oberlin College] for ten, and I don't see enough attraction in the combination to lead the kind of life Adlai is pursuing so madly." I then observed that it was not much to 1922's credit that of the 27,314,992 people who voted for Ad in 1952 only a comparative few were classmates.

After urging those present to support Adlai thereafter, I confessed my own stake in seeking his election to the presidency. Mentioning that Ad had been a beau of my wife years before I had met her, I expressed the hope that he would marry one of my daughters so that after he had become President I could introduce him by saying "Have you met my son-in-law, the President of the United States?"

By the time that the 1956 election approached, Ed DeLong, our classmate who was Director of Public Information at Princeton and a staunch Democrat, asked me to write a piece for the *Princeton Alumni Weekly* about Adlai's qualifications for the presidency. It appeared in the issue of October 26, 1956, under the heading "A Tribute to Adlai Stevenson." My appraisal stressed Ad's honesty, integrity and character; his courage, especially in expressing his convictions forthrightly; his feeling for people, belief in them and desire to serve them—hence his sincere faith in democracy. I also mentioned Adlai's comprehension of world problems and his vision of future trends and possibilities, characteristic of the statesman who is a humanitarian as well.

In referring to two of the greatest Princetonians of all time, I said by way of conclusion:

I think that Adlai's claim to fame, like that of Madison and Woodrow Wilson before him, lies not so much in specific achievement as in his attitude toward his fellow men. This respect and concern for them, as well as his affection for Princeton, are demonstrated by these words from his address at the Senior Banquet of the Class of 1954: "For here at Princeton, which for more than two centuries has transmitted from one generation to the next the riches of Western civilization, you have acquired some grasp of the basic principles on which our culture is founded—the concept of the supremacy of the individual, the worth of a human being, and the necessity for a climate of freedom in which these values may find means of expression."

Through the years Ad frequently demonstrated his love of Princeton and loyalty to 1922 by attendance at dinners, games, reunions and other similar occasions. He presented most of his personal papers to the university and told several friends that, upon his retirement, he intended to make his home in Princeton.

An avid tennis enthusiast—he was a member of the team at Choate, his prep school—Adlai brought his tennis racket to our fortieth class reunion in 1962. Most tennis-minded classmates were content to play only a game or two, but Adlai played many sets, kept busy by all those who wanted to boast after returning home, "I had a tennis game with Ad Stevenson!"

Over the years, my family and I enjoyed our friendship with Adlai through occasional personal meetings or through correspondence. He visited us in Oberlin several times, once to speak and receive an honorary degree. While those contacts, far too few as he became ever busier, always exuded gaiety and friendship, they also were meaningful because deep concern was felt about world problems as we discussed them. So our relationship with Ad was a great source of stimulation and inspiration to us.

In 1952 Adlai sent us a copy of Noel Busch's biography of himself inscribed with that light, modest touch so characteristic of him: "For my dear friends—Bill and Bumpy Stevenson—who will probably not recognize the subject of this volume any more than he does!" In 1954 we received from him a copy of his "Major Campaign Speeches" inscribed: "With the affection of the author of these interminable mouthings." After the 1952 campaign Adlai sent me a large box of book matches on the covers of which "President Stevenson" was embossed in gold, a premature gift to Adlai from an overoptimistic adherent. Adlai passed them along to me as the only "President Stevenson" of his acquaintance.

When in 1956 our elder daughter, Helen, became engaged to Robert Meyner, then Governor of New Jersey, the press frequently identified her as a "cousin" of Adlai. Actually, despite the name "Stevenson" which we shared, Adlai and I were not related. By a coincidence, however, my wife was a distant relative of Adlai's by marriage. When asked by reporters to establish the connection, she would say, "It's very simple. My mother had a sister who married a man who was Adlai Stevenson's father's double first cousin!" That was too complicated for the press, so they boiled it down to "cousin."

During the fall of 1956 my daughter Helen was increasingly advertised as Adlai's relative. So I wrote him that since he was getting all the publicity he ought to pay for the wedding, and the engagement announcement should read: "Adlai Stevenson announces the engagement of his distant relative by marriage to Robert Meyner. P.S. Her parents consent." Adlai replied by postcard: "The only engagement I would like to announce would be Helen's to me!" We were all very gratified that Adlai was able to attend the wedding, where, needless to say, he was a star attraction. Even before we left the church the photographers took dozens of pictures of Adlai kissing the bride while her new husband, her father, and the guests patiently waited—a situation which Adlai relished.

In August of 1961 Adlai, then at the UN, wrote me at our home in Aspen, Colorado: "I keep getting inquiries about hot jobs in the government and I am constantly thinking of you languishing on your ample derriere in comfortable spas while the rest of us are doing the same in less comfortable places." He then asked if I was interested in a Washington assignment. Later that year I was appointed Ambassador to the Philippines, and took up my duties there early in 1962.

The fact that Adlai and I were "Ambassador" concurrently led to some confusion. We both happened to be weekending at Under Secretary of State George McGhee's lovely home in Virginia when a long-distance call came for "Ambassador Stevenson." Cecilia McGhee found amusement in asking, "Which Ambassador Stevenson?" She pointed out afterward how unique the situation had been. Far more serious was the flash report my son-in-law Bob Meyner received last July that "Ambassador Stevenson had died suddenly overseas." He knew that I was abroad and didn't happen to know that Adlai was.

Even as I took my leave of the State Department in the summer of 1964 our careers had a relationship. At my farewell appointment with Secretary Rusk (at which I had looked forward to discussing several matters which I considered of special importance) there was only time for pleasantries as the Secretary,

Mr. Stevenson at the wedding of Governor Robert Meyner to Helen Stevenson in Oberlin, Ohio, January, 1957. Left to right, Governor Meyner's mother, the Governor and his bride, and her parents, Mr. and Mrs. William E. Stevenson.

through most of our meeting, kept his attention on television bringing us a speech by Adlai at the UN.

In my extensive travels abroad in recent years I have found whenever I met new people that they invariably asked if I was related to Adlai Stevenson. This brought home, as nothing else could, the universal esteem and affection in which he was held throughout the world.

Because I respected Adlai's judgment and opinions and enjoyed his company as much as I did, I regretted that, after my return from the Philippines to the States, our paths weren't crossing more often. Since we had both been actively involved in international affairs, there was so much to discuss. So last June, the month before his death, I wrote Ad suggesting we try for a meeting in New York City late in June or in July. In his reply of June 19 (my last letter from him) he said a June date was "out" because of other commitments, but maybe "we can have a proper talk" in mid-July "if I don't have to go to Europe." As I returned on July 14 to New York from a trip to Russia for the American Red Cross, I hoped to find Adlai in New York and see him. But on the plane flying home from Paris, George Ball, who was also aboard, received in mid-Atlantic the shocking message that Adlai had succumbed that very day in London. We were grief-stricken and neither of us could speak.

As we think back about Adlai's many worthwhile accomplishments, there emerges, I think, the pattern of a man who, throughout his life, had the intelligence, the character, the courage and the faith to be himself. He applied his exceptional abilities, as well as his extraordinary range of interests and knowledge, to human betterment.

No one can ever replace Adlai, and those of us who were privileged to know him will never forget him. We will remember him as a conscientious, responsible citizen of the world, a staunch, loyal friend, a man of unusual personal charm, a person who lived a full and glorious life—one who, in spite of some big disappointments, maintained a cheerful countenance and attitude where resentment might have shown in others. Adlai Ewing Stevenson amply demonstrated what a civilized human being should be like and could be like.

The final tribute of 1922 to Adlai was short and simple. Heading the class column in the *Princeton Alumni Weekly* of September 21, 1965, it read:

ADLAI EWING STEVENSON '22

1900–1965

The record of his life and deeds,
His thoughts, his hopes, and his ideals,
Is inscribed in the annals of the nation he served,
For the ages yet to come.
We his classmates stand silently by,
While men of goodwill throughout the world
Pay homage in their hearts and minds,
Claiming him as their own.

Politics and R & R

I AM SURE that no American will ever forget any detail of his personal experiences on December 7, 1941. For me, there is a special reason, not connected with the attack on Pearl Harbor, for the vivid recollection I have of that day. My wife and I were concluding a weekend visit with the Stevensons in Washington, at their house on R Street, and Adlai was driving us to the Union Station to catch the eleven o'clock train for Baltimore, where we were making a luncheon stopover on our way back to Chicago. I had intended to order a cab, but Adlai said there was an important matter he wished to discuss with me.

As he drove us along Massachusetts Avenue, he said that some of the "old Horner crowd," in particular Lloyd Lewis of the Chicago *Daily News*, Adlai's close friend and Libertyville neighbor, were urging him to run for the Senate in 1942, when "Curly" Brooks would be up for re-election. To promote his candidacy, this group was planning to set up some speaking engagements in Illinois which would put him before Illinois voters. Due to Brooks' strong isolationist position, in contrast with Adlai's service as

Hermon Dunlap Smith of Chicago, head of the insurance firm of Marsh and McLennan, Inc., was a life-long friend of Adlai Stevenson and an intimate adviser in his political career.

28

chairman of the Chicago chapter of the William Allen White "Committee to Defend America by Aiding the Allies," a significant debate could result if a confrontation could be arranged.

Adlai expressed grave doubts as to the possibility of getting the nomination, however, both because of not being well enough known and because of his lack of experience in politics. I urged him not to turn down this suggestion without further study, and promised to look into it carefully, immediately on my return to Chicago.

In a few minutes, I was on the train for Baltimore, and within a few hours had heard the news of the attack on Pearl Harbor over the radio. This put an end to any thought of politics on Adlai's behalf for the time being.

The date of our conversation should be noted. In the minds of many persons, Adlai's political career was a postwar development, but its origin was deep-seated. He had a heritage of politics, he already had served a hitch in Washington in the early days of Franklin Roosevelt's first administration, and many of his deepest interests were in the area of public affairs.

I don't recall my exact reaction to his disclosure, but I do know that I wasn't surprised.

It was not until over five years later, in the early summer of 1947, that he again seriously mentioned the possibility of running for office, although it had obviously been much in his mind. One afternoon at Libertyville, after a tennis game, he took me aside and asked if I could help "get the heat off" him from a man by the name of Lou Kohn, who was "pestering" him to run for the Senate in 1948. Adlai said he did not recall ever having met him, but that the man was pursuing him with frequent telephone calls. He said that Kohn was obviously so sincere in his interest that he did not like to refuse to see him, and that he thought the best procedure would be to refer him to me, if I were willing. Before long, my telephone started ringing, and I had agreed to talk with Lou Kohn.

I am afraid I was not entirely helpful to Adlai, because within a month or so I agreed to head a Stevenson-for-Senator Committee, the other two members of which were Lou Kohn and Steve Mitchell. By December I found myself involved in a number of meetings with Jack Arvey and Adlai, the outcome of which was Adlai's reluctant agreement to be a candidate for Governor rather than Senator, his endorsement by the Democratic Central Committee, and his election as Governor in the fall of 1948 by a record-breaking margin—an outcome which surprised me probably more than any other person in the entire state!

Certainly one of the most dramatic and vivid memories of my life was election night, November 2, 1948. I went to campaign headquarters late in the afternoon, joined the Stevensons for dinner, and then went back to headquarters, where we were greeted by a newsboy selling the early Chicago *Tribune* "election special" with the screaming headline "Dewey Landslide."

Adlai soon retired to the tiny corner room which he used as his office, where he asked Lloyd Lewis and me to join him. There we three sat, listening to the returns come in, with occasional interruptions as staff members popped in with special bulletins. Gradually it became evident that he might win, and then that he *had* won! Lloyd was working on the draft of an acceptance speech, but he kept emphasizing and re-emphasizing to Adlai the importance of caution. "If we give the impression we've won, the Democratic watchers downstate will go home, and they'll count you out—it's been done before!" By this time, the group of workers who had served so loyally during the discouraging campaign were jubilant with certain victory, and we all celebrated together, winding up with a visit en masse to Democratic headquarters at the Morrison.

The great upset victory of November 2, 1948, was, of course, a major turning point in Adlai's career, and started him on the road which led to the two presidential nominations and the United Nations ambassadorship. As this still somewhat obscure lawyer was suddenly placed in the limelight as Governor-elect and became sought after by important business leaders who previously had had no hesitation in referring to him as a "lightweight," I thought back over his remarkable development during the many years I had known him.

My first recollection of Adlai was as a boy at Charlevoix, Michigan. Just what year we met, I could not say, but we were both taken there as infants in the summer of 1900, when he was six months old and I was three months his junior! I remember him as an agreeable but not remarkable boy, and I always enjoyed our contacts during our formative years, not only in Charlevoix but at the H F Bar Ranch in Wyoming, and on my occasional visits to Princeton as a Harvard undergraduate. I did not see him regularly until he moved to Chicago as a young lawyer in 1927.

From then on our ways crossed very frequently, not only because of our many friends in common but because of our interests in common. I remember, for example, being invited to a small luncheon at the Chicago Club at which we were both asked to become trustees of the Illinois Children's Home and Aid Society. During this period, he became more and more active in functions which involved appearances before the public, such as the Council on Foreign Relations, where he showed early indications of his remarkable eloquence and wit.

Due to his assumption of various responsibilities in Washington—such as his term as Special Counsel to the Agricultural Adjustment Administration in 1933 and 1934—his reputation in Chicago was limited to his personal friends and to those who shared his main interests, such as the Council on Foreign Relations, the William Allen White Committee, and his various philanthropic activities, including Hull House, the Immigrants' Protective League, the Illinois Children's Home and Aid Society, etc.

Accordingly, when Lloyd Lewis suggested his possible candidacy for the Senate just before Pearl Harbor, Adlai's doubts that he was well enough known to secure the nomination were well founded. This opinion was confirmed shortly thereafter. Although as Special Assistant to the Secretary of the Navy he could not actually seek the nomination after war was declared, he had retained hopes that he might be drafted. However, these were short-lived, as indicated by a letter he wrote me on February 9, 1942: "The political pot has been boiling, and I have been conferring with a stream of Illinois statesmen. But the organization wouldn't have me—'not well enough known'—so they took one of the boys."

As the war approached its conclusion, Adlai was able to resume his interest in other areas, and was especially fascinated by the opportunity to buy the Chicago *Daily News*, which arose from the death of his Navy "boss," Frank Knox. With the support of a number of friends, he organized a syndicate for this purpose. He was given virtually a "blank check," but he hesitated to commit his associates to a price he felt unrealistic. I had lunch with him at the Attic Club the day the bids were to close, and I remember urging him to raise our bid. This he was reluctant to do, because, as he wrote his backers on October 19, 1944, his figure was "conceived with a view to insuring the preservation of the integrity, character, and traditions of the *News* in accordance with Colonel Knox's will, and not to compete on price with all other bidders." It is interesting to speculate what the effect on his political career would have been had he become publisher of the *News* at that time. Certainly, he would not have become a candidate for Governor in 1947.

The successful bidder in 1944 was the Knight Newspapers, and, with John S. Knight as publisher, the *News* vigorously backed Adlai for the governorship in 1948. In 1959 the Knight interests sold the *News* to Field Enterprises.

In the last months of the war Adlai became actively involved in the preparatory work of the United Nations, going to London in September of 1945, where, due to the illness of Edward R. Stettinius, Jr., he took over as chief of the United States delegation to the Preparatory Commission.

The following spring Stettinius resigned as head of our UN delegation, and with Adlai's approval, I launched an immediate campaign to secure his appointment to this office, seeking the backing of Mayor Kelly and a number of influential Chicagoans. The group I was able to approach was augmented by the fortuitous circumstance of my going east to my twenty-fifth Harvard reunion, where, in the locker room of the Essex County Club, I solicited the support of three classmates who represented an incredible combined circulation and influence: Roy Larsen, executive of *Time, Life* and *Fortune;* John Cowles, of the Cowles newspaper-magazine family; and Ralph Henderson of *Reader's Digest.* There was insufficient time to launch a national campaign, however, and President Truman promptly appointed Warren Austin to the post, despite my fervid telegraphic plea to him: "Strongly urge appointment Adlai Stevenson of Illinois to succeed Stettinius on U.N. Security Council. He is uniquely qualified by reason of his native ability, his experience at San Francisco and London meetings, and especially because he has respect and confidence of Soviet delegates." At a later date, Adlai remarked that the latter qualification had become perhaps a doubtful political asset!

A little more than a year later, the political pot, although not boiling (as he had described it in February, 1942), was beginning to simmer. At a Sunday luncheon in Lake Forest on July 19, 1947, I happened to run into Adlai's cousin, Loring Merwin, editor of the Bloomington *Pantagraph*, and we started discussing Adlai as a possible candidate for the Senate. Loring volunteered to send letters to the editors of twenty-five downstate newspapers, asking "how well, if at all, Stevenson is known in your district, and whether you think he might draw any substantial number of Republican or independent votes there in a race against Senator Brooks." These letters drew the reply that might have been expected—that Stevenson was generally not known—but from a few came a mildly favorable reaction. In the meantime, Lou Kohn had been working strenuously on his own, until we were brought together by Adlai's call to me, and joined forces.

From this point on, an increasing number of others were brought into the Stevenson orbit—workers in the Illinois campaign, state appointees, presidential campaign staff and associates at the United Nations. Recollections of these events are well covered in this book by others who played a part in them, but, because of my long and close friendship with Adlai, I have been asked to touch upon aspects of his personal life—those moments, increasingly rare as his burdens mounted, devoted to relaxation with friends.

I believe I was first aware of his extraordinary charm and wit at his bachelor dinner, comprising a very small group gathered in a dining room in the somewhat dreary H-Y-P Club on Plymouth Court in Chicago. This could easily have been a dismal affair, but it was enlivened throughout by the original and sparkling humor of the groom, who is generally expected at this occasion to be in a sort of nervous stupor rather than to shine brilliantly. Again I remember a summer evening, sitting under the stars on the open deck of his home on the Des Plaines River, being regaled by a brilliant and witty three-cornered conversation, the three corners being represented by Adlai, Robert M. Hutchins and Lloyd Lewis. Today, probably thirty years after the event, I can recall little that was said, but I know I never laughed so hard and long in my life, before or since!

After Adlai built the low, slate-roofed house on his farm on the Des Plaines, south of Libertyville, this became his home for the remainder of his life, a home to which he was attached by the strongest ties of devotion, ties which seemed to strengthen the longer he was removed from it by his political and governmental responsibilities. The principal tie was to the soil, which he looked upon as a bit of Illinois farmland and prairie, where his sheep could graze, his Dalmatians—"King Arthur" ("Artie" for short) and later his successor, "Merlin"—could run freely, and where, following an afternoon tennis game, he could relax with a drink, watching the sun set behind the magnificent sugar maples which surrounded the house and lined the distant river bank. He was also devoted to the house, which seemed ideally suited for his needs, with its ground floor study to which he could withdraw for private conferences, the comfortable living room with adjoining screened porch, and the dining room looking west toward the river. In the basement was a "rumpus room," which became the display room of various campaign memorabilia, as well as the center for festive parties, with New Year's Eve a favorite occasion for celebration. When the supposedly "fireproof" house burned to the ground in 1937, he rebuilt it very much as it was before.

Even when "in residence" elsewhere, he seemed to draw strength and security from his love of "the farm." There seemed to be a steady stream of foreign dignitaries of every creed and color, as well as American politicians and just sight-seers, who would wander across the lawn at a crucial moment in a game of tennis, at which point Adlai would withdraw to welcome them, mumbling something about a vague recollection that he had said something in New York about stopping by on "Saturday afternoon."

Of course, the best-known *regular* relaxing event was *The Birthday Party*, which became a kind of ritual occasion. The first of these birthday parties started most casually at the Governor's Mansion on Saturday, February 4, 1950, the eve of his fiftieth birthday. It was planned by three of his former law partners and their wives—the James Oateses, the Edward McDougals and the John Derns—and also included the Ed Days, the Loring Merwins, Jim Mulroy, Jane Dick and the Smiths. The law partners presented him with an inscribed silver tray, accompanied by appropriate oratorical eloquence, and there were two songs especially written for the occasion—one by Ed Day, "The Gov Is a Wonderful Guy" (to the tune of "I'm in Love with a Wonderful Guy"), and the other by Ellen Smith, "He Is the Very Model of an Illinois Governor" (to the tune of "I Am the Very Model of a Modern Major General"). The former was revived and sung a number of times at succeeding parties, but the latter was destined to a very brief career, no doubt hastened by the fact that when Ed Day arranged to have the song recorded as a remembrance of the evening, the WTAX singers undertook to sing it to the tune of another Gilbert and Sullivan favorite, "I Am the Captain of the *Pinafore*," which proved to be a quite impossible feat.

Following the dinner festivities, we all removed to the Lake Club, where Hildegarde was performing. She, of course, singled out the Governor for special attention, questioning him about his occupation. The preceding victim having been in the groundstone business, he replied, "I'm in the grinding business, too; I pulverize the public!" Returning to the Mansion, we all repaired to the attic, where we searched in the dark for a mysterious "ghost." Meanwhile, my wife had slipped away unobserved, and we soon heard soft melodic music, excerpts from *La Bohème* and *Manon*, drifting upstairs from a phantom source.

It was an evening to be long remembered, and it was remembered in a series of annual birthday parties. After the return from Springfield, these were held in the homes of friends in Lake Forest, with some special feature always planned. One year it was in the Edison Dicks' game room, with not only the professional talent of Burr Tillstrom, who put on a specially composed "Kukla, Fran and Ollie" skit, but also some highly skilled amateur talent depicting incidents in Adlai's career. The most remarkable performance was a scene in which Ed Day was Adlai as a young law clerk asking for permission to go to Washington, with Jim Oates in the role of his stern employer.

Another year, all the guests came to our house prepared to enact, in costume, brief scenes from Adlai's recent trip around the world.

In 1957, on the birthday following his second presidential defeat, we decided to hold a special gala, and a group of friends came from New York for a full weekend of festivities.

Following his move to New York, the party was held several times in the embassy in the Waldorf Towers. One such party coincided with the great snow of 1961, and some of the Chicago group were grounded, but held their own separate celebration in Lake Forest. Those who had reached New York had the unforgettable experience of walking to the party through several feet of snow along a deserted Park Avenue.

In 1963 (following the Cuban missile crisis) he wrote: "I am asking only the old hawks to my birthday party, the veteran hardline celebrants of this annual occasion from Illinois, and a few local doves. Please come."

As the party grew in size, it became increasingly cosmopolitan, but less intimate. It was a wonderful, exciting occasion, but had lost some of its special charm. The 1965 party was arranged by the James Oateses at the River Club, with much brilliant and original poetry recited, followed by a long poem, to which all the guests had contributed, and which was read by Rosalind Oates, with pictorial accompaniment. Adlai mentioned late that evening that he felt this party should be the last, and even the entreaties of some of us to come back to Lake Forest in 1966 appeared futile. It *was* the last of a remarkable and truly unique series of parties!

These parties provided a recurring, special and wonderful, though brief, period of recreation and gaiety, but for continuous and uninterrupted days of complete rest and relaxation, there is no doubt that his favorite spot was the lovely country of rocky islands and blue water at Desbarats, in Ontario, near the Canadian Sault. He first came here to visit our camp in 1930, and for thirty-five years returned every summer, with only an occasional omission for special reasons, as in the campaign year of 1952, when he wrote us: "How I wish I was up at Desbarats this very moment, but they have forbidden me to leave the United States, and it looks as though my two or three days' holiday will be in Wisconsin, if at all."

In glancing through our guest book, I find the theme which recurs most frequently is his brief comment of 1951: "Again and again!!" and in 1955: "Better than ever!"

On September 7, 1956, in the middle of his second presidential campaign, he wrote from Libertyville in longhand:

Thank you, dear Ellen, and all the beloved Smiths, and the Canadian allies! for that blessed note. The balsam brought tears to my eyes— perfume I pine for! and I dreamed a moment of sunset on the wee porch at Point Cottage with the drinks—or on the porch at the big cabin with the children! Early in the morning I'm off again—for two months—and the dreams of many, many years of blue skies, blue waters, and gay sounds of Desbarats will come back again and again.
—Much love,
ADLAI

It is pleasant to think that these annual summer visits brought both gaiety and peace to Adlai, because he brought so much to our camp—and I mean our *entire* camp: ourselves, our children, our grandchildren, our guests and our staff, all of whom he treated as his old and dear friends. Every year our grandchildren would inquire, "When is the Gov coming?" and "Is he bringing anyone with him?" For we also gave him carte blanche to include members of his family or a friend, who, without exception, would prove to be a congenial and charming addition, as well as an enthusiastic partner at mixed doubles in the pine-encircled tennis court. Perhaps even ahead of tennis, Adlai's favorite activity was canoeing, but, as suggested in his letter, his favorite occupation was relaxing in the sun—or the sunset, depending on the time of day.

The very special position which he held in our family group

AES boating with the Smiths at Desbarats in 1951.

was well expressed by our eldest daughter in an article she wrote for the Bethlehem *League World*:

A great quality of his was his genuine interest in children and their ideas. Often he took the time to sit down with them individually to discover their opinions of topics ranging from fishing holes to the United Nations. And my eldest daughter will never forget the time last summer when he took her aside, asked her to play a Beatle record, listened intently to several songs, and asked her to explain her feelings about the music.

With Adlai III and his wife Nancy and two of his grandchildren at Libertyville in January, 1960. Borden is at left.

My first memories of "the Gov" date back to a picnic in Desbarats thirty years ago. I'll never forget watching him go down to the water's edge to fill a bucket, slip on the mossy rock, and continue to slip gradually into the lake, keeping only the bucket high and dry. Needless to say, he had a good laugh at himself, which is more than I can say for many others who have had the same inglorious experience.

Just thirty years later he wrote in our guest book: "The 30th anniversary of my visit to Desbarats. It is as lovely, and the Smiths as young, and I fell in *again!*"

But no one else can express his feelings for Desbarats as well as he did in his own magic words. After his last visit in 1964, he wrote:

MY DEAR, DEAR SMITHS,

The summons has come, and I'm off to N.Y., Malaysia and Cyprus, in a few minutes, without even time to write you a proper letter of thanks for perhaps the best R & R I've ever had! And, thinking of 35 years of Desbarats, that's saying a lot. Maybe it came just when I needed it most; but I suspect the largest component was the Smith family—three generations—and their mysterious gift for hospitality—and quiet repose in that lovely, tranquil environment. And this time even the journey down was painless and on time! But what a pity to waste any part of a blue and white northern summer day in an airplane.

I send you blessings and thanks from the heart, head and sinews.

Love always,
ADLAI

Before he left for Europe last July, we made definite plans to meet in Desbarats on August 18 for his annual visit. Knowing the happiness that his visits there had brought him, it was consoling to hear that as he was walking down the London street on July 14 he was discussing plans for his return to Desbarats within a month.

It also was consoling to think of Robert Louis Stevenson's words:

And does not life go down with a better grace, foaming in full body over a precipice, than miserably straggling to an end in sandy deltas? For surely, at whatever age it overtake the man, this is to die young. The noise of the mallet and chisel is scarcely quenched, the trumpets are hardly done blowing, when, trailing with him clouds of glory, this happy-starred, full-blooded spirit shoots into the spiritual land.

Friend of the Family

WHEN I was thirteen I met Adlai's great-aunt, an impressive old lady who had been president of the DAR. When I was seventeen Adlai's grandfather, the ex-Vice President, spent an afternoon on the porch of my family's summer home in Ephraim, Wisconsin, telling yarns of the Old South. Like their cousin, Senator Alben Barkley, the old gentleman was a famous raconteur, and I was so fascinated that when he left I tried to write the stories down. Next day I went to see him to clarify some details I had forgotten, and was captivated by the courtly gallantry with which he encouraged a young person to develop an interest in politics and history. Many years later I found those notes, and most amusing they were. I wish I had them now, but I gave them to Vice President Stevenson's grandson when he was Governor of Illinois.

I mention this background of Adlai's political family partly to show why talk of "the reluctant politician" has always seemed nonsense to me. Politics was not only in Adlai's blood, it was in his genes. And partly I think it was natural for me to begin my recollections of Adlai thus before I knew him, not only because

Harriet (Mrs. John Paul) Welling has been active for many years in Chicago civic and cultural affairs.

our family backgrounds were in a way similar (Virginia-to-Kentucky-to-Illinois, and my forebears were political, too) but because both politics and family were always part of our friendship.

When Adlai first came to Chicago in the twenties, I knew him only slightly, as a friend of my younger brother who worked hard and went to dances, too. But the charm for women, later so famous, must already have been there. For I remember giving a debutante lunch at the old Casino Club for the daughters of some of my family's friends, where the girls (drinking only sherry but smoking incessantly) argued hotly as to who was first with Adlai.

Then he married the daughter of a close friend who was also a young friend of mine, and I knew him a little better. But my husband and I were older, so we didn't see much of the young Stevensons together. And I only got to know Adlai really well when we worked together on the board of the Chicago Council on Foreign Relations in the mid-thirties. It was Hitler who brought us together, for Nazism and isolationism were both growing worries, and most of us on the Council Board saw eye to eye about the dangers of both; although, true to the Council's policy of impartial coverage, we tried to get speakers to tell both sides of these intensely contested issues.

When Adlai became president of the Council in 1935, I was vice president, and it used to be my lighthearted boast that I gave him his first job, because I was on the nominating committee that picked him. It seemed an obvious choice at the time, but in looking back now I realize what a rapid rise he had made in only eight years, from a recently graduated young newcomer to a public position of prominence and distinction that had hitherto been held by eminent older lawyers.

As all the world now knows, that was his first platform experience. All the world knows, too, of the instant success of the witty, urbane introductions that seemed to flow so easily and spontaneously from his lips. But once when I was asked to see that he insert some new fact about a speaker into his introduction that day, I called Adlai about an hour before the lunch, and he replied, a bit disconcerted, "Well, I'll try, Harriet, and I will if I can, but you know I learn these things by heart." Remembering the true spontaneity with which that same high quality of sparkling speech later *did* flow from his lips, it seems to me a lovely illustration of how the great can grow.

Perhaps a capacity to continue growing is a true mark of greatness. Certainly, Adlai's early jobs were each a little big for him at first. He mastered each quickly and had outgrown it before he moved on to the next. And there was never any hesitancy in the courage with which he spoke up for what he thought was right. I remember my admiration for his daring to be chairman of the Midwest branch of the William Allen White Committee to Defend America by Aiding the Allies. I was a little scared myself at the idea of lending England the fifty overage destroyers, but the wisdom of it was perfectly clear to Adlai, and he calmly said so, although isolationist feeling then ran so high that there were men who refused to sit on the same platform with him. It was said that some of his more conservative partners were vastly relieved when in 1941 Colonel Frank Knox invited him to Washington to be Special Assistant to the Secretary of the Navy. Indeed, his old law firm always seemed to be torn between pride in his increasing prominence and wishing he wouldn't act that way.

While Adlai himself had no compunctions, then or ever, about taking a prompt and positive political stand, he felt acutely the inevitable price a man in public life must pay in time spent away from his family. I have a letter from him in Washington in March, 1944—when they were all in Libertyville—missing "the children." "I haven't had them in 3 long summers and an endless winter. And any moment they'll be grown up and gone. Damn this war!" If he only could have known how closely he would "have them" when they finally *were* "grown up and gone"!

But with his great feeling for family each further public commitment then bothered him; and I remember, when after the war there was talk beginning of the Senate or governorship, our standing on the corner of Monroe and LaSalle after some meeting, and his asking me if I thought it would be better for his family life if he didn't consider either one. This characteristic balancing of alternatives—so often misinterpreted as indecision, but actually the result of a sort of panoramic vision that saw all sides and considered others' interests, too—in this case showed I think, the great weight he gave to the importance of his family. He loved them warmly as individuals—including, of course, his sister and her family—and he so deeply respected the dignity and privacy of the family as an institution that with the reticence of impeccable taste he was able to maintain both with quiet poise throughout his public life.

As time went on he could give the boys extraordinary opportunities in companionship with him at home and abroad, and happily as time went on he was extraordinarily lucky in the family—daughters-in-law and grandchildren—he acquired. In 1956 I remember his enthusiasm over his son Adlai's charming new wife Nancy. "She's a terrific campaigner—everywhere we went in Florida they wanted her back." He professed a comic dismay that the expected baby would stop her campaigning, but his first statement on November 6 ended with: "As for me, let there be no tears—I lost an election but I won a grandchild." And referring to Nancy several years later he said, "As far as I'm concerned she's practically perfect. She's *wantless*"—to me the happiest word he ever coined.

My husband had a stroke in early 1947, so I couldn't do much in any of Adlai's campaigns, but after the 1948 election, following his divorce, Paul and I invited Adlai to stay at our house whenever he had to be in Chicago for the night. And from then on for sixteen years—except for a couple of years when he stayed with Bill Blair's family, in the block next to ours—Adlai had a room of his own in our house, where he could sleep (ours was a quiet street) and be undisturbed if he wanted to write a speech.

We treated him in a very non-VIP and "familified" manner, which I hope was relaxing for him. The whole household adored

Courtesy, William Calvin

Governor Stevenson with his Aunt Julia Stevenson (Mrs. Martin D. Hardin) when she visited the Executive Mansion. At left, Mrs. Ernest L. Ives, his sister.

him, not so much because *he* was important as because his consideration, charming manner and remembering everyone by name made *them* feel important. This interest in others and a total lack of pomposity with anyone was, I believe, a large part of his charm with everyone, from children to his most elderly friends. Once when we had finished breakfast and Adlai was chatting with me, resting his cheek on his hand, my granddaughter aged about five wandered into the dining room and, approaching his chair to say good morning, quietly removed his elbow from the table. Horrified, I exclaimed, "Anne! You mustn't do that to a grownup, especially to a guest!" But she firmly replied, "He knows perfectly well that he shouldn't put his elbow on the table." And Adlai, though slightly startled, was more entertained than shocked by the complications of teaching manners to the very young.

Sometimes if I were reading when he came in, he would have a brandy or a highball, but just as often if he looked tired I would shoo him straight up to bed and a good night's rest. Sometimes if he were late, I wouldn't even see him until breakfast. I thought then that these half-hour visits were brief, but later when I stayed a week at the Waldorf and saw how endlessly he was surrounded from breakfast to midnight, I realized how relatively long the visits were. In the days of the governorship he would reluctantly rise from the breakfast table, pat his lower ribs with both hands (a funny little gesture he had) and groan as he turned to the door, "Well, back to the salt mines!" And off he would go, grumbling good-naturedly, in what he called "my big black poe-litical limousine."

As I'm sure he did of all his friends, he would often ask what I'd been reading, and if it had relevance to his concerns would borrow it. I remember sending him off with a first-printing paper pamphlet of Vannevar Bush's *Modern Arms and Free Men,* which dealt with the future of missiles ten years before our government had begun to consider them, and which eventually I clamored to get back. When it couldn't be found he sent me a copy in hard covers inscribed by Vannevar Bush himself. And other books like *Parkinson's Law*—I don't think he read them, but he got the gist by his own kind of osmosis and made it grist for his mill. I remember in the McCarthy days showing him a bit from Douglas Southall Freeman's *Life of Washington* in which George at seventeen wanted to be County Surveyor. He was first directed to swear allegiance to the person and government of the King. Then, under oath, he disclaimed all allegiance to the issue of James II, or any person professing descent from James. Next, George took the oath of nonbelief in transubstantiation, and finally the special oath of Surveyor! "That was in 1749," I said to Adlai. "You see we've been at it [loyalty oaths] a long time." Instantly Adlai exclaimed, "And it shows the utter futility of oaths. He was the leader of the Revolution!" And he copied the passage down, as he so often did, to use later.

I have spoken of Adlai's capacity to grow as a mark of greatness. The world realizes now, I think, the achievement of his continuing to grow in defeat, taking it as a challenge to strengthen the party and working, speaking, until the huge deficit of the 1952 campaign was wiped out. His increase in stature during the Eisenhower years was unique in a man out of office. His even greater growth in stature world-wide in the UN years was unique in a man in that office. That was, I think, just a matter of the whole world "getting to know" him.

It seems, in closing, presumptuous to quote myself instead of that most quotable man, but one couldn't get a kind word about him from any quotation of his! His familiar wry way of turning a compliment into a deprecation was a habit springing from genuine modesty sparked by wit—as when in 1952, at the height of the McCarthy hysteria, I wrote to congratulate him on his veto of the Broyles bill, which would have required loyalty oaths of state employees and a state inquiry into the activities of "subversives." My note said, "Those people had been out to get your scalp," and he replied: "Thanks for your note. My scalp is firmly in place, as all can readily see, unhappily."

The other day I found a copy of a letter I wrote him in 1952 on the Sunday between the end of the campaign and Election Day. One paragraph read:

The poetic close of your speech at last night's rally so expressed my own passion and hope for America that I realized more clearly how and why the people who had scarcely heard of you in July now think they feel as close as all of us who have loved you from way back for yourself alone! It is the sense of intimacy of a deep faith shared—that is the basis. And on that foundation you have made yourself a symbol of what America is about.

A Gold Nugget
in Your Backyard

Mr. arvey, you have a gold nugget in your own back-yard. His name is Adlai Stevenson."

This was the first time I ever heard the name of Adlai Stevenson in connection with politics.

The time was the summer of 1947, the place Washington, and the speaker James F. Byrnes, one of the most influential Democrats in the country, a former Supreme Court Justice who a few months before this conversation had resigned after two years as Secretary of State.

I was to hear much more of Adlai Stevenson, and to come to know him intimately. But up to this time he meant to me only an upper-crust Chicago lawyer who had been connected with the founding meeting of the United Nations and previously had been assistant to the Secretary of the Navy, Frank Knox, another Chicagoan.

Colonel Jacob M. Arvey, a native Chicagoan and senior member of a law firm there, has been Illinois Democratic National Committeeman since 1950. He attained his military rank during World War II service overseas.

Mr. Byrnes and I were chatting at a luncheon given by Senator Scott Lucas, who had told him that my mission to Washington in my capacity as chairman of the Cook County Democratic Central Committee was to discuss the appointment of a U.S. attorney for the Northern District of Illinois.

I was looking for a man who was a Democrat, highly endowed with qualifications, but not too intimately identified with the Democratic organization.

It was then that Mr. Byrnes mentioned Adlai Stevenson. "I have had many dealings with him," he said. "He is an ideal man for this job."

Subsequently Mr. Byrnes' estimate was confirmed and his availability mentioned by many friends, among whom were the late Judge Harry M. Fisher and Abraham Lincoln Marowitz, now a Federal Judge. Judge Fisher brought me and Mr. Stevenson together for the first time.

Just when I became aware of it I can't remember, but it gradually became evident that a Stevenson boomlet was in the making.

Forty-seven years old, with Washington and international experience and twenty years in the practice of law behind him, Stevenson was a man of maturity, ability and stature. He was obviously already qualified for high position.

The U.S. District Attorney post went to a younger man, Otto Kerner, a soldier with a fine record in World War II. Kerner was to go on to bigger things as Governor of Illinois.

Stevenson's name was first formally proposed for political office when a delegation came to me to suggest him as a candidate for U.S. Senator.

It is interesting that one of the visitors, Hermon Dunlap "Dutch" Smith, an insurance executive, was not even a Democrat. Like many prominent Chicago businessmen, he resided in a northern suburb and was an enrolled Republican. Three of the others, Laird Bell, Stephen A. Mitchell and Louis Kohn, all attorneys, were enrolled Democrats, but not exactly celebrated for activity in the party organization.

Their call on me came soon after a chance encounter I had had with Dutch Smith on the New York-bound *Twentieth Century*. We chatted on the train, and I told Mr. Smith about my quest for a new type of candidate, a man, as I remember putting it, "without any scars," one whose integrity was unquestioned, and one who could defeat the incumbent Governor of Illinois, Republican Dwight (Pete) Green.

My companion didn't hesitate a minute before naming a man who happened to be on the same train that night. I knew enough about the gentleman to say eagerly, "Dutch, that's exactly the type of man I'm thinking of."

After a little reflection it dawned on us that our candidate was a Republican, which naturally ruled him out.

Dutch Smith and his associates probably had this in mind when they came to see me. I listened to them, and we arranged for Dutch to have me meet Adlai Stevenson again.

When I met with Adlai alone, he insisted that in no circumstances would he be a candidate for any office other than that of United States Senator; that if he had any qualifications, experience and know-how, it was in the area of foreign affairs; that he had never held an executive position and that he would prefer not to try public service in that capacity. He made it clear that he would be a candidate only if he were the overwhelming choice of the Democratic party, and without a serious primary fight. I explained to him that our minds were already well made up as to the choice for United States Senator, and it was my belief that the organization would select Professor Paul Douglas, a former Independent alderman, for that office. I explained that he, Adlai, would be ideally suited as a candidate for Governor as a contrast to the scandal-plagued administration of Governor Green.

The claim has been made by many cynics that Adlai Stevenson

and Paul Douglas were chosen as the candidates in 1948 only because we felt we could not win, and that if sacrificial lambs were needed, they might as well be men who had good public images. This is an untruth. That there were many who doubted Stevenson's ability to win, and some who thought that he had no chance whatsoever, made it easier to procure an almost unanimous approval of his candidacy. The fact remains, however, that most members of the organization felt that we had a chance, a better than even chance, of winning.

The scandals to which I have referred, and the facts that this was Governor Green's eighth year in office and that he was unpopular with some members of his own party, afforded us a great opportunity to break Republican control of the state with a man whose reputation was unblemished and who could attract wide Independent support.

We felt that we could hold the organization votes, and that both Stevenson and Douglas would win almost all of the Independent Democratic vote and much of the Independent Republican vote. Our entire campaign was based upon that theory; that we were thinking along the proper lines was proved by the overwhelming vote which Stevenson and Douglas received. The organization acted as the base of our activities, and the leaders of our party concentrated all their efforts and energies on mobilizing the full strength of our organization. The independent organizations set up by Stevenson and Douglas and their friends, plus the work that we did along those lines, started the snowball rolling and implemented the work of our regular organization.

Stevenson was a very cooperative candidate. He did not consider himself superior to leaders of the organization, he sought their advice constantly, and he worked with them. He appreciated and took advantage of the fact that many of these men had been in politics for many years and had been involved in a great many political campaigns, and he was a quick student, good listener and, above all, an effective campaigner.

I shall always remember the first time I was exposed to his rare speaking ability. It was on a train en route to Springfield, where the Illinois Democratic Committee was to meet that night to add its endorsement to that of the Cook County Democratic Committee, which had been given that morning, and he inquired whether he was expected to make a speech. When I said yes, he reminded me that he had never made a political speech before and asked whether our publicity director, James "Spike" Hennessy, who was with us, could "dash off" something for him. We suggested that he try it himself and then if necessary Spike would edit it. Editing was unnecessary because, when he came back ten or fifteen minutes later and read to us what he had scribbled on several telegraph blanks, we knew then that this was a new style in political speaking and it was bound to make an impression upon all those who heard him. It would be unique yet effective. Events proved we were right.

I am greatly amused at the stories that Adlai Stevenson was indecisive. He was not a superficial man. He insisted upon knowing everything about his subject. He did not do things impulsively. He did not make impulsive decisions, but wanted to know every facet of a problem before he decided upon action.

I had one experience with his decisiveness, as well as his courage, and uncomplimentary as its reference is to me, I must recount it for history's sake.

We had not had a Democratic governor for years, and therefore when the newly elected Democratic Governor asked me to visit him at the Mansion one night to unfold to me his plans to take away patronage in the state police highway system, and withhold hundreds of job appointments from the organization, I was stunned and distressed. He proposed to install a merit system for the state police organization.

To accomplish this, he planned to ask both the Republican and the Democratic organizations to share equally the initial appointments, which meant that the Republicans would retain about three hundred men, who by custom would have been ousted. His program provided that once men put on the uniform of highway patrolman they would renounce all political identification and promise not to participate thereafter in politics. This stunned me because every Republican governor who succeeded a Democrat discharged all the Democrats and put Republicans in their place. I not only argued but pleaded with him, and asked him why we should suffer patronage-wise because of his political victory. I had in mind particularly hundreds of men in downstate Illinois. In little villages and small towns practically the best patronage job available was that of highway patrolman. I asked whether he wouldn't consider instituting a civil service system.

You may have guessed the end of the story. All my cajolery went for nought. He was decisive and he was courageous as well. This was his idea, this was his conviction; and I finally found myself pleading with the legislature to enact Adlai Stevenson's program, the removal of politics from the state police system.

The system as established set up a state police merit board entirely independent of the State Director of Personnel and Civil Service Commission as regulated by the Illinois Personnel Code. I believe members of two political parties would agree that it has been a success; in any event I know of no serious effort to overturn what Governor Stevenson accomplished.

Another example of his courage was the case of a man appointed factory inspector right after the Governor took office. The day after his appointment was confirmed by the State Senate, one of the leading newspapers of Chicago—and one, incidentally, which had endorsed the governor—disclosed the fact that this appointee had been convicted when a young man for some misdemeanor and editorially asked the Governor to discharge him. To this were added the demands of the Republican Senators. Characteristically, the Governor responded that he had appointed

Burke and Dean, Chicago

AES with Chicago Democratic leaders en route to Washington in 1949. At his right, Cook County Committeeman Albert J. Horan; on his left, Colonel Jacob M. Arvey, State Senator William Connors and Alderman Matthias (Paddy) Bauler.

this man on the basis of what had been reported to him as to his qualifications and integrity. He said, "I mean to judge him by what he does now as my appointee." That his judgment was good and that his faith did not go unrewarded is proved by the fact that two years later when he was reappointed to the same position this man received a unanimous endorsement from a Republican-controlled Senate.

As I look backward from the year 1965, Adlai Stevenson's nomination for the presidency in 1952 seems to have had a kind of inevitability about it, but few party leaders could have sensed this when he took office as Governor in January, 1949.

President Truman may have foreseen it, for Adlai Stevenson meant something special to the President. Stevenson's crushing gubernatorial victory by 572,000 in Illinois undoubtedly was what gave Truman his own plurality in the state (he won by some 30,000), and the 28 electoral votes from Illinois were a sizable percentage of his winning edge of 114 in the electoral college.

The governor grew steadily in public stature during his four years in Springfield. Long before the 1952 convention his picture had been on the front pages of the news and picture magazines. He had been analyzed and dissected by the Washington pundits and exposed to radio and television audiences.

Naturally as Democratic National Committeeman (elected in 1950) I was very conscious of this development.

I suppose millions of words have been written about how Adlai was drafted in 1952. I read hundreds of thousands of them, I suppose. Here is my own recollection.

As it became apparent that the Governor was presidential timber, many newsmen began to approach me on the subject and I gave every encouragement and impetus to the thought.

Governor Stevenson had been called to Washington to a secret meeting with the President. He told the President that he did not want to be a candidate. He later discussed the matter at great

length with me and told me he did not want me to do anything
to aid in the movement to make him President, that he was
satisfied the way he was. He further said that it appeared that
Eisenhower would be the Republican nominee and he did not
think that Eisenhower could be beaten, that the American people
were a hero-loving, worshiping breed, and that we had been in
office—the Democratic party, that is—since 1932, had made many
enemies, that our mistakes had been unduly emphasized, and that
whoever the Democratic nominee was he would inherit all the
criticism that had been leveled at the Democrats for twenty years.
I told him that I would respect his wishes, that I would make
no effort to get delegates, but that I felt obliged as a citizen and
as a member of the Democratic party to answer questions truth-
fully. If I were asked whether he would make a good President,
I would have to say "Yes," and if I were asked whether there
was a chance of his being nominated, I would be obliged to say
"Yes," and I did just that.

In Washington, however, people in the know felt that President Truman would run for re-election, and the Stevenson talk
was based on the remote possibility that the President would retire. Then at a banquet on March 29, 1952, in Washington, the
President announced, to the consternation of his confidants and
aides, that he would not seek the presidential nomination that
year. Newspapermen hurriedly left the side of the hall where
President Truman was seated and rushed to the other side to
surround Governor Stevenson. They bombarded Stevenson with
questions; cameras flashed incessantly for many minutes. It was
there and then that I determined that every possible aid should
be given to the draft movement.

I was frequently asked by the then Mayor David Lawrence of
Pittsburgh, and other leaders around the country whom I knew
well, about Stevenson's availability. I had to tell them what I
really felt, that if he were nominated he would accept. I felt that
his inherent sense of patriotism and his dedication to duty would

produce only that kind of an answer, that he could not in good conscience turn down the nomination.

I recall that Mr. Stevenson was asked to appear at a meeting in New York at which all presidential hopefuls were to speak. Included were W. Averell Harriman, Stevenson, Senator Kerr, Senator Kefauver and Vice President Barkley. Governor Stevenson by this time had issued a forthright statement in which he said that under no circumstances would he permit his name to be presented at the convention, that he was not a candidate and did not want to be considered as a candidate.

That did not end the matter for the press and it did not end it as far as I was concerned, even though Mr. Stevenson wrote to Paul Fitzpatrick, Democratic State Chairman, saying in view of his determination not to be a candidate he felt there would be no point in his appearing on the program. Furthermore, he said his appearance might be construed as a refutation of his statement to get out of the race.

They called me in Florida, where I was staying, and pleaded with me to get Mr. Stevenson to change his mind. I thereupon called the Governor in Springfield and asked him whether he would not attend the meeting because his appearance had been advertised and his failure to participate would hurt attendance. The meeting was for the purpose of raising badly needed funds for the Democratic party, and inasmuch as he had accepted I thought he should go through with it. He agreed but later insisted that I also attend.

To my surprise, when I arrived I was seated directly behind the speaker's microphone in the second row, and I was the only one in a crowd of perhaps four or five thousand people who did not have on a dinner coat. I did not know it was a black-tie affair. The point of the story is that Stevenson and I did get together and then I learned why he wanted me there. He wanted me to meet him after the dinner to go to Mr. Harriman's home and said frankly that he hoped to procure my support of Harriman for the nomination. I told him that I would—and then the banquet started and the speaking started. Governor Stevenson was so impressive in his remarks and he so captured his audience that Harriman's speech was lame by comparison. The marked contrast between the two men that night prompted Congressman Celler to say to me after the affair, when we met in the corridor, "Jack, *you must make this man run.* It is unthinkable that any other man should be the nominee of our party at this time. He wouldn't have a chance."

When Governor Stevenson and I left the banquet hall, I told him very frankly that that evening would not be a very good time for my meeting with Harriman because I was uncertain that he could adequately or successfully represent the Democratic party at the election. Stevenson reluctantly abandoned the matter for that night.

Later, as everyone knows, the demand for Stevenson came from many sources. From all over the country leaders telephoned me to ask whether Stevenson would accept the nominations and I said, "Yes, he would—he would not ask for it, but I doubt that he would refuse to accept."

A few weeks before the convention Frank McKinney, Chairman of the Democratic National Committee, telephoned me from Washington and said that the President had explored, in view of Stevenson's reluctance, the idea of a new candidate, and asked what I thought of Vice President Barkley. Well, of course, I was in love with Mr. Barkley, for to me he was the true image of an American. If I were asked to pick a typical American, I would pick either Barkley or Harry S. Truman. By that I mean a man of plain, common stock, not highbrow, not lowbrow, not rich, not poor, but an intense patriot with a fine background. The President wanted me to ask the Governor to place the name of Barkley in nomination. Although the Governor was an ardent admirer of Barkley, indeed distantly related to him, he felt that he could not desert Harriman. However, he indicated that he would sup-

Al Howard Studio

Vice President Alben W. Barkley shakes hands with Colonel Jacob M. Arvey as AES stands by.

port Barkley with enthusiasm and vigor if he obtained the nomination.

What I want to relate now is very interesting. I believe it shows that the American people respect some people, even love them, but that they are very discerning in whom they pick for public office. Sometimes the greatest admiration in the world will not guarantee a favorable vote.

A great many delegates and leaders objected to Vice President Barkley because of his age, with the result that he withdrew his candidacy. In doing so, he made one of the most emotional speeches I have ever heard at a convention—or elsewhere. He spoke for over forty minutes in telling why he had decided to pull out. His speech was greeted with wild acclaim. Men and women cried and cheered, waved pennants, threw away their hats and became hysterical. The ovation lasted many, many minutes. This induced Les Biffle, Sergeant at Arms of the U.S. Senate, and an intimate friend of the Vice President, to formulate plans for a crash campaign to nominate Barkley. Approached on the matter and asked for my support, I replied, "No." I could have and would have been for Barkley, but inasmuch as he had withdrawn I had made plans for Stevenson's nomination and I was going to stick with that despite Stevenson's saying, "I won't take it."

When the voting commenced, the same crowd that had cheered Barkley so enthusiastically just a day or two before voted against him. They appreciated all he had done for the party, they regarded him with great affection and admiration, but they did not think he would make a suitable presidential candidate because of his age. This is a lesson in politics: sometimes you can be fooled by the applause of the crowd. It may mean affection, it may mean sympathy, it may mean genuine respect, but it does not always mean support. This is what happened to Stevenson at the 1960 convention.

To get back to the Chicago convention. After a meeting Sunday night Governor Stevenson asked me where we could go and talk for a while. This was on the eve of the opening of the convention. We came to my home about one o'clock Monday morning, and for two hours Governor Stevenson asked me to undo what had been done. I shall never forget one of his phrases. He said, "You got me into this, now please get me out. I don't want to be the nominee for President." And I recall saying to him, "Governor, this is out of your hands, this is out of my hands, and I don't know that you will nominated—but if the convention nominates you, there is nothing you can do but accept it."

I thought of this the next day when Governor Stevenson, as the governor of the host state, made a stirring welcoming speech in which he referred to Illinois as the state which had had three Democratic governors, one a Catholic, one a Jew and one a Protestant. It was a short speech, but it was in the Stevenson style and the crowd ate it up. I wondered how a man could be so insistent that he not be selected as a candidate and yet stir an audience the way he did. It was inevitable after that. There were a couple of inconclusive ballots, and then during an interval we had a dinner party in the Stockyards Inn, adjacent to the convention hall, at which the guest of honor was President Truman.

One of the ushers came to the door and told me there was a man outside asking for me. It was Paul Fitzpatrick of New York. We went into a side room and he told me that Mr. Harriman was ready to withdraw and throw his support to Mr. Stevenson. I walked back into the room where the dinner party was being held and told President Truman of the development. We invited Speaker Rayburn to join us and decided on the procedure and the timing for making it known to the audience. At the convention, Mr. Harriman withdrew and threw his support to Stevenson. Massachusetts then changed from Dever to Stevenson, and other states began changing their votes. The die was cast, and Stevenson became the nominee of the party.

Now as to the draft. There was no organized draft. If it could be called a draft, it was a spontaneous draft and it sprang up in several parts of the country, with different people and different organizations.* All I can say is, I did not discourage support for Stevenson; I just kept reiterating that he would be a candidate if he were nominated. I saw to it that as many people as possible knew of it. I do not think that the preconvention campaign cost me more than a couple of hundred dollars in telephone calls or in trips made from here to there, but it was a hit-and-miss proposition, without preparation, without organization, and had not the rank and file of the Democratic delegates at the conven-

* For a discussion of this point, see Walter Johnson, *How We Drafted Adlai Stevenson* (New York: Alfred A. Knopf, 1955).

tion wanted Stevenson, he would not, could not, have been the nominee.

He was the nominee of the 1952 Democratic Convention because the majority of the delegates wanted him to be—and even where state delegations were for their favorite sons. Many in the delegations preferred Stevenson and said so quite openly and frankly.

Once he accepted the draft, he campaigned vigorously and with distinction, but who can tell whether he ever expected victory? In the wee hours of the very morning the convention opened he had told me he considered General Eisenhower unbeatable.

First, he cited the war hero image; then, a new face on the political scene; third, the fact that the Democrats had been in power twenty years; and fourth, he feared that the party had been hurt by the tarnished image of some of President Truman's appointees.

One personal memory of the campaign will always stand out in my mind. It was the night General Eisenhower in a radio speech pledged that if elected he "would go to Korea." My reaction was intense and instinctive, and I said to Mrs. Arvey, "That's the speech that will beat us."

The ironical thing was that Governor Stevenson had long before made the same decision, that he would go to the South Korea war front and to other troubled areas of the world immediately after his election. But he believed that such an announcement by him might adversely affect the foreign policy of our country, and he refused to make public his intention.

Another memory—and this makes me smile—is of a half-serious suggestion I made to the Governor one day. It may be recalled that Vice President Barkley was one of the most loved men in public life, and his marriage to an attractive widow a year or two before increased the nation's affection for him.

"Adlai," I said, "why don't you get married? That would really give the campaign a lift."

"How could I?" he answered. "I'm not in love."

Would Adlai Stevenson have made a good President? How can one tell?

Knowing him as I did, observing him under fire, watching him make decisions in moments of tension, aware of his profound knowledge of foreign problems and conscious of his high integrity and mindful of his passionate love of peace for all men in all nations, my conclusion is that it was a great loss to the world that he was not given the opportunity to prove himself a great President and world leader. I know of no other man who was *not* President who had as much influence and commanded as much respect throughout the world.

This was the Adlai E. Stevenson I knew.

STEPHEN A. MITCHELL

Adlai's Amateurs

ADLAI STEVENSON was truly a charismatic leader. He "got through" to people, and nearly all admired him.

He had vision, idealism, courage, wit and style. As a friend he was warm, agreeable, sympathetic, convivial.

He had enormous integrity; he also was an instinctive politician who understood but did not speak the language of ward professionals.

He was enormously informed in national and world affairs, but completely naïve in such popular American areas as moving pictures and baseball. He spoke with educated eloquence, but his heart and feet were at home in the prairie farmland he loved.

He was resolute and diligent; at times he also was profoundly melancholy, even cynical. He was fastidious in taste and choice of friends, realistic about politics and politicians, and resolutely idealistic on issues.

He was an inspiring leader but a demanding taskmaster. His profession was the law, but it never seemed to have priority in

Stephen A. Mitchell divides his law practice between Chicago, where he formerly made his home, and Taos, New Mexico, where he and Mrs. Mitchell now spend most of their time. He was an early backer of Adlai Stevenson and served as Chairman of the Democratic National Committee from 1952 to 1955.

his heart. His deepest and most abiding interest was in foreign policy. He was not a proficient executive, but his personal output of work and ideas was enormous.

In short, he was an immensely complicated man, whose life was compartmented into many different levels and areas, all veiled by a basic inner reserve.

His personality had many layers, and I did not see them all. But as friend, admirer, amateur politician and early backer I had an inside view of Adlai.

In 1940 when he headed the Committee to Defend America by Aiding the Allies (William Allen White Committee) I marked him as a man of great courage. In isolationist Chicago it took great courage for a La Salle Street lawyer to fight the Chicago *Tribune*, General Robert E. Wood and other powerful isolationist forces of high business and social standing.

Looking back to 1947 when our triumvirate—Lou Kohn, Dutch Smith and Steve Mitchell—started the ball rolling that was to win him the nomination for Governor, I should have realized that he was well known to and highly regarded by a large number of Chicagoans.

When our first Stevenson-for-Senator letter went out December 3 there were seventy-nine names on it. They included Ralph Bard, William McCormick Blair, Edison Dick, Marshall Field, Jr. (Marshall IV), Meyer Kestnbaum and Samuel W. Witwer, Jr., probably more Republicans than Democrats, a good many Independents. Nearly all were influential persons. Later many others rallied to us, probably influenced by Stevenson's work for the Council on Foreign Relations and the William Allen White Committee before the war and his wartime career and postwar work in the UN and Department of State.

But in early meetings when I reminded my co-workers that we needed enrolled Democrats who could vote in the primary, Bill Blair said, "But I don't know any Democrats."

Bill got to know a great many; he was to join them shortly, and his contribution to Adlai, the Democratic party and the nation has been immense.

My friendship with Adlai developed during the war. He was variously in the Navy and State departments, and I served first in Washington and Paris in the Lend-Lease Administration and later in the State Department as adviser on French economic affairs.

In 1944 he made an impressive report to some twenty of us in the economic affairs area on his survey of Italy. We saw each other occasionally after that and Illinois politics always came up. It was obvious this was a deep-seated hereditary interest.

In 1946-47 Adlai was winding up his UN work. He was restless about the future and preparing his return to Chicago. We discussed my work in forming a new law firm. There were some indications that we might become associated in the practice of law, but politics was our common interest.

In 1947, in the improbable Republican setting of the Union League Club, Adlai first told me of the efforts of Louis A. Kohn, member of a prominent law firm, to induce him to run for Senator. I hardly knew Lou. Like Adlai and myself, he had just returned to Chicago after wartime service (in the Army). A Democrat of some personal means with a substantial income from his law firm, he was a stranger to Adlai when he began his personal campaign because of his conviction of the need for new and good political leaders. He believed that Stevenson filled the bill —a fine speaker, a supporter of the UN, and a gentleman of quality and good name who could be nominated and elected.

Adlai asked if I would work with Kohn and Hermon Dunlap (Dutch) Smith, perhaps his oldest friend in Chicago, in his behalf and I agreed very readily.

I remember noticing that day that Adlai, who habitually wore white, button-down collar shirts, wore his cuffs turned up a bit. This permitted the economy of wearing the same shirt in the evening without revealing the grime of the day. (I thought in later years this was a symbol of his only partial embrace of "politicians." When he relaxed with friends in the evening he shut out the grimy details of political activity.)

Adlai's sartorial tastes, which presumably had developed at Choate or Princeton, ran to the Brooks Brothers type of clothing long before this became popularly known as the uniform of the Ivy League. The professional Democratic politicians in those days were likely to affect wide-lapeled, double-breasted suits and white-gray hats, and they were uneasy about Adlai's button-down shirts and a beat-up slouch hat that looked like a newspaper reporter's. When the late Governor Paul Dever of Massachusetts called on me in 1952 to appraise my acceptability as National Chairman, he turned back as an afterthought to inspect my attire, saying, "O.K. You don't wear button-down shirts." He was wrong. I frequently did—and do.

After that Union League Club lunch I met with Adlai and Lou Kohn, and the Stevenson-for-Senator Committee was born.

Politicians, like presidents and soldiers, must start as novices. No matter what their experience and advance study, they must learn as they act. We were no exceptions; we all were amateurs.

We never had a chairman. Dutch Smith, a suave, literate, wealthy head of a large insurance firm, Lou Kohn and I were the first members, but Kohn was the wellspring.

He was as indispensable to the Stevenson nomination as Stevenson himself. But for his personal dedication, high purpose and stubborn persistence we others never would have had a rallying point or a candidate to sell to the Democratic Central Committee of Cook County, which runs the Illinois Democratic party.

As to the other two: Dutch Smith was a resident of exclusive Lake Forest, a Republican, with a family tradition of social service and civic interests. A Harvard man, he had been a friend of Adlai's since childhood.

Apparently I was chosen because I was interested in politics, had many friends among the Cook County party leaders although never accepted as a clubhouse Democrat; because I had been a friendly adviser to Adlai and because of my Roman Catholic religion. I enjoyed amicable relations with Cardinal Stritch, and the Catholic influence in Chicago politics is of great importance. My religious affiliation and Adlai's personal confidence were paramount in my selection six years later as Democratic National Chairman.

Actually, I did not meet Dutch Smith until November of 1947 after we announced our Stevenson-for-Senate Committee.

From then on we moved fast.

We got newspaper publicity, issued statements by prominent citizens backing our man, and we sent out a letter bearing the names of the pioneer seventy-nine members of our committee.

Paul H. Douglas had been campaigning most of the year for the Senate nomination. Stevenson's appeal as a competing candidate was brought home to me soon after we started our publicity. A Douglas aide said, "You papered the state and in no time you caught up to us."

Then we went to see Colonel Jacob M. Arvey, chairman of the Cook County Democratic Central Committee, one rainy afternoon in the Arvey law office.

He ran his eyes down the list of names on our newly printed letterhead and said, "H'mm. This is a new list. I don't remember seeing any of these names on a political committee before."

He was courteous and seemed to enjoy the novelty of our approach. He was quite willing to have us continue our efforts; what did he have to lose?

The Democrats were in deep trouble in Cook County at the time. Nationally the Truman administration was in trouble, too. Who could have expected in 1947 that President Truman would be re-elected?

In Cook County the 1946 elections had been a shattering setback. The head of the ticket, Richard J. Daley, later the highly successful Mayor of Chicago, had been defeated for sheriff; a

Republican had been elected president of the Cook County Board. The organization had lost critically in power, patronage and political "clout." In 1948 the powerful office of Cook County State's Attorney was at stake; it would be even more serious to lose this office, which can be both a political sword and a shield.

The public was chafing against postwar meat shortages and rationing, but shrewd politicians knew there was deeper resentment in Chicago because of a series of shocking murders. The twelve or fourteen ward leaders who ran the Democratic machine recognized that drastic steps must be taken. Already they had eased Mayor Edward J. Kelly out of City Hall and his party leadership, replacing him as mayor with a respected businessman, Martin H. Kennelly, in April, 1947, and making Arvey party leader.

To win the county in 1948 the leaders knew they needed another "blue ribbon" ticket, and who could fill this bill better than Adlai Stevenson, backed by "blue bloods," and Paul Douglas, a war hero college professor already well known as an independent and articulate alderman?

There is no doubt in my mind that when Colonel Arvey and his fellow slate-makers announced their ticket in January, 1948, they fully expected that Stevenson and Douglas, and President Truman as well, would lose.

They were placed at the head of the state ticket to give luster, quality, character and integrity to the entire slate and elect the county ticket. The strategy worked and contributed greatly to the election of a Democratic state's attorney (who was denied renomination four years later).

Political memories are short, as nations are ungrateful. I remember a Chicago politician saying in 1953 after Adlai had redeemed his party and won fame as Illinois' Governor and candidate for President, "We're better off losing if we can't win with one of our own."

While our campaign was gaining momentum that fall Adlai was

in and out of Chicago, still assisting the Secretary of State, General George C. Marshall. We were delighted one day when the general came to Chicago to speak on the Marshall Plan, and Adlai got wide coverage in the papers with his introduction.

The following day Kohn and I were distressed to find our candidate in one of his Hamlet moods, to which we were occasionally exposed. He seemed melancholy and uncertain about his Senate race.

"Maybe," he said, "I'd better haul off and issue a statement taking myself out of the whole thing."

I almost hit the ceiling. I heatedly told him we were doing great, his prospects were excellent, and further that he had a deep obligation to go through with his effort, first as a public duty, but also, and I made this very emphatic, to keep faith with the people who had worked hard to support him.

Adlai was vague about expressing his feelings, which may just have been a mood of discouragement, but I felt his hesitation was related to his wife's lack of sympathy toward his political career. He did not refer to her very often to me, but once he said that she had a strong jealousy of him, and it was obvious that her attitude, which eventually led her to obtain a divorce, brought him many burdens and heartaches. Anyway, he finally agreed that day that we should continue.

We held more meetings that fall with party leaders, and I suspect that Jack Arvey had very early made up his mind that the ticket would be Stevenson for Governor and Douglas for Senator. Douglas, the war hero, would be a natural to oppose the right-wing Republican C. Wayland (Curly) Brooks, who was well known for recounting the horrors of World War I, from which he had emerged wounded and bemedaled.

On the other hand, Stevenson, with a Bloomington background and experience in farm affairs and rural communities, would attract downstate votes and serve as a balance against Douglas, a university professor. Stevenson's appealing personality and humor, as much a part of him as his integrity, would also be more palatable to the professional politicians, in the unlikely event of his election, than the rather formidable austerity of Paul Douglas. Colonel Arvey deserves full credit for his 1948 decision on the ticket as well as for loyal support of Stevenson in 1952 and 1956.

But the facts are that Adlai would not have been named for Governor except for: (1) the obvious merits of Stevenson himself; (2) Lou Kohn; and (3) Democratic party troubles.

Once the slate was picked, Adlai made a brief campaign in the primary. Victory was a formality with organization backing. He proved witty and adaptable, and I could feel the good will of Democratic ward audiences going out to this man who was not one of their own. I heard one man to whom politics was both a living and a way of life say, "He's got class. We can go with him."

Going with Adlai, however, wasn't much of a commitment until late in the campaign of 1948.

From the outset Arvey and George Kells, State Chairman, made it clear we were on our own financially. Arvey did relieve us from paying the usual candidate's levy to the Cook County Committee, which would have cost us $10,000, but we paid the State Committee $2,400.

We were to operate as an independent Stevenson-for-Governor Committee and to develop support, money and publicity as best we could.

They would coordinate Stevenson's appearances with downstate caravans in the late summer and fall and would insure support from the Democratic organization in Chicago. Many times Adlai asked, in effect, "Will the Chicago leaders deliver for me?"

Looking back I realize that compared to campaigns today, which are budgeted in millions, our spending was frugal. It cost us only $135,000 to elect Stevenson, though after the election we did raise more funds (thereby hangs a tale to which I shall refer later).

Many substantial contributions were confidential, but since they were made public later in connection with the 1952 presidential campaign with permission of the donors, there is no indiscretion now in recalling a few. John Hay Whitney, later owner of the Republican New York *Herald Tribune*, was a contributor. So were Phil Wrigley, John Stuart of the Quaker Oats family, Lester Armour and Colonel Leon Mandel. Many wealthy Republicans were in our camp through personal friendship.

Marshall Field, Jr. was our largest contributor in cash. The Field family's *Sun-Times* supported us, but in those days its influence was just beginning to develop. Mr. and Mrs. Edison Dick helped financially and personally; Jane Dick in particular was an enormous help as head of the women's organization. The money given and advanced by Adlai's sister, Mrs. Ernest Ives, was indispensable, and other relatives and family friends in downstate Illinois were generous.

Marshall Field III was a devoted friend of Adlai. (In 1952 the *Sun-Times*, of which his son Marshall, Jr. had been made publisher, supported Eisenhower, to the distress of the senior Field. Presumably he could have overruled his son, but in his gentle way he limited his public expression to writing a letter to the editor, which of course occasioned much comment and attention.)

Field also made available to us our campaign manager, James Mulroy, former managing editor of the *Sun*. He had vast knowledge and contacts in the field of publicity and news channels; he was also unfailingly cheerful and tireless. He became the nerve center of the 1948 campaign.

Mulroy joined us in the early autumn, and soon hit the panic button. We weren't getting anywhere, he warned. We needed money, the campaign was ineffective, and finally he feared that Cook County workers would trade off Stevenson votes in return for support for state's attorney and other local candidates.

Mulroy may have been overstating for effect, for it was about this time that some shrewd observers began to see a chance for Adlai. Harry Barnard, the biographer of John Altgeld, who had been through Governor Henry Horner's underdog campaign in 1936, said, "Adlai's sincerity is getting through."

But Mulroy roused us to action. At Adlai's suggestion I canvassed various Democratic leaders asking them to intercede with Arvey to mobilize an aggressive campaign in Chicago for Stevenson.

One of these, Federal Judge Michael Igoe, told me as early as October 9 that our candidate could win. He put me in touch with Edward Fleming, who was knowledgeable in politics and owned a coal company and a race track. On the basis of his personal poll of certain working men's groups, Fleming judged Adlai's chances to be good. He made two substantial gifts and also disclosed he was betting large sums on Stevenson at eleven to one and on Truman at even higher odds. Adlai was so impressed that he suddenly asked Fleming to make a bet for him, and gave him his personal check for something like $1,500. Fleming laughingly told me later he made the bet with his own money, holding the check because it might have caused embarrassment to Stevenson. Adlai, he said, didn't know the way of bettors.

All Fleming asked in return was that Stevenson telephone him at his apartment on election night. Adlai kept that promise.

By this time a few other Democratic insiders in Chicago were joining the band wagon.

Former Mayor Kelly gave me a cash contribution, smaller than Fleming's, from another race-track owner, Benjamin F. Lindheimer.

The former Mayor insisted on a receipt, commenting, "Ben might think I didn't give the money to you."

Our supporters prodded Arvey, and the Colonel went to work in the last days before election, when efforts counted most. In my presence he called Congressman William Dawson, the South Side leader, who was in a distant city, asking his support. "Bill," he said, "come home. I need you."

Dick Daley, later to become Adlai's director of finances and still later Mayor of Chicago, was a strong supporter. Even Mayor

Kennelly warmed up a little from his aloof attitude. But Stevenson, Douglas and Truman were underdogs until the very end, and there were no public polls predicting even close races.

Organization funds remained hard to get. A few days before the election Colonel Arvey turned down Dutch Smith and me cold when we asked for $4,000 for radio time.

We were heartened by many last-minute developments, but we all were still wary, and probably discouraged by fatigue, as election day neared. On the last day of the campaign, November 1, I drove Stevenson home. We talked about what would happen the next day, and I said I thought the election would be close and that Adlai would win or lose by less than fifty thousand votes. Adlai refused to state a figure, but clearly he thought he would win.

His victory, of course, turned out to be overwhelming, the largest in the history of Illinois.

Adlai won by 572,067 votes. Douglas likewise had a tremendous margin, about 407,000 and Harry Truman, who didn't have a chance, carried the state by 33,612. The Chicago *Tribune,* it may be remembered, was so unprepared for this result that it carried a headline announcing the victory of Thomas E. Dewey.

But the *Tribune* was not alone.

I never in my life saw men more surprised by election results than Jack Arvey and the other leaders at headquarters on election night in November, 1948.

What elected Adlai, in my opinion, were four factors:

1. The candidate himself and his campaign.
2. The weakness of the Republican incumbent candidate, the late Dwight Green.
3. The massive and sustained support of the St. Louis *Post-Dispatch.*
4. The support of the Chicago *Daily News,* then owned by John S. Knight, and various downstate newspapers.

Adlai Stevenson made a distinguished Governor of Illinois, and

The day after his inauguration as Governor in January, 1949, with (from left) Stephen A. Mitchell, Louis Kohn, Hermon Dunlap Smith and Edward McDougal.

one of the best things he did was to raise its Supreme Court from low to high quality. A notable contribution to this was his nomination of Walter V. Schaefer, a Northwestern University law professor, to the court in 1951.

Wally Schaefer is an able and upright scholar of the law, and he was an early Stevenson supporter. I mention him at this point because the very day after Stevenson's election Schaefer, with a number of associates from the campaign, launched a project for the Governor-elect. We transformed our headquarters into a research center.

Adlai realized that none of us had any experience in government at the state level—actually at any level—and he was determined to be prepared when he went to Springfield. He sought advice, experience and ideas from every quarter. Wally Schaefer gradually took control of the research project, and he was one of those who accepted appointments when the new Governor took office. He became counsel to the Governor. The everloyal Lou Kohn was another. He was named secretary, and he loved the opportunity to help and watch.

Adlai offered me several appointments, including the plum of attorney to the public administrator, which would have brought in legal fees as high as $100,000 a year, but I was making a good living from my own law practice and preferred private life. In 1951, however, I was happy to accept when he nominated me to the nonpaying position of member of the board of the Chicago Medical Center.

Otherwise I functioned privately and informally as friend and adviser. Along with other friends I wrote opinions on various matters, visited him whenever I was in Springfield, and acted as his representative in various delicate negotiations such as the resignation of one of his appointees who had been cut in on a somewhat malodorous race-track stock deal. The appointee protested there was nothing wrong, but Adlai—I think properly— nevertheless insisted that he resign.

It is interesting to note that another of those who received this stock, Paul Powell, was a Democratic power in the legislature at that time. He remained in state office and some years later was elected Secretary of State of Illinois!

I recall with strong feeling even now that Powell refused to support Stevenson for the presidential nomination in 1956, but that didn't stop him from prominently displaying himself at Adlai's funeral services at Bloomington as well as at Springfield. I wish I could have heard the Governor's comment on that.

As Governor, Stevenson revealed facets that may have surprised many people. I have said that politics was in his blood. He had campaigned independently, and on a high plane of idealism, but he proved a realistic administrator and politician. He recognized that practical politics required organization, clubhouses, jobs and money.

But Illinois soon learned it had an independent Governor who was running for re-election. His decisions and appointments brought a high moral tone to the capital. Many Republicans and Independents accepted his call to state service. His party's leaders were disappointed by lack of patronage.

Governors as well as candidates nearly always have trouble about money, whether it be campaign funds, expense accounts or state budgets. In spite of Biblical dicta, it is not necessarily the "love of money" but the shortage thereof that causes the trouble.

After the 1948 campaign our first hasty audit indicated we had a deficit, and we welcomed a number of "late contributions" which poured in in the wake of victory—and declined quite a few, too. With these we were able to repay certain loans and out-of-pocket expenses (Adlai, his sister and Lou Kohn got back some $15,000), and we found ourselves with an eventual surplus of about $23,000.

I proposed that this fund be held and disbursed at the Governor's discretion. Adlai was beginning to realize the problem of getting quality talent at the low state salary level, and this situation was in our minds. To carry out the plan, I developed the idea of Gifts for Illinois, Inc., a charitable corporation with a board of estimable citizens who would receive and pay out the funds as additional compensation to certain state employees on the Governor's recommendation. The Internal Revenue Service ruled that contributions to Gifts for Illinois, Inc. would be tax-deductible only if the state legislature approved the procedure. This would create a political problem for the new Governor with a jealous state legislature, and a decision against "action this session" was reached by the Governor, counsel Walter Schaefer and me in June, 1949. The Governor did use the surplus campaign fund to supplement salaries for certain aides, and it was enlarged with gifts from old friends and trusted supporters such as myself, whose sources and purposes were clear and above suspicion.

After the revelation of the "Nixon Fund" which provoked the famous "Checkers" speech and came close to forcing Richard M. Nixon off the GOP ticket, the Republican counterthrust was aimed at this "Stevenson Fund," as the Gifts for Illinois became known. I personally was sorry it had not been revealed publicly several years before.

The Stevenson "draft" of 1952 is discussed in many sections of this book by his friends. From early March until the convention I saw his struggle only from a distance but in sharp relief. He really wanted to be re-elected Governor of Illinois, but I did not expect things would turn out that way.

In January, 1952, the Governor asked me to join a meeting in his Chicago office to "establish a planning group to organize an independent campaign committee" for his renomination and re-election as Governor. President Truman at that time was believed still a probable candidate for re-election. He soon took himself out of the race, however, and the national spotlight focused on Stevenson for President. But we went ahead with the Governor committee, hired a manager and rented offices.

In February of that year I was offered the post of counsel to the Chelf Committee, which had been created by the House of Representatives to investigate the U.S. Department of Justice. The circumstances compelled me to accept.

Even though many loyal Democrats could not bring themselves to admit it, there *was* a mess in Washington at that time. The Department of Justice stood charged as a malefactor and conspirator with the Internal Revenue Bureau. I was urged by wise and trusted friends in extremely high places to take the counsel's job and help the cleanup. Several officeholders in the department were later removed from office by President Truman, and his new Attorney General, James McGranery, redeemed the department by far-reaching changes that were accepted and carried forward by his Republican successor, Herbert Brownell.

I did go to Washington but first resigned from the new committee for Stevenson's re-election.

We were in frequent contact that spring and summer about the pressures on him to seek the nomination for President, and we agreed on the position he took. When the crisis approached in mid-July, after talks with George Ball and Dutch Smith, and a long phone conversation with Adlai in Springfield, I leaked a story to Arthur Krock of the *New York Times,* then in Chicago, for the convention, as to Adlai's actual state of mind. This led the paper's political correspondent, Jim Haggerty, Sr., to write a story prominently displayed on page one in which on the authority of two of the Governor's friends (unnamed) the paper said Adlai could be drafted.

When I read parts of the story to Dutch Smith from Washington, he quipped, "Who's been reading my mind?"

By Friday, July 25, the day of the balloting at the Democratic convention, the nomination was certain. The Governor spent the early evening working on his acceptance speech with Carl McGowan, and I saw him for the first time that week. We had snatches of conversation and he indicated Senator Sparkman would be his choice for Vice President.

After his nomination I did not see the Governor. I passed the word through Dutch Smith that I was very willing to do anything I could to help.

By Monday I was back in my Chelf Committee office and, aware that my activities were viewed dimly by certain Democratic party leaders, as well as by the Republican members of the Chelf Committee, I did not expect to take an active part in Adlai's campaign.

But on Friday, August 1, Adlai telephoned. For a moment I did not recognize his voice and I remember his saying, "It's Adlai, the candidate."

He went on to discuss the national chairmanship, mentioning several persons who might succeed Frank McKinney. He felt he must replace McKinney to dissociate himself from past party leadership so that (a) he could not be in the shadow of someone else and (b) the party machinery would have a new look. He mentioned he had chosen Wilson Wyatt as "personal manager," and the new National Chairman would head the "quartermaster corps" to supply money and campaign materials and maintain contact with the party leaders.

Dropping names of possible candidates as he went on, he said he wished to continue the recent Democratic tradition of having an Irish Roman Catholic as chairman, he wanted to make sure the wounds of the convention were healed, and he finally said he wanted an independent man of close ties with old party leaders who was also "close to me."

Stephen A. Mitchell, Senator John Sparkman and AES.
Allen Grant, Life Magazine © *Time Inc.*

"I want you," he finally said.

All my immediate impulses except friendship and loyalty to him were to refuse. I told him I had little experience, that certain professional politicians wouldn't want me. He assured me he hadn't consulted them, and indeed I don't know that he had consulted anyone. I urged John M. Bailey (now Chairman by selection of Presidents Kennedy and Johnson) as a better choice on his record, but he said, "I don't know him. I must have someone I trust." I asked him when he had first thought of appointing me and he replied, "While I was on my pillow after the acceptance speech." This meant he had been agonizing over the matter for a week and had settled on his original choice.

After getting my wife's reluctant consent and clearing with my law partners, I sought advice from my politically wise friend, Monsignor John Fitzgerald, secretary to Cardinal Stritch, and got strong approval from Congressman Frank Chelf, with whom I had been in close harmony on his committee's operations. I was able to call Adlai in a few hours and accepted with only one condition, that I wanted him to "butter up Evelyn [Mrs. Mitchell]" because she did not like the idea of my being a "professional politician."

He laughingly answered, "You'd better get to be a professional in a hurry, and tell her that if the job was good enough for Cordell Hull, it is good enough for you."

The appointment was kept secret while insiders were being sounded out, and I got the word that President Truman was "negative" about me. I was an amateur, of course, and also was counsel for the Chelf Committee that was investigating one of his departments.

Like any losing campaign, that of the Democrats in 1952 produced a certain amount of acrimony on the losing side. President Truman in his memoirs some years later indicted our leadership on several counts and Governor Stevenson loyally defended his associates. This is not the place for me to recount the campaign in detail.

Wilson Wyatt was to manage Adlai, and he did so ably. I was to coordinate the campaign from Washington, and the Governor was to operate from his Springfield base. There was no friction between us; we became close friends and still are.

In retrospect, I think no candidate could have defeated General Eisenhower that year. In the state of the nation in 1952 there was great demand for a change, and a change to so magnetic a national hero as Ike was irresistible.

Adlai Stevenson recognized Ike's appeal and he knew what he was up against. I think it is greatly to Stevenson's credit that even though he did realize it he never for a moment shrank from the fight once he had been nominated. He made a distinguished campaign and made a personal impression on his countrymen and the world that will never be forgotten. And he changed the Democratic party to his image and paved the way for the election of Kennedy and Johnson in 1960. Without Stevenson as our spokesman and symbol from 1952 to 1960, the Democrats would still be out of the White House.

I remember thinking: we should have had two elections, one in which the voters could have indulged their hero worship for Ike and vented their spleen against the Truman administration, and another in which they could have voted for Stevenson and themselves.

My contacts with the candidate were sporadic during the campaign. He was on the hustings and I was in Washington.

But defeat brought us together.

The day after election the Democratic National Committee was beaten, busted and benighted.

Our campaign deficit was estimated at $830,000; we had a large staff on the payroll, and had taken a fearful beating. Even Goldwater in 1964 was better off—he had money in the bank.

My agreement with Adlai was to stay through election day,

or "maybe through Inauguration Day." But as I sat in my Washington office in an atmosphere of combined gloom and shock, it became clear that things were not that simple.

Somebody would have to pay off our debt, someone would have to start rebuilding the party after its first national defeat since 1928. Who could lead this effort better than Adlai Stevenson? He was our greatest asset. The late Sam Rayburn, who had then been reduced to Minority Leader of the House, was among the first to see this and supported Stevenson strongly. Senator Lyndon B. Johnson took little interest in the National Committee at that time. He, like Senator Robert Taft in an earlier and similar situation, looked on Congress as the base for rebuilding the national party. So he moved quickly to insure his election as Minority Leader of the Senate. I recall he telephoned me to make sure the National Committee would not take sides in the Senate leadership contest—and that Senator Estes Kefauver, his opponent, telephoned three days later asking for help.

This was my first proposal to Adlai after the election. I would stay as National Chairman, I promised, if he would continue as national leader.

He consented at once, and he never, it seems to me, gave a finer demonstration of his principles of responsibility as a citizen. He felt it was his duty in defeat to carry on in the party leadership he would have exercised in victory. Without hesitation he was ready to launch a new campaign—to rebuild the party.

We lost no time. He addressed a fund-raising dinner in New York City on February 14, 1953, and I made the first of many trips to the Democratic South in December, 1952. And we recruited Katie Louchheim, who later became vice-chairman of the committee and one of the chief factors in our success.

One of Adlai's first steps was a formal visit to Washington on February 15, 1953, as early as a decent interval after the inauguration of President Eisenhower would permit.

The visit was triumphal. We staged meetings with all Democratic leaders and receptions for party faithful and their wives. People of all kinds lined up for blocks waiting to shake the Governor's hand. I can think of no sharper contrast to this outpouring of affection and respect to a defeated leader than the acrimony and venom which overtook the Republican party after the defeat of Barry Goldwater in 1964. Stevenson's popularity was undiminished by defeat. He was enthusiastically saluted, and all could see he would be the key to our financial and political recovery.

Soon after, the Governor left on a trip around the world. Before he returned I was able to send him a report dated May 28, 1953, saying the standing of the Democratic party with the public at large was improving and "Your own standing in the country generally as well as in the Party is higher than at the time of the election," I wrote, ". . . the respect and confidence that people have in you is growing."

In September, 1953, the Democratic party had a national meeting in Chicago—a "Tribute to Stevenson" lasting two days (one dinner for the "Regulars" and one for "Adlai's Amateurs"). Throughout the balance of 1953 and 1954 Adlai's efforts were gratifyingly fruitful. He made numerous appearances at party meetings at which any fee less than $100 per plate for dinner was considered niggardly. His speeches were masterly and influential, and the money rolled in.

Many prominent Democrats of today were not too cooperative in those hard days or were entirely unknown to me. Mr. Joseph P. Kennedy told me in 1954 in a phone call from Hyannis Port, "I am not going to give you any more money." In 1952 he and other members of the Kennedy family had been substantial contributors, and when I reported their gifts to Adlai, he said he hoped I hadn't made any promises to Mr. Kennedy, that "He wants to be Secretary of the Treasury."

The party regained self-confidence and unity and in November, 1954, Democratic candidates regained control of the House and Senate and in nine state capitals. "Mr. Sam" Rayburn again became Speaker of the House and Senator Lyndon Johnson Senate Majority Leader.

At a Victory Dinner in New Orleans in December, 1954, Adlai, clearly the party's hero, tacitly laid down his party leadership to resume his private life. My resignation as National Chairman was accepted, and for the first time in memory the members of the National Committee made their own choice for National Chairman—Paul M. Butler—instead of rubber-stamping the nominee of a presidential candidate or accepting the dictation of a few big-city leaders.

Adlai flatly refused to take any part in the jockeying for a new chairman, and I am sure former Governor David Lawrence of Pennsylvania, Carmine DeSapio, former party leader of New York, and Colonel Arvey could never understand or forgive my refusal to "pass the word" for the election of their choice for national chairman—the late Jim Finnegan (who became Adlai's campaign manager in 1956).

Back in Chicago to pick up the pieces of my neglected law practice, I enjoyed a lull from politics. But it didn't last long. I doubt that Adlai ever had a respite, even on his tours abroad. It was truly said, "If we could count the foreign vote, Adlai would have been elected." I went around the world for the State Department in 1965 and found that Stevenson's name was known hardly less than "Kennedy" and more than "Johnson." Several times I was introduced to audiences as "Mr. Stevenson."

Early in 1955 a "Stevenson Steering Committee" was set up, and many of the practices we developed in earlier years were adopted. A separate bookkeeping account was established on the records of my law firm, with a separate bank account. I had followed this practice scrupulously in the past in financing Stevenson operations and always had complete records as answers to any questions raised by critics. Adlai wanted things done that way. He was insistent that all money matters be handled with honesty, economy and a full record.

The 1956 steering committee organizers were Wilson Wyatt, Hy Raskin, former deputy chairman of the National Committee and an experienced professional, Bill Blair and I. (In 1958, with Adlai's specific blessing, Hy Raskin joined Senator John F. Kennedy's inner circle which planned and carried out his capture of the Democratic nomination for President in 1960.) Our work was separate from, but vaguely coordinated with, several brain trust groups directed by Thomas K. Finletter and Arthur M. Schlesinger, Jr., which were preparing position papers for Stevenson. Our committee was confidential and our purpose was to prepare the way for a Stevenson nomination in 1956 and for the campaign of that year. Between June of 1955 and November, when the Governor announced he would be a candidate for the presidency in 1956, we collected some $50,000 and made good use of it in promoting Adlai's second nomination, which was won easily.

Soon after the candidate's announcement the "Volunteers for Stevenson" were formally organized and took over the office space and functions of our steering committee. My wife was vice-chairman of the Illinois section of the women's committee, and a good one. Her committee organized the ladies who sold those lapel pins in the shape of a shoe with a hole in the sole.

It is a footnote to history that in the autumn of 1955 one of the problems facing us was the rival aspiration of Lyndon B. Johnson to the presidency.

At this time Johnson was still recovering from his heart attack suffered in July, 1955, but I wrote to Stevenson (October 24, 1955) that the Senator was "disregarding his own health and is so intent on his own plans that if he should run and die the day after election he would justify that for, as one of his friends says: 'Lyndon seems to feel that if he is not going to be president why should he live?' "

In retrospect the situation is academic, but the files reveal that we took the matter very seriously for some time. Sam Rayburn, a Stevenson supporter, was embarrassed by the situation for, as he put it, his fellow Texan's move "put him in a bind."

Long before convention time the following year the Johnson presidential ambitions had been eased to the shelf for a few years, although the Texas delegation in 1956 wore yellow streamers saying, "Love that Lyndon." Finally, he and Mr. Sam went along with Adlai.

The 1956 convention and campaign are covered in other articles. Wilson Wyatt and I were "advisers." These scattered items may help fill out the picture.

In August, 1955, there was a conference of state governors at Chicago with many important national personalities and issues on the agenda. Stevenson was then living quietly at Libertyville and commuting to his office in Chicago. He dominated the news, however, and the activities of the governors' conference, and the papers were full of visits made by various Democratic governors to the Stevenson home. His personality and the coming 1956 presidential race overshadowed the conference; this was indicated by the attendance of nearly all the national news writers and TV-radio commentators at a dinner in honor of Adlai which I gave after a news conference. The news coverage of it established Stevenson as the leading Democratic political personality in the nation in spite of his hard defeat in 1952 and his lack of any official position or organization.

There were two crises in the 1956 convention, one generated by the now notorious Governor, George Wallace of Alabama. He was then a state judge and member of the state delegation to the convention. He seized on a TV statement by Stevenson to denounce Stevenson's position on the civil rights plank, which had been hammered out with great effort before the convention by party leaders from all parts of the country. Wallace waved "the bloody shirt" of white supremacy and was clearly determined to fight for political recognition on the race issue. The second crisis came in a clash between Speaker Rayburn, who was chairman of the convention, and Stevenson regarding the latter's proposal to throw the convention open for the free choice of a vice presidential candidate.

Stevenson went before the convention over Mr. Sam's vehement protest and declared "hands off" in the race for the vice presidential nomination. The close, tense race between Senator Kefauver and Senator John F. Kennedy, and the all-night maneuverings before it, brought Senator Kennedy and many Southern politicians together as comrades and had a good deal to do with his capture of the nomination for President four years later.

Perhaps Stevenson's greatest personal trial and political danger in the 1956 campaign came in the spring when Senator Kefauver beat him badly in the Minnesota primary. I had been concerned by many reports that Stevenson was too diffident and remote from party people during his primary campaigns. Charlie Bartlett, an astute observer and Pulitzer Prize winner, told me before the Minnesota primary that Kefauver would win largely because of his earthy, friendly manner and close contact with crowds and because Stevenson's handlers were keeping him away and apart from the party faithful. After the Minnesota defeat I wrote the stark facts as I saw them to Adlai in a memorandum March 22, 1956, saying:

"Your campaign has been badly damaged and your dominant position in the race is precarious . . . you are failing to communicate to the average person. . . . People don't want to admire you from afar—they want to know you. . . . Your speeches are not selling Stevenson as a human being. . . . You can win." I told him he must win in Florida by a good margin in order to avoid defeat in California, and he could win in Florida only if he would "give the voters . . . a true clear picture of the man you are."

I don't recall any personal reaction from the candidate. But he must have decided that he had to "go out and extravert," and he did in fact throw off his reserve and his coat and went to the people of Florida with a handshaking, folksy campaign, won the primary and broke Kefauver's prospects. Here, as in other trials, Stevenson showed his gameness, the deep competitive urge that lay beneath the surface, and the physical endurance and mental toughness that made him the fighting campaigner he could be when he thought it necessary.

In late October Stevenson insisted upon pushing the control of nuclear weapons as a campaign issue. To my mind this was the only example of the criticism that "Stevenson talks over the heads of the people." I don't think most of us knew what he was talking about and the dreadful importance of the issue, but the opposition did know how to add to the confusion and cast Stevenson as a visionary, impractical "no-winner." The "nuclear weapons issue" helped lose the 1956 election, but Stevenson's courageous stand paved the way for the nuclear test ban treaty which was a crowning achievement of the Kennedy administration.

After the election of President Kennedy, Stevenson went to the limit of his persuasive ability to bring recognition and high office to many men and women who had worked with him. I know of no case in which he failed or refused such a request for his help, and I do know he tried his level best to encourage my appointment to the Federal Bench.

Our visits were infrequent in later years because of the heavy UN burdens he carried in New York and my change of residence to New Mexico. But I recall the tingle that went down my back one day as I walked in the town plaza of Taos and heard that unmistakable voice coming out to the sidewalk from a radio set in denunciation of the Soviet record as Stevenson marshaled the facts before the United Nations in October, 1961.

During the 1964 Democratic Convention at Atlantic City it was typically thoughtful of Adlai to invite my son and me to join with his family and other friends for a luncheon. He was ever warm, compassionate and deeply touched by acts of loyalty to him, although he was not given to extravagant praise or effusive thanks. It is enough for me that he said to me during the end of our struggles in 1954, "You are doing a good job and a lot of the credit is rubbing off on me." I knew then and know now it was the other way around.

As I look back now over seventeen years of political association and friendship, my eyes turn toward a silver cigarette box on my desk. He sent it to me as a Christmas present in 1952, just after the bitter defeat of November. I wrote him a note of thanks and in it said: "I am most appreciative of your gift, not only for myself, but for my heirs, who will know by it that their ancestor was associated with a great and good man." So he was.

J. EDWARD DAY

Pictures on the Wall

FROM TIME IMMEMORIAL it had been customary in Illinois for every state appointee, high and low, to have a picture of the current governor prominently displayed on the wall of his office.

There is nothing unusual about this. It is done at all levels of government, even in the big federal departments. The pictures are as much standard equipment as crucifixes on the walls of Catholic schools.

When Adlai Stevenson took office as Governor, he promptly passed the word that he preferred not to see his face on display in every state office he entered.

In part this was modesty; in part it was his deeply ingrained aversion to the trite and the stereotyped. But most of all it was a symbol of his devotion to forthrightness—of his revulsion against the gimmicks and claptrap which are supposed to be standard operating procedure in the world of politics.

J. Edward Day was associated with Adlai Stevenson in law practice in the Chicago firm of Sidley, Austin, Burgess and Smith, whose Washington office Mr. Day now heads. He was a member of Governor Stevenson's Cabinet as Director of Insurance and was President Kennedy's Postmaster General.

93

It has often been observed that Adlai Stevenson made politics respectable. He gave a lifetime interest in politics and government to hundreds of thousands of fine people who had always before scorned politicians.

Many of those people are or have been among our most distinguished public servants. But for every one who ran for or was appointed to office there were thousands who just continued to go about their usual business, but with a new conviction that truth and politics did not necessarily have to be incompatible.

I am convinced that the great majority of Americans are always vaguely groping for frank and fair and forthright leadership, never really giving up no matter how often they are disappointed. In Illinois in 1948 the voters sensed they would find that kind of leadership in Stevenson, and they gave him the greatest majority any candidate for governor there had ever received. He ran more than 500,000 votes ahead of the party's candidate for President, Harry Truman.

I emphasize Stevenson's forthrightness and unwillingness to hedge on integrity because it is a trait that transcends ideology. Too many subscribe to the pernicious view that the end justifies the means, and that it does no harm to slant and shade the truth if it is supposedly for a good cause.

Stevenson could, in 1949, have ducked giving the deposition attesting to the reputation of Alger Hiss for integrity, loyalty and veracity. It plagued him endlessly in his later campaigns. The circumstances surrounding it were misrepresented and misinterpreted.

I thought at the time he made a mistake to give it. He was not obligated to Hiss by close ties of friendship. But long ago I realized Stevenson's insistence on going ahead with the deposition was another proof of his special quality. Later he said of his decision: "I think it will be a very unhappy day for Anglo-Saxon justice when a man in public life is too timid to state what he knows or has heard about a defendant in a criminal case for fear that defendant would be ultimately convicted. That is the ultimate timidity."

As head of the state insurance department I was in an especially advantageous position to observe Stevenson's no-compromise honesty. At times, before his administration and after, the insurance department was a political and financial playground where money and influence bought official decisions. The insurance department's exercise of its power to grant licenses for small-loan offices has in more than one administration been particularly suspect.

Not only did the tradition and potential make the insurance department a sensitive responsibility, but the numerous rough-and-tumble operators in the Illinois insurance industry were ready to try anything to get their way.

The circumstances of my appointment as head of the insurance department illustrate Stevenson's concern with independent, non-political performance rather than mere politics and patronage in making his choices for top state positions.

Insurance is unique among major businesses in that, although it is highly regulated, it is, by act of Congress, almost totally exempt from supervision by the federal government. This means that regulation at the state level is not only extensive but is particularly vital for the protection of the public interest.

This is especially true in Illinois, which is the home-office state for many very large and some very controversial insurance companies. More insurance companies are licensed to do business in Illinois than in any other state but Texas. Illinois has had more than its share of bad actors and scandals in the insurance industry. As in any state, there are many factions and antagonisms within the insurance industry: stock companies vs. mutual companies, "bureau companies" vs. companies charging their own independent rates, etc.

In the early summer of 1950, when I was working at the Mansion as a legal and legislative assistant to the Governor, he and my wife and I went to his home town of Bloomington, sixty miles north, for a small dinner party at the home of the Governor's sister and brother-in-law, Mr. and Mrs. Ernest Ives. Among the guests was the president of the giant State Farm Insurance group of companies, a man with the same first name as the Governor, Adlai Rust. I had never met him before.

In the course of the conversation the Governor disclosed some information that was entirely new to me even though I was close to most important things going on in the administration. Stevenson said Harry Hershey was resigning as head of the state insurance department to run for the Illinois Supreme Court, and he asked Rust how he could find a man who knew insurance to take his place.

Rust replied: Don't try to find a man who knows insurance. Find a smart young lawyer who has no ties to the insurance industry and who isn't allied with any of its factions.

Stevenson rode back to Springfield that night with Mrs. Day and me in our Dodge. Before we left Bloomington we stopped at the home of one of his relatives and picked up an oil painting of some member of the clan which he wanted to hang in the Mansion in Springfield.

As we drove along toward Springfield with the Governor and the portrait in the back seat I said, "That man Mr. Rust described as the best kind for insurance director sounds like me."

Shortly after that I was appointed.

My predecessor had once been the Democratic candidate for Governor. My successor was the brother of the Attorney General. But I had no political connections and practically no political background. I had been, since my graduation from Harvard Law School in 1938, an associate in the substantial Chicago law firm in which Stevenson was a partner up until 1941 and with which he resumed a connection for about a year after World War II. I had worked with him on a few legal matters, had become acquainted with him socially and, of course, supported him in his campaign for Governor.

My appointment to his cabinet didn't bring one new vote to the party. What is more, I was notably independent-minded and the Governor knew I would—and expected me to—call the shots as I saw them in running the department.

When, as Director of Insurance, I proved to be an aggressive and unyielding stickler for decency, a few of the rough boys hurried to the Governor's office to try to get him to slow me down. But it did them no good. He refused to intervene and they soon gave up.

The number of small-loan licenses granted dropped to a modest figure despite the advice of some politicians that every new license could be good for a hefty contribution to the party.

I don't want to indicate that the job of Director of Insurance was exactly a plum. In 1950 cabinet members (called "Directors") in Illinois were paid $8,000 a year. This was not too surprising considering that the Governor's salary was only $12,000.

The incredibly low-level salaries for state executive posts serve to highlight the problem Stevenson had in attracting good people for full-time positions, particularly if they had to move to Springfield. It also may explain in part why some Stevenson appointees let him down badly by succumbing to financial temptation and causing the scandals involving horse meat and race-track stock.

These unrealistic salaries caused Stevenson to seek some means of supplementing the pay of some of his top officials. Typically, he talked frankly and forthrightly about the problem and about his effort to alleviate it. A bitter Republican partisan who heard the Governor during a dinner table conversation describe his procedure of paying money from unexpended campaign funds to certain state officials released the story during the 1952 presidential campaign. By putting the worst possible interpretation on this "Stevenson Fund" the man succeeded in starting a furor intended to dilute the "Nixon Fund" charges some Democrats were making at the time.

While the "Stevenson Fund" was receiving intense press attention, Stevenson announced he would release his federal income tax returns for several years back. Ernest Ives and I were assigned the task of locating the returns in Stevenson's inactive files and making them public. Nothing was held back.

The names of the donors to the campaign contribution were also released. This revealed that whereas I had received $2,000 *from* the fund my father-in-law had given $2,000 to it.

I remember during that 1952 campaign a special instance of Stevenson's deeply ingrained tendency to economize to the point of penny-pinching. He had always gone about the Mansion turning off unneeded lights with a vengeance, and he used a state limousine that dated back to the pre-World War II days of Governor Henry Horner. In 1952, since he felt that his first duty, even during the presidential campaign, was to continue on the job as Governor of Illinois, he decided his national campaign headquarters would be in Springfield. I went out on short notice and rented a residence, suitable for office use, near the Mansion. It had perhaps ten or twelve rooms and the rent was reasonable. But when he saw it Stevenson said we could save money by setting up beds and having some of the campaign leaders sleep in this house. Needless to say, with the shortage of working space that soon developed, this idea was never carried out.

It was particularly irksome to Stevenson, tightfisted as he was, to be constantly attacked by the Chicago *Tribune* for allegedly wasteful spending as Governor.

The vitriolic approach by the *Tribune* toward his administration is hard to exaggerate. The *Tribune* reporter who dealt most with the Governor's office had, as it happened, been one of my intimate public school and church school friends while each of us was growing up in Springfield. But because I was working for Stevenson this man never uttered one friendly word to me from the time I returned to our home town in 1949 to be on the Governor's staff. He even resigned later from the First Presbyterian church in Springfield where both of us had been active in young people's work, because the minister, Richard Paul Graebel, became such an outspoken admirer of Stevenson.

Even after I moved from the Governor's personal staff to his official cabinet, I continued to attend the meetings of his kitchen cabinet as well as the meetings of the department heads, the latter much less frequent and almost always held in the evening. The discussions of both groups were free-wheeling and down to earth. At the staff meetings in 1952 I was one of those who strongly urged the Governor to make a strong and open bid for the presidential nomination.

Stevenson's friends and foes alike, for thirteen years, have tried to live his political life over again by speculating endlessly on what might have been.

The common refrain has been that he should have saved himself for another, more favorable election day by refusing to run for President in 1952. This approach goes on to say that he should have run for Governor again.

I have always had several arguments with this theory.

For one thing, I am not at all sure he could have been re-elected as Governor in 1952. True, he had had an excellent record as Governor. But in a presidential year straight-ticket voting is a powerful factor. Without Stevenson at the top of the Democratic ticket in 1952, the Eisenhower landslide, in my opinion, would have been so shattering that the same thing would have happened in Illinois to an excellent incumbent Democratic Governor seeking re-election that happened in New York in 1964, as a result of the monumental Johnson landslide, to an excellent incumbent Republican Senator seeking re-election.

To estimate objectively what the Eisenhower landslide might have been in 1952 without Stevenson as his opponent, one must take the further step of supposing who the Democratic nominee would then have been. Elections are not decided in a vacuum but by a choice of alternatives. Truman's choice, when he thought Stevenson could not be persuaded to run, was Alben Barkley, who was seventy-five years old and lacked the support of labor. Others who sought the nomination included Senators Kerr, Kefauver and Russell.

Any other Democratic candidate than Stevenson would, in my belief, have been a very weak alternative indeed—such a drag on the ticket, in fact, that no state-wide candidate on the Democratic ticket in Illinois, not even Stevenson, could have pulled through.

Despite Eisenhower's incredible popular appeal, Stevenson ran such a respectable race that he saved many a candidate at the courthouse, state and Congressional level from being defeated. Nothing happened to Democratic local tickets in 1952 comparable to what happened to Republican local tickets in 1964, when voters turned out in droves to vote *against* the Republican presidential candidate.

The Democratic party incurred a mammoth debt to Adlai Stevenson in 1952 for saving their state and local officeholder strength from wreckage.

In 1956 Stevenson had to run. I say this not just for the usual reasons that he was again by far the strongest candidate the Democrats had or because he "owed" it to his party to be a sacrificial offering in their time of desperation. I say it because he had to be true to his devotion to forthrightness and to "talking sense." To him the Eisenhower performance was an infuriating exercise in Madison Avenue gimmickery. Stevenson had to speak up against what to him was drift and blandness. In 1956 he was not a reluctant candidate.

To suggest that he should have sat back, refusing to run, hoping to get the nod in 1960, is to ask that Stevenson should have been something he wasn't: cunning, contriving and highly adjustable in his convictions.

The 1956 battle was by no means in vain. Many of the great issues Stevenson pressed became the pattern for the bold steps of the 1960's. The test-ban treaty is but one example.

Those who say Stevenson should have saved himself for 1960 never tell us how he would have kept himself in the public eye all those eight years so as to have been able to prevail against the Kennedy onslaught.

I prefer to think that Stevenson lived his career to its fullest potential. I see no point in letting wishful thinking prevail in second-guessing his choices.

If Stevenson had been twice the man he was, he still could not have won against the military-hero, time-for-a-change combination. So how futile it has been to speculate so often that he didn't win because he was "indecisive," because he was "too funny," because of his divorce and all the rest.

AES with Mr. and Mrs. J. Edward Day at their vacation home in 1950.

I am convinced that if he had been elected he would have been an effective President. He would have brought an excellent group of men into his administration just as Kennedy did. He would have been imaginative, idealistic, conscientious and decisive just as he was as Governor.

Stevenson was modest and self-deprecating, as his honesty and his sense of humor required him to be. But he was ambitious. He wanted to be Governor. He wanted to be President. He no doubt wanted to be Secretary of State.

Stevenson was warm and kind.

He knew my children as toddlers, ages six, two and six months, when I moved to Springfield in 1949 to be on his personal staff and later to be a member of his cabinet.

Many men, particularly in politics, ask "How are your children?" as a standard conversational gambit. Often as not they don't even listen to the answer. Stevenson not only listened; he always, through sixteen years, remembered my children's names and whereabouts, and by his follow-up questions showed he was interested in their doings.

Adlai Stevenson was genuine in his devotion to his friends and in his interest in people.

His staff parties at the Governor's Mansion in Springfield were not just stiff, routine exercises in dutiful hospitality. The guests included his chauffeur, his housekeeper and his secretaries, plus members of his family and of his official staff. Adlai joined with the assorted guests standing around the piano singing old favorites. Relaxed informality prevailed.

Each year, beginning in 1950, a group of Stevenson's closest friends put on a relaxed, happy birthday party for him with songs, poems and humorous performances. For the 1950 party I had written lyrics to the tune of the *South Pacific* song, "A Wonderful Guy." We all sang it that year and at many later birthday parties, including the last one, at the River Club in New York, in February, 1965. The words were as follows: *

> He's as honest as Abraham Lincoln;
> He's a man no money can buy.
> He has a heart but, to boot, he is smart;
> The Gov is a wonderful guy.
>
> Political hacks are now in a dither,
> With a patronage light in their eye,
> But you will note there's a lump in their throat
> When they speak of that wonderful guy.

---

* *Based on* A Wonderful Guy, *copyright* © *1949 by Richard Rodgers and Oscar Hammerstein II. Used by permission of Williamson Music, Inc.*

> The Senate they gave him was really a daisy,
> A bit to the left of Marie Antoinette.
> The Senate's idea of good legislation
> Was—how shall we say it?—all wet!
>
> The Gov is as honest as Abraham Lincoln;
> Even Republicans hold his name high.
> We acknowledge his worth on the day of his birth;
> He's our Gov, he's our Gov, he's our Gov,
> He's our Gov, he's our Gov,
> He's a wonderful guy!

As his fame grew, from his performance as Governor and his skill as a speaker, glamorous people from the great world—the pundits and the international experts and the liberal rich—sought his company and his time. But he always seemed to prefer his old Illinois friends.

Stevenson was considerate. But by that I do not mean that he was never irritable or edgy, because he was. He craved time alone to collect his thoughts, to concentrate on his paper work and, most of all, to write or polish his speeches. But the fate of every executive and of every candidate is to live from interruption to interruption. In his absorption with trying to do his office work well, Stevenson often forgot, as most men will, that his secretary was not a machine. But he never postured or pontificated or acted self-important. He just wanted to do so much so well, and there weren't enough hours to do it in and to stay rested too.

His warmth was not the hail-fellow-well-met variety of the gregarious office seeker. His was the warmth of a man sincere in his regard for others, regarding them never as pawns to be manipulated for his gain but as humans deserving of his thoughtfulness.

To my knowledge, every person who was ever once his friend remained his friend.

The same cannot be said for many men.

In 1960 at his Town House Hotel suite during the Democratic Convention at Los Angeles, I was made to feel welcome each evening when the Stevenson insiders gathered, even though I was a firmly committed Kennedy delegate. (Arthur Schlesinger, Jr. was similarly included easily and warmly in those nightly gatherings even though he too was committed to Kennedy.) By convention time Stevenson vaguely hoped that lightning would strike again and that the nomination would come to him again. But I had made my decision for Kennedy the previous February when Stevenson told me he would not be a candidate and when he even urged me to persuade his friends to stop talking about his running again.

Timing is everything. For Stevenson the timing was not right, and nothing could make it right. But we have had many American greats who were never President. And we have had many Presidents who were far from great.

His ultimate legacy is not his list of accomplishments or the issues he voiced or the eloquence with which he voiced them. His legacy is the reassurance it gives idealists to know a public figure can indeed talk sense to the people and thereby achieve a special place in history.

WILSON W. WYATT

What I Think
Is Still What I Thought

SHORTLY after the second Stevenson campaign I met James MacGregor Burns, the biographer of John F. Kennedy, at Williams College. In acknowledging our introduction he revealed himself as an admiring Stevensonian with the comment: "The '56 election I think I understand, but the '52 I'm not prepared to concede." We were in agreement: Stevenson was a great new spirit on the American scene.

A campaign manager comes to know his candidate well, and that was my good fortune with Adlai Stevenson. Through the crises of a presidential race the soul of the candidate is laid bare to his inner circle of advisers. The finest judgment on Stevenson, the man, is that his close associates in both campaigns admired him ever more as they saw him move from challenge to challenge.

His rigid integrity was evident at his very first campaign press

Wilson Wyatt was the campaign manager of the Stevenson presidential campaign of 1952. A corporation lawyer, he has served as Mayor of Louisville, Lieutenant Governor of Kentucky, Housing Administrator under President Truman and special emissary of President Kennedy for the Indonesian-American oil negotiations in Tokyo in 1963.

conference in Springfield in 1952. A group of us had done the usual skull practice. This was to be his first encounter with the national press since his nomination. It seemed clear that the result would be a national headline, and we wanted this national headline to be on a predetermined affirmative issue. We waited hopefully.

Governor Stevenson entered the press session at the St. Nicholas Hotel and made a preliminary statement. He then opened the field for questions, and soon came a shocker. A reporter asked whether he would send an ambassador to the Vatican. The Governor hesitated in deep thought, then announced that he was uncertain that he would do so. An audible murmer swept the room. Instantly it was clear—this would be the big news from his press conference. Big headlines proved it the next day.

The question that triggered such an explosive press reaction might be termed loaded. The Vatican ambassador issue was of utmost political delicacy and had just provoked a struggle between President Truman and the Senate in which the President was to come out second best. Myron C. Taylor, who had been President Roosevelt's, and later President Truman's, personal representative at the Vatican, and our first envoy there in nearly a century, had resigned. His appointment never had been accepted in certain religious circles, but Mr. Truman had nevertheless decided to replace him with General Mark Clark. Such was the reaction that the Senate adjourned without taking action and Mr. Truman finally withdrew the nomination at the request of General Clark.

Governor Stevenson could have evaded or temporized on this political hot potato. Had he done so, he would have avoided the diversion of attention to the Vatican from his own news. Instead, he chose a course that could be described as either courageous or naïve, or both. In the face of a long tradition that unqualified omniscience is expected of a candidate on every subject from baby care to relations with Afghanistan, he dared flatly to say he didn't know—and left the obvious implication that he might not appoint a Vatican representative.

In the postconference critique everyone asked him, "Why did you scoop yourself? Why did you deliberately choose to scuttle the big news announcement that you had prepared?"

He answered very simply that the question had been asked directly and he thought it best to give at once a frank answer.

It is interesting to note that Presidents Eisenhower, Kennedy and Johnson all handled the situation negatively. None saw fit to follow the lead set by FDR and President Truman.

This was the first of almost daily demonstrations of Governor Stevenson's candor, his integrity, his sense of honor. Others might fence with the press. Others might dissemble adroitly. Others might side-step the issue. But not Adlai Stevenson—even when he could, with honesty. It was always his course to deal directly and forthrightly, come what may.

Early in the same campaign I was present when a small delegation of powerful party leaders met with him at the Governor's Mansion in the Illinois capital. They were urging a position important to their region. He was not in accord. He thought it failed to serve the national interest. Finally in desperation, but with confidence that he had the unanswerable argument, the absolute trump of trumps, one of them said, "But otherwise you can't win." Coldly Stevenson responded, "But I don't *have* to win."

The delegation shook their heads and left the room. What kind of a candidate was this? Was he going to follow his convictions even when it might cause his defeat? With Stevenson the question was not winning or losing, but doing what he thought he ought to do and letting the chips fall where they may.

But it was not all serious. As the manager of the campaign I was almost daily cautioned I was not giving the candidate enough rest, that I was pushing him too hard. Usually, "they" would add that one member of Eisenhower's staff was actually a masseur and that his services were incomparably beneficial. "They" urged that

I arrange the same for Stevenson. I responded that our candidate simply would not agree.

Finally one day Senator Symington gave me the same argument. I gave him the same response: Adlai wouldn't agree. Then Stu told me he knew a young Puerto Rican who was incomparable in the rubdown art. He had been most helpful in the recent rugged Missouri campaign from which the Senator had emerged the winner. He said he was sure he could arrange for the masseur to be available for the Stevenson campaign.

I told him it was pointless, that the Governor wouldn't agree. Then a bright thought occurred to me. I said, "Stu, our candidate winds up next week's itinerary in your home city. On Saturday morning he starts in Jefferson City, then goes to Kansas City at noon, and then takes the traditional motor circuit around East St. Louis and St. Louis in the late afternoon. After a rest and dinner at the hotel he is to deliver a national TV hookup from St. Louis that evening. Why don't you have this accomplished masseur go with you to Stevenson's suite at the end of that long and fatiguing day, just before dinner? Then tell him what you have told me, bid him adieu and leave the masseur with Stevenson. The Governor will then learn from experience how much a rubdown will relax him and our problem will be solved."

The Senator agreed. We both thought the plan a masterpiece.

The plan worked—up to a point.

The next Saturday night at headquarters I watched Stevenson on TV. He looked fine. The speech was another outstanding success. At midnight I went to the Springfield airport to meet the returning caravan. I rode with the nominee to the Governor's Mansion. I anticipated his warm expression of pleasure over this new-found relaxation. Not a word. We entered his office, and the two of us discussed the past week and the plans for the coming week. Still not a word about the big event at St. Louis.

My curiosity could no longer be repressed. I asked, "Did you see Stu at St. Louis?"

Then came the torrent. Adlai said, "I had the most excruciating experience I have ever endured." He said the rubdown relaxed him so utterly, so completely, that when he appeared before the television cameras he could scarcely suppress a whole series of yawns. Under the heat of the klieg lights, he grew even more relaxed. Finally, he said, it was only with heroic effort that he was able to keep his eyes open and complete his speech. He said it was agony.

That ended all plans for Stevenson's "relaxation through rubdowns."

Stevenson had a deep sense of responsibility. It was typically demonstrated by an occurrence in the latter days of the '52 campaign. He was concluding a whistle-stop journey from Pennsylvania, through New Jersey and into New York. His crowds were enormous. He was in the populous East, where the electoral strength could well be decisive.

At midnight, on the next to last day, he telephoned me from the campaign train. I was at the New York headquarters, completing the elaborate arrangements for his major appearances the following day in New York City, which were to conclude with a significant television appearance.

He told me that the prisoners had rioted at the Menard State Prison at Chester, Illinois. He had said nothing about the problem to those who were with him on the campaign train. He wanted to leave quietly and without their knowledge, to fly at once to the prison where the state police and state officials had already gathered. He asked for me to arrange for Senator Fulbright and others to fill his speaking engagements throughout the next day and expressed the hope—but only the hope—that he might be able to return to New York in time for the television speech the following evening. This would mean his failure to appear for campaign addresses believed to be critically important. And then he added the statement which showed his deep sense of personal responsibility.

He said that, after all, he was still Governor of Illinois and the entrance to the prison was going to be accomplished at daybreak even if it became necessary to use extreme force. He said that some of the guards were being held as hostages. Then he added, "This is a situation in which there might be loss of life, and this is a responsibility which I cannot delegate."

He returned to Illinois, the entry to the prison was successfully accomplished, the guards were rescued, and order was restored. He missed all his speaking engagements that day.

Actually, the Governor's role was unspectacular. Soon after he arrived about 5 A.M., a plan which he previously had approved by telephone was put into effect and the mutineers yielded when threatened by a state police siege.

Characteristically, Stevenson chose not to steal the spotlight and take over the operation. As planned, the state public safety director delivered an ultimatum to the convicts.

The Governor visited the seven released guards in the prison hospital, spoke consolingly to their shocked wives and children and soon afterward boarded a charter flight for LaGuardia Airport. It was delayed by fog and had to be sent to Philadelphia for refueling.

An hour before TV time it was nip-and-tuck as to whether he could make it to the television theater in time. The New York sponsors decided they couldn't risk it, that I should prepare at once to substitute. Hastily I put a speech together, finishing the last lines as the taxicab pulled up at the auditorium. I went backstage. Adolf Berle, who was to introduce Stevenson, quickly revamped his script to introduce me. Like an old-fashioned melodrama, just as we were walking out on stage, the doors burst open and in rushed Governor Stevenson. The ovation was tumultuous.

I told Adlai afterward that he had just ruined the best speech I "almost" ever made.

It had been a frantic day in the campaign, but there was never a moment's hesitation in Stevenson's mind about what he should do; the Menard responsibility was one he could not delegate.

Adlai Stevenson spoke great thoughts with rhythmic beauty. But like Lincoln he always had a ready twinkle and a ready wit.

In speaking once of an opponent, he said he was reminded of the little old lady who didn't know what she really thought until she heard what she had to say.

And he gave a thrust at what he called the archaic platform of the opposition by recalling the story of the Australian bushman who was given a new boomerang, and then spent the rest of his life trying to throw the old one away.

Shortly after Election Day, 1952, four of us (Carl McGowan and his wife, my wife Anne and I) vacationed with Governor Stevenson at a "dude ranch" in southern Arizona. On the first morning we rode horseback over the Mexican border to the little town of Nogales. No sooner had we arrived than all the town turned out. They swarmed around him with true Latin enthusiasm. His immediate response was a twinkling exclamation: "I ran in the wrong country!"

In early 1957 he sent me an autographed copy of his book *What I Think*, a book which had been published prior to the '56 campaign. His inscription to me read: "This has been sitting on my desk for a *year*. But something happened to that year! Anyway, what I *think* is still what I *thought!*"

How typical, and how true. Regardless of the vicissitudes of campaigns, politics and crowds, regardless of the possible lure of votes, whatever he thought was still what he thought.

Of course I shall never forget election night in 1952—but one occurrence especially. All will recall his constant humor in virtually all his speeches. Many thought (but not I) that it was politically hurtful.

The one-sided returns poured in. State after state conceded. Finally, toward midnight, I telephoned him on our private line from the presidential headquarters at the St. Nicholas Hotel to

Wilson W. Wyatt and AES at the Executive Mansion in Springfield, July, 1952.

the Governor's Mansion a few blocks away. I said simply, "Adlai, I think the time has probably come for a statement." Just as simply he answered, "So do I. Suppose you come by for me."

We drove together to the television room at the hotel, which was jam-packed with reporters and enthusiastic adherents. On the way he showed me the statement he had dictated a little while earlier. And as we neared the hotel he said, "I thought I would add a little story."

"But," I asked, "is this really a night for a story?"

Then he told me he had in mind the now famous Lincoln anecdote and I heartily agreed. And the one statement everyone recalls from his concession that night to President Eisenhower was that story: "Someone asked me, as I came in, down on the street, how I felt, and I was reminded of a story that a fellow townsman of ours used to tell—Abraham Lincoln. They asked him how he felt once after an unsuccessful election. He said he felt like a little boy who had stubbed his toe in the dark. He said that he was too old to cry, but it hurt too much to laugh."

And he became a hero in defeat.

His sense of history was typified by an occurrence about six weeks before the end of the '56 campaign. One evening, in Washington, after a long session with a group of his advisers, he asked me to remain after the others were gone. When the last had left the room, he looked at me and, with a twinkle, said, "Wilson, the one thing for which we are unprepared is victory."

He then recalled the fact that there was no precedent for the transition from the Republican party to the Democratic, under the new and very different circumstances brought about by the Twentieth Amendment, which requires the President to take office on January 20 rather than on March 4 and which, even more significantly, provides for the Congress to take office on the third of January—seventeen days prior to the inauguration.

This produced a major change. Before the ratification of the amendment in 1933 (it became effective in October of that year) Congress did not come into session until months after the President's inauguration unless, as was frequently the case, the President himself called the Congress into a special session. Prior to the amendment, therefore, a newly elected President was able to wait until after his inauguration to make the final decision as to his Cabinet and to evolve and state his policies, since Congress did not convene until the President was ready for them to act.

Since the Twentieth Amendment, however, Congress waits impatiently from January 3 to January 20 for the new President to be inaugurated, to announce his Cabinet and to send his legislative program to the Hill, with the result that it is now imperative for a new President to be prepared to act at once, from the very moment he takes the oath of office. All of this Governor Stevenson realized.

He asked me if I would research the problem and prepare for him for Election Day a full, confidential memorandum of all the steps to be taken, from the moment the President's election should be announced on election night through to the day of inauguration. This involved, as he knew it would, a complex consideration of timing, of personalities, of officials to be appointed and of policies to be announced.

On election morning in Illinois I delivered to him the detailed volume which I had captioned, "The Transition."

The events of election night made the volume unnecessary. But once again Stevenson had been before his time. Four years later, in early August of 1960, the Brookings Institution telephoned me to request a copy of the volume, "The Transition," for their use as they formulated a report for what became the Eisenhower-Kennedy transition in January, 1961.

Again, Stevenson helped prepare the way.

It was clear that Adlai Stevenson had brought a measure of greatness to the twentieth century. He had, in truth, elevated and inspired, through his part in the political "dialogue."

His was the eloquent voice of conscience as he gave expression to the aspirations of man.

His was the integrity that raised the moral tone of our country.

His was the wit, and charm and wisdom that caused him to be called the most civilized American since Benjamin Franklin.

His was the idealism which Woodrow Wilson would have smiled upon with warm and admiring approval.

His was the buoyant hope that spoke with clear vision of the "revolution of rising expectations."

His was the faith that would admit of no defeat in the upward struggle of mankind toward the dawn of a better world, and toward the time when our swords might be turned into plowshares, and man might be at peace.

His was the *quality* that has inspired youth to turn, with dedication, to the honorable calling of public service.

This was the time for Adlai Stevenson. Not in the formal toga of the office of the presidency, but in the more enduring toga of the spirit, in giving leadership to the aspirations of free men everywhere.

I frequently glance at his inscription on a photograph on my office wall—one he sent to me shortly after the election in 1952, the election in which there was so much discussion about his reluctance to be a candidate. This inscription showed his modest habit of jesting at his own expense. Stevenson had endorsed it to me as "A cruel taskmaster and dear friend whose heart is always high, from his reluctant dragon."

Let's Talk Sense
to the American People

As the democratic National Convention came to order on Monday morning, July 21, 1952, in Chicago there wasn't the slightest doubt that a substantial number of delegates wanted to make Adlai E. Stevenson their candidate for President.

There also wasn't the slightest doubt in the minds of many of us that Governor Stevenson honestly and sincerely did not want the nomination.

I admired Mr. Stevenson's record as governor. I had been impressed by his earlier achievements in helping form the United Nations and then in representing our country before that fledgling body. I had talked with him a couple of times on the eve of the convention. But he was strongly on record as not wanting the nomination—and I took him at his word.

That morning as the Governor delivered Illinois' welcome to the convention I didn't give the slightest thought to a Stevenson-Sparkman ticket. His nomination was most improbable, I thought, and though my name had been casually mentioned in the press

John Sparkman, United States Senator from Alabama since 1946, was the running mate of Governor Stevenson on the Democratic ticket in 1952.

for Vice President I didn't take the matter seriously. In my meetings with the Governor he had never given me the impression that he would accept, and he never gave me any indication that he would select me as his running mate.

His own welcoming speech, however, gave tremendous impetus to the pro-Stevenson movement he so strongly disclaimed.

It sparkled with humor, insight and great common sense, and it made a profound impression on the convention and the public in general. I am sure he did not intend to, but he helped fuel the Stevenson fire.

The Democrats met just a week after the Republican convention had left Chicago, and the country was still reeling with the charges and countercharges that the GOP leaders had hurled at each other.

Governor Stevenson took witty note of Republican caterwauling:

"After listening to this everlasting procession of epithets about our misdeeds," he said, "I was even surprised the next morning when the mail was delivered on time. I guess our Republican friends were out of patience, out of sorts and, need I add, out of office.

"But we Democrats were by no means the only victims here. First they slaughtered each other and then they went after us. And the same vocabulary was good for both exercises, which was a great convenience. Perhaps the proximity of the stockyards accounts for the carnage."

He ended solemnly and with dignity:

"My friends, the constructive spirit of the two great Democratic decades must not die here on its twentieth anniversary; they must not die here in destructive indignity and disorder. And I hope and pray, as you all do, that we can conduct our deliberations with a businesslike precision and a dignity befitting our responsibility and the solemnity of the hour of history in which we meet."

As I have said, the speech made a profound impression, and by Thursday, when names were placed in nomination, there was no doubt of the strength of the "Draft Stevenson" forces. With Senators Richard Russell of Georgia and Estes Kefauver of Tennessee he was oné of three top recognized contenders.

When the first ballot was taken the results were: Kefauver, 340; Russell, 268; Stevenson, 273; others, 347½. Required to nominate, 616.

The second ballot went: Kefauver, 362½; Russell, 294; Stevenson, 321½; others, 241½.

The third ballot was: Kefauver, 275½; Russell, 261; Stevenson, 617½; others, 73.

A motion was immediately adopted nominating Adlai Stevenson by acclamation.

I should note here that our Alabama delegation was unpledged and unbound by the unit rule. No more than fourteen of our votes went to any one man on any of the three ballots, and our fellow Southerner, Senator Russell, got those on the third ballot.

On all three ballots, the record shows, Governor Stevenson received a half-vote from the Alabama delegation. It was cast by L. L. Patterson.

After Governor Stevenson was nominated, President Truman, who had arrived in Chicago late that afternoon, strode onto the rostrum and delivered a speech reminiscent of his 1948 whistle-stop campaign. As he finished, he introduced the nominee, who was greeted with thunderous applause. The draft was genuine; it was also tremendously popular.

In his acceptance speech the Governor again spoke of his reluctance. But his was a complete acceptance, and a pledge to give his best. His speech electrified his listeners and those who read it. Here, Americans thought, was another Woodrow Wilson, a master of the English language and a finished artist in the expression of his thoughts.

He spoke solemnly to the American people:

The ordeal of the twentieth century—the bloodiest, most turbulent era of the Christian age—is far from over. Sacrifice, patience, understanding and implacable purpose may be our lot for years to come.

Let's face it. Let's talk sense to the American people. Let's tell them the truth, that there are no gains without pains, that we are now on the eve of great decisions, not easy decisions like resistance when you're attacked but a long, patient, costly struggle which alone can assure triumph over the great enemies of man—war, poverty and tyranny—and the assaults upon human dignity which are the most grievous consequences of each.

Better we lose the election than mislead the people. . . . I ask of you all you have. I will give you all I have . . . in the staggering task that you have assigned to me. I shall always try to "do justly and to love mercy, and to walk humbly with my God."

As I listened to these ringing words I had no idea that I would be Adlai's running mate. I soon received the word, but Governor Stevenson never did tell me why he selected me. I believe these three factors played a part in the final selection:

1. I was a member of the drafting subcommittee of the Resolutions Committee. We had a most difficult time in drafting a civil rights plank. We had both extremes. Several of us wanted very badly to see a plank that both the South and the North could accept. Our work was arduous, our sessions long, even running all night. I worked very hard trying to find a solution to this problem. I believe Adlai knew it and was impressed.

2. From the time of the establishment of the Senate Small Business Committee in 1950, I had been chairman. We had done some excellent work. Adlai was interested in a program for small business and took note of my activity in that field.

3. He felt, as I did, that the time was right for bringing closer together the North and the South. His principal competitors for the nomination had been Senators Kefauver and Russell, both Southerners. Selection of me, a Southerner, as running mate, would help unify the party geographically.

The notice came to me about four o'clock Saturday morning. Frank McKinney, Chairman of the Democratic National Committee, called me at my hotel soon after Mrs. Sparkman, our daughter, Mrs. Tazewell Shepard, and I returned from the convention hall.

When I was nominated early Saturday afternoon, I was called to the platform. Governor Stevenson met me there and in a very brief speech presented me to the convention.

On Sunday at the request of our presidential nominee I met with him at the home of Mr. and Mrs. William McCormick Blair, Sr. in Chicago, and we discussed a good many problems we had ahead of us. I was greatly impressed by his grasp of the problems and the incisive manner with which he handled them.

As soon as we were able to pull things together we met for a weekend in Springfield, Illinois, to make plans for the campaign. There were some twelve or fifteen of us, including the Governor; Oscar Chapman, who was to handle the Governor's itineraries; Wilson Wyatt, who was to be Governor Stevenson's personal campaign manager; Stephen A. Mitchell, the new National Committee Chairman; Mrs. India Edwards, head of the Women's Division of the National Committee; W. Averell Harriman, close adviser; Senator Earle Clements, Chairman of the Senate Democratic Campaign Committee; Congressman Mike Kirwan, Chairman of the House Democratic Campaign Committee; Bill Blair, Executive Assistant to Mr. Stevenson; and Edd Hyde, my Executive Assistant.

We spent the whole time, morning, afternoon and night, in discussing different matters pertaining to the campaign—campaign strategy, scheduling, staffing, just about everything one could conceive.

One could not sit through those days under the leadership of Adlai Stevenson without feeling a tremendous admiration for the character of the man and the clarity of his mind and expression.

When it came time to stop on Saturday night the question arose: What time shall we start tomorrow? The Governor immediately made it clear that time would be taken out for church.

He invited any who wished to do so to go with him to church, but named the various churches conveniently near. In connection with this he told us that he did not propose to do any campaigning on Sunday. I do not know whether or not Governor Stevenson was able to keep that resolution throughout the campaign. I broke it only once—to attend an ox roast in Cuyahoga County, Ohio, an annual event regularly given on Sunday.

Another characteristic that came to the top in these conference sessions was his abhorrence of demagoguery and his determination that we should avoid it.

I recall one thing in particular. Just a few days before, the head of one of our great radio and TV networks had revealed his desire to have the two principal candidates debate on TV and radio. Someone brought up the subject with the suggestion that our candidate send a telegram forthwith accepting the invitation and challenging General Eisenhower to join him. Governor Stevenson rejected it immediately with a statement that he did not propose to embarrass General Eisenhower by asking, in effect, for an opportunity to ride on his coattails. He pointed out that to a great part of the United States he was unknown whereas Eisenhower was a household word in practically every American home.

In the course of the campaign there were other instances when he refused to give way to what he considered demagoguery. For instance, when questioned about the "Nixon Fund" he gave quite a practical answer devoid of demagoguery, when it would have been so easy to give a different answer, joining the clamor that the very existence of the fund was a disqualifying evil.

Another, and perhaps the most outstanding, example had to do with "going to Korea." Just a few days after his nomination he disclosed to close friends that if elected he would immediately go to Korea, and also to Japan and India, countries he felt were of crucial importance in the Far East struggle against Communism. He felt that to publicize this intent would look

William Calvin

Governor Stevenson and Senator Sparkman at Lincoln's Tomb, Springfield, at the start of the 1952 campaign.

as if he were trying to make political capital out of the Korean War and that it also might compromise future negotiations.

Again, one with lesser determination might have given way to temptation. He was speaking to a Marine Corps graduating class in which his oldest son, Adlai III, was being commissioned. When someone on his staff suggested that he point out in his speech what a strong personal reason he had for ending the war, he rejected it quickly. By the way, young Adlai later commanded a tank platoon in Korea.

Because of the necessity of his being in Springfield to attend to state affairs, Governor Stevenson decided to set up his campaign headquarters there. The National Committee remained in Washington. My campaign headquarters were in Washington. We had separate staffs, which coordinated activities constantly with each other and with the National Committee. His choice as chairman, Steve Mitchell, did an excellent job.

Shortly after the convention, President Truman invited Governor Stevenson and me to visit him at the White House. This we did on August 12. We discussed all phases of the campaign with President Truman and heard from him some of his own experiences in campaigning. We had lunch with President Truman and later enjoyed a complete tour of the White House. He accompanied us to every room on every floor including the basement and the attic. President Truman was most congenial and cooperative. He assured us of his desire to do whatever he could to help in the campaign.

It may be recalled that very early Governor Stevenson had received a telegram from the editor of an Oregon paper asking, among other things, what he proposed to do to clean up "that mess in Washington." In his reply Governor Stevenson used the same phrase "that mess in Washington" without quotation marks. Immediately much of the press played up his reference to "that mess in Washington," seeking to produce a rift between President Truman and Governor Stevenson. It was explained that he simply omitted using quotation marks in replying to the editor's telegram. It gave the Republicans much to talk about in the course of the campaign, but apparently President Truman accepted fully the explanation that Governor Stevenson gave to him personally.

During the campaign Governor Stevenson and I, according to plan, worked in different parts of the country—when he was North I was South; when he was East I was West. From the time I left him on the weekend of the conference in Springfield until election eve, we did not see each other. We did use the telephone considerably, exchanging ideas, making suggestions, discussing situations as we individually saw them.

Governor Stevenson was always receptive to new ideas, and from time to time he gave many very helpful suggestions.

Right at the very beginning of the campaign Governor Stevenson and General Eisenhower both spoke the same day at the National Plowing Contest at Kasson, Minnesota.

Not long thereafter I was at Worthington, Minnesota, on their Turkey Day Festival. While I was there and in neighboring Iowa and in other farm areas, many people spoke to me about the Kasson Day speech, saying that neither the General nor the Governor struck fire in their Plowing Contest addresses. Among those who campaigned with me throughout Minnesota were Senator Hubert Humphrey, now Vice President of the United States, and Governor Orville Freeman, now Secretary of Agriculture. They both felt that the farm question was not handled in a completely adequate manner. In fact, comment was quite general to the effect that nothing had been given to the farmers in which they could "sink their teeth."

I called Governor Stevenson within the next few days and told him of the reaction that I had received generally to his speech at Kasson and asked him if he was going to have another farm speech opportunity. He told me he was and gave me the date. I believe he took the suggestion seriously, for in his later speech, at a pancake day rally, I believe, he bore down heavily on the practical pocketbook issues involved in agricultural programs.

On another occasion Governor Stevenson called me while there was much turmoil regarding the "Nixon Fund" and in the course of the conversation stated that he believed all four candidates should make a disclosure of their income tax returns. My reaction was negative for I felt that this was a highly personal matter and that disclosure should not be required. I told him that mine would be by far the smallest and perhaps I was prejudiced against disclosure for that reason. But I agreed to go along if he really felt that it should be done. Both Governor Stevenson and I made full disclosure of our individual returns. As I recall, each of the Republican candidates released some kind of auditor's statement. I well recall that in my case newspaper reporters were invited to my office. They went over my files item by item.

On election eve Governor Stevenson and I flew into Chicago to appear together in a nationwide television program. I rode in with him from the airport, just the two of us. He rather amazed me by starting to talk, as soon as we were on our way, of prospective members of the Cabinet. I am not superstitious, but I did feel a little strange discussing such things ahead of time. I asked him if he felt confident of election. His reply was "I am as confident as I can be." He certainly seemed sincere in his statement, but I have often wondered if he really believed we were winning or if he was simply trying to bolster my feelings.

Before going on television, we had carefully gone over our parts. The Governor had his script prepared. He read it over and timed it accurately. We were careful in the program to make certain that sufficient time was left for him. Somehow, however, he seemed to read very slowly and he was "cut off." All of us who took part in the program would gladly have given up all our time for him to have completed his statement. Hurried arrangements were made for a retake, and in at least some parts of the country the complete statement was made available.

His final speech was brief but in characteristic phraseology and thought. It follows:

In this city of Chicago, in the early hours of a July morning last summer, I accepted the nomination of the Democratic party for the presidency of the United States. By the calendar that was just fourteen weeks ago. That is not so long as time is measured, but to one who has spent weeks, as I have. writing, traveling, yes, and listening, to countless thousands of the American people, it has been a long, long time.

The end has now come, the cheers and jeers, the tumult and the shouting are almost over, and these are the last words I shall speak to you before the balloting begins tomorrow morning.

Anyone who runs for office wants to win. I want to win, of course; but, win or lose, if I have kept faith with myself during the campaign, then I can await tomorrow—and the day after—and all the days after that—in good temper and sober contentment. . . .

I said when I accepted the nomination, Let's talk sense to the American people. . . . Talking sense is not easy. It means saying things that sometimes people don't like to hear; it means risking votes, and candidates are not supposed to do that. It means saying the same thing in all parts of the country and at all stages of the campaign. . . .

Win or lose, I have told you the truth as I see it. I have said what I meant and meant what I said. . . .

I have asked you for your support for my candidacy. I ask you now for support of our common faith in this country. The confidence we've inherited is our greatest wealth, the source of our strength.

Whatever the electorate decides, I ask that we close our ears, once and for all, to the cowardly voices of hate and fear and suspicion which would destroy us; that we dedicate ourselves, each one of us alone and all of us together, to that belief in ourselves, that trust in each other, on which the greatness of our country rests. For believe me, the future of the world depends on it.

On election night Governor Stevenson was in Springfield; I was in my home town of Huntsville, Alabama. Sometime before midnight he telephoned me stating that it appeared to him to be definite that we had lost and that if I agreed he was ready to make a statement of concession. Shortly thereafter the country heard him say:

. . . The people have rendered their verdict and I gladly accept it.

General Eisenhower has been a great leader in war. He has been a vigorous and valiant opponent in the campaign. These qualities will now be dedicated to leading us all through the next four years. . . .

I urge you all to give to General Eisenhower the support he will need to carry out the great tasks that lie before him.

I pledge him mine.

We vote as many, but we pray as one. With a united people, with faith in democracy, with common concern for others less fortunate around the globe, we shall move forward with God's guidance toward the time when His children shall grow in freedom and dignity in a world at peace.

He added that he felt like the boy in the story Lincoln told about who stubbed his toe and said he was too old to cry but it hurt too much to laugh.

I am sure that he received many messages, as I did, citing that story and ending with the statement, "Well, I am not too old to cry—I'm doing that right now."

The Governor's sister, Mrs. Ernest Ives, in her excellent book *My Brother Adlai,* says that when it was all over and he had gone to bed she asked him, "How are you?" To this he replied, "I've no regrets. I didn't ask for any of this, and I've done the best I could." He made a tremendous race. He received the largest number of votes that any candidate for President had ever received before that time with the single exception of Franklin D. Roosevelt in 1936. He consistently "talked sense to the American people." He was conscientious, hard-working and, what proved to be true afterward, a man of destiny.

PAUL SIMON

Young People Loved Him

Memories crowd in on those of us who have had the opportunity to know, respect and admire Adlai E. Stevenson. This collection of memories is from one who was not an intimate, but perhaps I speak for the thousands—at least—of a younger generation who were moved by the man and his message.

One of the things I remember most vividly was his appeal to youth and his interest in young people. A look at his staff or his law associates showed this; a look at an audience he addressed evidenced the same. His appeal was particularly noticeable on a college campus, among both the students and faculty. Here they recognized his rare talent for the right phrase and for incisive thinking.

He had many followers among young people, and also some worshipers. The latter sometimes proved a source of embarrassment to him. At the 1960 Democratic Convention in Los Angeles I recall a bearded, pale young man walking around the lobby of the convention hotel carrying the sign: STEVENSON OR ATOMIC DEATH!

Illinois State Senator Paul Simon publishes several weekly newspapers in Illinois and is the author of several books. A frequent contributor to national magazines, he makes his home in Troy, Illinois. His article is adapted from one he published in Spirit *magazine.*

128

Through unusual circumstances, at the age of nineteen I found myself leaving the campus of Dana College in Blair, Nebraska, to take over as publisher of a small weekly newspaper in Troy, Illinois. That was 1948, the year Illinois voters turned out en masse to oust Governor Dwight Green and bring in a man who was little more than a name to most: Adlai Stevenson.

I saw Governor Stevenson occasionally at these "Hello, who are you?" affairs where the aim of the Governor's staff is maximum exposure and minimum conversation. But because of special circumstances in our county—described later—the Governor found that he appeared to have few friends in our heavily populated Democratic county. I was among those who sided with him and soon I had an invitation to have lunch with the Governor. I was not yet twenty-one, and it impresses me more now than it did then that he should have taken time out to have lunch with someone not even old enough to vote.

In my correspondence file I have two more indications of his amazing and sensitive interest in youth. When I was twenty-two the Army beckoned, and I received this heart-warming send-off:

I hear today from Carl McGowan that you are shortly to be inducted into the Army. I find myself of two minds: I am delighted on the one hand that you are going to be serving in the armed forces, and disappointed on the other hand that your emphatic and clear voice is going to be stilled hereabouts for a while. I hope it will not be long before you can resume your very important and helpful contribution to the revival of law enforcement in Illinois.

During most of 1952 I was stationed in Germany and followed the presidential race via the *Stars and Stripes* and the European editions of the *New York Times* and New York *Herald Tribune*. I still remember the thrill that went through me listening to the radio at some weird hour while the Governor accepted the Democratic nomination. That will always remain, in my mind, his most eloquent hour.

Deeply moved, I scraped together everything a private first

class could and sent it as a donation; I don't believe it totaled more than $50.

In response I received a note from the presidential candidate himself:

> I am touched more than I can say by your letter—and your contribution. I can well imagine that the salary of a private first class is not such as to give him much room for leeway, and that a political contribution comes at the very bottom of the priority list. I can only say that I shall value this contribution much more than many larger ones I will receive.

He added a few paragraphs which made clear that it was Stevenson who dictated the letter, and not some aide. I would guess that not often in the history of presidential campaigns has a major candidate taken time out to acknowledge a letter from a "pfc."

As I look back on it now, Stevenson appealed to youth and had an interest in them because he was always young himself, always growing, always eager to explore and probe untried paths.

Professional gambling with all its underworld links constituted a major problem in many counties in Illinois. My county of Madison, across the river from St. Louis and north of East St. Louis, was no exception. We had a system which permitted bookies and gambling casinos to operate freely though illegally. Every three months they were simply haled into court, found guilty and given fines of varying amounts, usually around $25 and court costs. Our county officials called this "common sense law enforcement." John McConnell, Jr., one of the few county leaders who openly disagreed with the policy, termed it more properly "nonsense law enforcement." Civic groups which might have been expected to complain were permitted to have bingo and slot machines and other forms of gambling; it was an effective way of bribing them into silence. County political campaigns were largely financed by the gamblers, and when I opposed this whole thoroughly rotten system in my small newspaper, one of the recurring responses was: "How can you have a two-party system if you don't have gambling?"

To those of us who saw the multitude of evils that arose from this situation—prostitution, gangland killings and control of law enforcement by lawless elements—there was only one hope of change: the state government. Governor Stevenson was known to be an honest man, and surely, we felt, no honorable governor could tolerate this situation.

Editorials urging the Governor to act appeared in my newspaper and other newspapers which had considerably more "clout"; special credit goes to the Granite City *Press-Record* and the St. Louis *Post-Dispatch*. I was also in contact with the Governor and his office regularly by mail and in person, making a pest of myself. Early correspondence shows a genuine reluctance on the part of the Governor to act. There was no tradition of such a move by the Governor, and his only police force, significantly called the highway police, by custom was confined to highway duties.

In the April, 1950, primary the candidates for sheriff of our county spent more than $130,000 for an office which at that time was limited to one four-year term and paid $4,000 a year. One possible key to such interest was the statement of a former sheriff who admitted, after the statute of limitations had expired, that he had made more than $250,000 during his four-year term in the mid-1930's.

A few weeks after that expensive primary I received a letter from James Mulroy, then the Governor's executive secretary. He said: "I am of the considered opinion that in a comparatively short time the better known gambling places in your county will be closed either due to action taken by your own authorities or by some other type of action." It was hardly clear what would happen, but my newspaper came out on Thursday with a headline: "Big County Gambling Places To Be Closed." Friday the paper reached our county seat, Edwardsville, and the story only brought laughs. "After all, a Democratic governor won't clamp down on one of the big Democratic counties in the state," was the confident consensus.

But that afternoon at 3:30 P.M. Illinois had its first state police raid on gambling, with fifty-one state policemen from the northern part of the state swooping down on our two big gambling casinos.

That day—May 12, 1950—marked the beginning of a new era for our county and some others in the state. Underworld sources of campaign contributions dried up, and suddenly counties found themselves talking about detention homes and park districts and other things with which a county should be concerned rather than the constant battle about which gang would control gambling.

The raids of 1950 and those that followed would not have been possible without taking the state police out of politics. Much to the distress of many of the political "pros," precinct committeemen and precinct captains no longer automatically emerged as enforcers of the law. The merit system lifted the whole vision and performance of the state police.

And yet I can remember a political leader being cheered vigorously at a party rally when he denounced Governor Stevenson for putting the state police on the merit system.

One other memory stands out in connection with those first momentous raids. I sat with other newsmen as the gamblers were brought into the state's attorney's office and arraigned. Seated next to me was the attorney for one of the casinos, a power in Democratic politics. He said to me, "That Stevenson is worse than Hitler ever was."

Two years later that same leader stood up in the Illinois caucus at the Democratic convention and said how desperately the nation needed Stevenson's leadership, and moved that the caucus go on record for Stevenson for President.

He—and some others—were for Stevenson for President just to get him out of Illinois. The Governor didn't "play ball," and all their grandiose plans for spoils were being blasted.

"What good is it to win if you end up with a Stevenson as governor?" many a would-be plunderer was heard to say.

Dr. Richard Browne, who delivered a eulogy for Stevenson at Illinois State University the morning of his burial, for many years served as the top executive for the Illinois universities that are frequently called our "teachers colleges." An official in the Democratic party came to Dr. Browne and told him that under the new (Stevenson) administration all classroom furniture in the universities would have to be purchased from a certain concern. Dr. Browne immediately went to Stevenson to find out if this was true. Stevenson told Browne, "Tell him to go jump in the lake. You buy your equipment wherever you can get the best price."

Early in 1952 I was serving in the Army at Fort Holabird near Baltimore, Maryland. While there in January I had the opportunity to meet two members of the personal staff of President Harry S. Truman who bombarded me with questions about Stevenson, and though they gave no clear indication why I was being questioned, it seemed apparent that President Truman might not run and that the Illinois Governor was being seriously considered. A few months later President Truman announced that he would not seek re-election, and the Stevenson talk which already had been growing then became regular front-page news.

To the credit of President Truman and his staff, it was clear from the questions put to me in Baltimore that their interest was in securing not just a good candidate but a good President.

And I shall ever regard it as our national loss that we did not find out how good a President he could be.

In 1956 Lawrence Irvin, a long-time Stevenson associate, had

Paul Simon on a Chicago platform as Governor Stevenson introduces Eleanor Roosevelt.

charge of Stevenson's personal suite in the Stockyards Inn in Chicago, next to the Democratic convention hall. I helped Larry Irvin in any way I could. It was my first national political convention and in many ways the most exciting.

When Stevenson received the nomination, instead of proceeding immediately to the convention hall, he first came to the suite and held a meeting with many leaders, including the Senator from Texas, Lyndon Johnson. He explained to them that, contrary to tradition, he planned to express no choice for Vice President, but leave the convention wide-open. While this meeting went on inside his suite, outside there was the biggest jam of reporters and television men I have ever seen. They all wanted to know what was going on. Soon Stevenson announced to the convention that it could make its own choice, and in a close race Senator Estes Kefauver received the nomination for Vice President over the young Senator from Massachusetts who had the suite around the corner, John Kennedy.

In 1962 the seat of Senator Everett Dirksen was on the election block, and I early indicated an interest in running against him. There also were others eager to make the race, but more tactful about their interest. For several months I was the only announced aspirant.

Chicago's Mayor Richard Daley one day announced that Stevenson, then Ambassador to the United Nations, might become the Democratic candidate for United States Senator. I immediately sent a telegram to the Ambassador pledging my support, perhaps a little like the mouse offering to help the lion. He sent this note in response:

I have been playing tag with you on the telephone and I am deeply distressed that we have not connected yet. I have wanted to thank you for your very kind and thoughtful telegram and I take this means of attempting to do so now.

I was flattered by your graceful and generous encouragement about the candidacy for the Senate. However, I hope—and believe—you will approve of the decision I made. Now you can continue your "personal efforts" without any anxiety about your old and devoted friend.

He had declined to leave his UN post for the Senate, and Illinois Democrats picked an outstanding Congressman, Sidney Yates, to make the ill-fated journey against Senator Dirksen.

Three personal characteristics I also remember about Stevenson.

One is a shyness and sensitivity on certain occasions which are seldom encountered in political life. I recall driving to the St. Louis airport with him after a political rally. His plane being late, we went to the airport restaurant to get a cup of coffee, and soon there were scores of people simply standing around watching us. I sensed that he felt uneasy. Other political leaders I know would have used this situation to wave at the crowd and make a handshaking tour.

A second characteristic was one he had in common with many Americans: difficulty with weight. He had a nervous habit of making sure that his suit coat covered his increasing girth. He was not a tall man, and the weight he added showed.

A third characteristic was to work constantly on the content of speeches until the last minute. If Stevenson received a long introduction, he often spent most of the time during it making last-minute changes in his remarks. Not surprisingly, he usually won the struggle to make words march to his command.

I last saw him at a dinner party for about twenty in Springfield. Among those present was his son Adlai III, now a distinguished member of the Illinois General Assembly. Governor Stevenson dropped in for a short visit. The conversation was gay and spirited. I remember particularly that he had some generous remarks about a biography I had written about Elijah Lovejoy. His final words to me that evening were in a lighthearted vein: "I spotted you in the audience as I sat on the stage. I couldn't help but recall the wars we fought together."

This took place in a harshly plain room above a small Italian restaurant in Springfield. As he descended the steep stairway I saw him for the last time.

In a sense he then left my world, but in reality he never will. It is difficult, sitting before a clumsy typewriter, to put into words the impact Governor Stevenson had on me and thousands of my generation. I leave it to those far more learned to discern his impact on national and world affairs. My view is provincial.

Part of the impact he had on Illinois and on me was the wave of able people he brought to Springfield: Carl McGowan, Newt

Minow, Bill Blair, Dick Nelson, Bill Flanagan, Larry Irvin, Leonard Schwartz, to mention just a few, as well as a man he brought to the national scene who is a real "Rock of Gibraltar," Stephen A. Mitchell.

And that is only part of the story.

Here was a politician who dared to think, who like the ancient god Janus looked both at yesterday and tomorrow, who matched compassion with wisdom. By being all this and more, he gave each of us a spark of hope which I trust never will be dimmed, even though we may often reflect that hope most inadequately.

Perhaps a battle-scarred Illinois legislative veteran who has served since the 1930's, Representative Lloyd "Curly" Harris, summed it up best when he told me, "You know, Paul, after I talk with Governor Stevenson I come away feeling a little cleaner."

All of us feel cleaner and finer for having known him.

With AES in War and Politics

ADLAI STEVENSON and I both arrived in Washington at the outset of the New Deal, he a refugee from a Chicago law firm and I fresh out of law school. Roosevelt's inauguration made Washington an irresistible lodestone for young lawyers with a mission.

The air was yeasty and rarefied. It seemed to offer little resistance to forward motion, and we were, all of us—to a greater or less extent—guided by two operational principles.

We were convinced that our predecessors had made a mess of it and that nothing done up to that point in history was much good. And we had the satisfying feeling that there was nothing we could not do.

Exposure to New Deal Washington left its mark on both of us —less perhaps on Adlai than on me, since he was ten years older and had more sense. But when we returned to Chicago at the end of two years, we both found the practice of law rather sterile, at least during the initial period of decompression.

For Adlai no activity could be sterile very long, since he had

George W. Ball, Under Secretary of State under Presidents Kennedy and Lyndon Johnson, is a onetime law associate of Adlai Stevenson and was his close friend and adviser for many years.

a remarkable sensitivity to the great issues of the time. For the first four years after our Washington interlude, he and I practiced in different Chicago firms. By 1939, when I had become an associate of the firm of which he was a junior partner, he was already deeply engaged in persuading a skeptical Middle West that isolationism was a ridiculous policy for a nation destined to lead the world.

In 1940 Adlai was commanding the barricades for William Allen White's Committee to Defend America by Aiding the Allies. By this time he had established an extraordinary local reputation by the wit and authority with which he presided over the proceedings of the Council on Foreign Relations.

The Council was a vital place in Chicago during that period of great national debate. It was an oasis of discontent in a complacent society brainwashed each morning by Colonel McCormick's insistent xenophobia. We watched with growing delight as leading citizens came in droves to overflow luncheons of the Council, to expose themselves to views that were not confined to the admonitory passages of Washington's Farewell Address. The attraction for many, the more cynical of us suspected, was hardly the wisdom of the speakers so much as Adlai's wise and scintillating introductions.

In those days Adlai was well on the way to becoming a respected local institution. But clearly that could be only a transient phase. The isolationist Middle West could not long hold a man who saw with clarity that the forces of evil were threatening the civilized world, and who believed passionately that America could not sit idly by. In June of 1941 he became Assistant to Secretary of the Navy Frank Knox. A few months later, at Stevenson's suggestion, I joined him in Washington as a legal counsel to the Lend-Lease Administration.

From the moment he arrived in the Navy Department, Adlai became a one-man recruiting office for the United States Government, exhibiting a quality with which I was later to become much more familiar—an unflagging zeal for helping even casual acquaintances find appropriate assignments in the public service. This was not merely an expression of his fondness for people, and it was certainly not the politician's instinct for patronage. It sprang from his deeply held conviction that the government needed and deserved the best talent the nation could produce.

After Secretary Knox's death in April of 1944, Adlai returned to Chicago. At about the same time I became the civilian member of an Evaluation Board of Air Force officers with a vague mandate to appraise the effectiveness of the air offensive in the European theater.

Paris was liberated in August, 1944, and the Board established itself there. Within a fortnight it became clear that we needed a much larger study by competent civilian specialists if we were to gain an adequate appreciation of the strategic air attack on Germany.

I returned to Washington for consultation, to find that others in the Pentagon had independently come to a similar view. As a result of the discussions that followed, Secretary Stimson created the U.S. Strategic Bombing Survey. Appointed a director of the Survey, which was to be based in London, I still retained my assignment as member of the Air Force Evaluation Board based in Paris. I therefore needed an alter ego who, for an interim period, could take over my duties on the Board while I worked with the Survey.

I telephoned Adlai and he flew to Washington two days later. He was more than ready to lend a hand, and at the beginning of November we flew to London together with the other members of the Bombing Survey. Ten days later Adlai and I crossed over to Paris, where he was to remain with the Evaluation Board.

It had been agreed that the Board should concentrate on studying the effectiveness of tactical bombing. This meant specifically a thorough examination of Allied efforts to interdict the Normandy invasion area by various types of air attack. The broader Bombing Survey, on the other hand, would direct its attention to a full economic and political appraisal of the strategic offensive against the German economy.

Adlai tackled the more limited assignment with curiosity and resourcefulness. As always when he faced a new problem, he talked to everyone who might have any information on the subject and filled dozens of yellow pages with his carefully handwritten notes.

In the course of his duties he made a tour of the Western front. He visited General George S. Patton and was at General Courtney H. Hodges' First Army Headquarters in Belgium the day before the Germans launched the Ardennes offensive. When he left the following morning to return to London through Brussels, Adlai did not know that the Battle of the Bulge was about to begin. His notes, gathered during his work in Paris and amplified and confirmed by the expert advice and eyewitness accounts he collected at the front, provided an invaluable addition to the store of information needed for the work of the Evaluation Board.

I have many memories of our weeks together in Europe. We shared a large apartment in a run-down villa in Saint-Germain-en-Laye, which, a few weeks before, had housed the generals commanding the veterinary corps of the Wehrmacht—and, Adlai strongly suspected, "their horses and other patients as well." The winter of 1944-45 was unusually cold and we had no heat. At night we faced a tough decision. Should we spend the evening with an American general who had a coal stove but who, in Adlai's words, was a "14-carat bore," or should we make out as best we could in our Arctic quarters?

One evening with the general provided a definitive answer. "I'd rather," said Adlai, "be frozen stiff than bored stiff." During the nights that followed, we pursued a consistent ritual. We put on our overcoats and placed a bottle of gin on the table before us. There was nothing to drink with the gin but tap water purified with halazone tablets. Yet we made out. After an ample number of drinks, we would each feel a sufficient illusion of warmth to go to bed.

Those long, uncomfortable nights taught me a great deal about Adlai Stevenson. Our conversation ranged widely, not limited to the work we were doing or the events of the day. We talked about our personal problems, our hopes and aspirations. Characteristically, Adlai asked as many questions as he answered. He was as much interested in my future plans as in his own. An evening with Adlai Stevenson was not necessarily a Stevenson evening.

A trivial recollection of that period sticks in my mind. One night when we were staying in Paris, Adlai and I were returning with a colleague from a very bad dinner in Montmartre. We were walking in the vicinity of the Place Vendôme—appropriately enough, as Adlai observed, on the rue Casanova—when we encountered American military police raiding an off-limits house. Field- and company-grade officers were debouching into the street in maximum disarray, protesting with spleen and outraged innocence at the affront to their dignity.

Adlai and I, although civilians, were in uniform (we each had the assimilated rank of colonel) and hence were indistinguishable from the culprits. This created a situation of some hazard, for Adlai· was enchanted with the spectacle of so many chagrined and choleric officers "whose expectations and consummations," as he said, had been abruptly interrupted. He insisted on seeing the show, and at least twice his curiosity led him so far into the crowd that he found himself shoved into a paddy wagon. It took all the advocacy my colleague and I could muster to establish Stevenson as a noncombatant and save him from the indiscriminate sanctions of military justice.

It was the kind of absurd situation he thoroughly enjoyed. Thereafter in my presence on several occasions he repeated the story with imaginative embellishment—generously substituting me for himself as the epic figure rescued from incarceration.

It gives me no comfort to have the last word now.

To Adlai

It's comforting to have you near —

Lyndon Johnson

Under Secretary of State George Ball, Ambassador Stevenson and President Johnson, photographed in the Cabinet room.

II

I did not see much of Adlai for some years after the war. He was in London for preparatory work on the United Nations, then he returned to Chicago while I remained in Washington. But we did have an occasional long evening of communion, both before and after his election as Governor in 1948.

Early in January, 1952, our paths again converged. I received a visit in my Washington law office from David Lloyd, who at that time was working in the White House as an assistant to the President's Special Council Charles Murphy. Lloyd told me that he and Murphy had talked with President Truman regarding the possible candidacy of Adlai Stevenson for the presidency. The President had not yet decided whether he would run himself. He had not commissioned them to sound out Stevenson but had indicated that he would interpose no objection if they cared to do so on their own initiative.

After several further conversations Lloyd called to say that he hoped I could arrange for Stevenson to come to Washington for a talk with President Truman.

I telephoned Adlai in Springfield but found him totally cold to the idea. Only a short time before, he had announced his candidacy for a second term as Governor. Running for President would be, he believed, an act of bad faith. He felt he had much unfinished business that he wished to complete during his next term. Above all, he was not going to let down his friends and supporters, many of whom were Republicans. He was not going to behave "like the garden variety of opportunistic pol."

After several telephone calls and considerable persuasion on my part he did, however, concede that he had official business in Washington that could provide the occasion for a visit. He wanted to meet with John L. Lewis and with the Secretary of the Interior to seek support for proposed measures for the federal inspection of coal mines in light of the Centralia mine disaster.

I talked further with Lloyd and an appointment was made with the President for Tuesday evening, January 22. It was understood, of course, that the meeting must be kept secret.

Stevenson was late in arriving in Washington from New York,

where he had made a speech the night before. He came to my house for a hasty dinner and found to his dismay that Carleton Kent of the Chicago *Sun-Times* had been calling and was already onto the fact that something unusual was afoot.

Dinner was hasty and Adlai droll but preoccupied. How could he best explain to President Truman that he wished to remain Governor of Illinois without seeming ungrateful or disrespectful of the office of the presidency?

I drove Adlai to Blair House, where President Truman was then in residence. I waited while he argued with the guards, who had never heard of him.

Adlai telephoned me the next morning. He had, he said, "made a hash" of his talk with the President, who had not understood his feelings at all and no doubt thought him a complete idiot. He was satisfied that President Truman had written him off as hopeless and that the incident was closed.

It was not an accurate appraisal, for I immediately began receiving calls from newspaper correspondents who had been alerted by the White House that Stevenson had spent the previous evening with the President.

During the weeks that followed I telephoned Springfield every few days, pressing the point that he should stop trying to resist the logic of history that made him the inevitable Democratic presidential candidate. Meanwhile I attempted, as best I could, to maintain uneasy communications between the White House and the Governor. I was not notably successful. Lloyd and Murphy were as convinced as I of Adlai's great qualities, but they knew the outer limits of the President's patience—and Stevenson was not behaving in a manner that made any sense to a seasoned man of politics.

Pursuant to his promise to discuss the subject further—and prompted, I suspect, by my persistent nagging—Adlai came to Washington toward the middle of March to try to explain his position more fully to the White House. Using an assumed name to avoid reporters, he flew in with his son John Fell on their way to Florida. They joined Murphy, another of the President's assistants, James Loeb, and myself for dinner at my house. One of my sons took John Fell to the movies while the rest of us talked late into the evening.

The discussion did not go well. Murphy told me later that he was deeply discouraged—reflecting, I assume, President Truman's own view of Stevenson's continued obduracy. Adlai spent the night with us, then took off the next morning. In the plane bound for Florida he wrote my wife a note, reporting wryly that "now we're approaching Jacksonville the miseries are melting away." Nevertheless, "the noose still feels uncomfortably tight about my neck and I wish I could see where the paths of self-interest and family interest converged with paths of duty."

But if the President was growing impatient, the country was becoming rapidly aware that a new political personality was emerging from Illinois. To catalyze the process, I wheedled Stevenson into letting me set up a small center of information in my law office. He reluctantly agreed but only if I made it clear that I was acting purely on my own initiative.

I raised several thousand dollars and hired some people to work up copy about Stevenson which we could begin to feed to the news media. I also sent a man to Springfield to review the Governor's papers, talk to his staff and try to develop some material that would bring out the achievements and dimensions of the man—stories about his family, his work as Governor, his principles and philosophy. In all of this, I was greatly aided by friends, Arthur M. Schlesinger, Jr. particularly. On one occasion I took another old friend, Bernard De Voto, to Springfield, where he stayed with Adlai for several days preparing an article for *Harper's Magazine*.

All of this activity began to worry the Governor, as "publishing" friends in the East let him know that they were being approached to print articles about him. He sent me several admonitory messages, addressing me teasingly as "The Earl of Warwick."

By that time, of course, a great number of people were starting to play a Warwick role, calling, writing and telegraphing to urge that he declare for the nomination. My principal anxiety was not that he needed to assert a positive intention, but that he might shut the door so tightly as to make it impossible for us to keep his candidacy alive. Whenever he considered drafting what might be interpreted as an irrevocable statement, I would insist that he hold off until I could talk to him on the spot.

I am not sure how many times, during the spring and early summer of 1952, I rushed to Springfield for long and searching talks in the Governor's Mansion. Those talks ranged widely over the whole problem of his possible candidacy. Occasionally, I could induce him to talk of what he would do "if he should be drafted." More than once he said to me, "If I do have to run, I must run on my own, with no one telling me what to do or say. I'm going to be myself, and the poor unfortunate electorate will have to take me for what I am. Every word I write or speak during the campaign must be mine. It must bear my own imprimatur."

He was always prepared to talk about the issues, particularly the great life-and-death issues of foreign policy. But—to my knowledge—even after his nomination, he shied away from any talk about how he would organize the government. He recognized quite clearly that one of the most difficult tasks for a President is to find the right people for the right jobs, and he worried about it. But he avoided the discussion of any specific appointments since he feared that any names he mentioned might become public knowledge and lead to the suspicion that he was promising jobs to gain support. I recall only one exception when, during a conversation alone with him in Springfield, he told me that he regarded John J. McCloy, a distinguished Republican, as the best man for Secretary of State.

During the months prior to the Republican Convention in July, it became clear that if Taft were to receive the Republican nomination Stevenson's choice would be made a great deal easier. He could campaign against Taft with the conviction that the issues were sharply defined. Taft meant a turning back toward prewar isolationism. But General Eisenhower was something else. He was an internationalist and Stevenson thought he might not make a bad President. Moreover, after twenty years of uninterrupted Democratic power "one could make a strong case for giving the Republicans a taste of responsibility."

But these doubts did not persist after July. Once the Democratic party had made its decision, Stevenson tackled the job of "educating the country" with zest and energy.

III

The 1952 campaign—not only for those who took part in it but for many Americans who played a merely passive role—was, I think, the highest achievement in Adlai Stevenson's career. He lighted up the sky like a flaming arrow, lifting political discussion to a level of literacy and eloquence, candor and humor, that tapped unsuspected responses in the American electorate. Most of us who participated in it had had no experience before in a national political campaign, and we loved every minute of it.

Adlai Stevenson loved it, too. Although he had no taste for the tedium of "political talk," by and large he liked the "pols" that he met in his campaign travels throughout the country. He admired their single-minded devotion to the business of getting votes and was amused by their total lack of interest in the issues involved. They were technicians plying a trade, displaying a cynical detachment he delighted to observe. What he could not stand were candidates who pretended a pious concern for the issues that they did not feel.

Once the campaign got under way he gave it his whole heart.

The draft at the convention absolved him from any remaining doubts about his obligations to the people of Illinois. The measured respect in which he held his opponents before the campaign was quickly dispelled by the handling of the "Nixon Fund" and the soap-opera character of the "Checkers" speech. He was shocked and outraged at Eisenhower's refusal to defend General George C. Marshall in the presence of Senator Joseph R. McCarthy of Wisconsin, who had vilified the General, Ike's former commanding officer. Adlai was in a fight. He had no doubt about the rightness of the policies he was advocating. He had a deep faith in the good sense of the American people—provided they were told the truth.

It has been often remarked that Franklin Roosevelt could have added a further dimension to his political effectiveness if, great actor that he was, he had had the use not only of radio but of television.

In many ways I think that Adlai Stevenson would have been a more effective politician if he could have fought his two presidential campaigns when only the radio was available. The 1952 campaign was the first in which television played an appreciable role, and for Adlai that was just bad luck. There was a vibrant eloquence in his words and in his oddly cadenced voice, but he obstinately refused to master the skills of the effective television performer. I know this well because I was, for my sins, director of public relations during the 1956 campaign. And while such brilliant virtuosos as Ed Murrow went to great trouble and pains to teach Adlai the tricks of an intimate television style, he resolutely persisted in reading speeches from a manuscript. "If they don't like me as I am, *tant pis!* I won't pretend to be anything else." His only concession to the susceptibilities of the television audience was an occasional nervous grin which, at irregular intervals, he would turn on and off too quickly.

Adlai's insistence upon working on his speeches to the last minute has become part of the legend. We used to tell him that "he would rather write than be President." On more than one occasion he completely missed press coverage by withholding his speeches for further polishing until after it was too late to make the morning newspapers.

Nor would he ever learn to keep his speeches within the Procrustean limit of thirty minutes. For those of us who followed a text of the speech in the studio or at campaign headquarters, the anxiety was always intense that Adlai wouldn't finish on time. The problem arose not only from the fact that he insisted upon inserting additional words, phrases, whole paragraphs at the last minute, but also from the curious circumstance that he had no established speaking pace. We never knew whether he was going to start slowly, then begin racing at the end of the speech when he discovered he was far behind, or start speaking quickly and then suddenly slow down. The greatest disappointment came on election eve in 1952, when he failed to finish on time and anguished friends frantically arranged to buy five additional minutes later in the evening so that the peroration of his speech would be known to the American people.

A constant quarrel that I had with him was his refusal to give his speeches a clear structure. "You are," I told him on more than one occasion, "a fine poet but a lousy architect. You say the right things and say them eloquently, but you don't let the structure of your speeches show through. Consequently, your listeners cannot recall what you have said or that you have recommended anything specific."

People, I insisted, think in schematic terms. Eisenhower's speech-writers regularly inserted in each speech eight, ten or twelve points, which the General would solemnly enumerate as the ultimate solution to a particular problem. Adlai would go to the heart of the matter but never tick off his recommendations in systematic form.

This kind of advice always annoyed Stevenson, and certainly he never accepted it. He had contempt for the pretentious pronouncement of obvious points as though "a list were a concept or a litany a program." That was, he felt, a cheap political device and he would have none of it. Besides, it offended his sensibilities as a writer.

IV

In spite of the problems, the failures, the heartaches, the testimony of the polls and the logic of circumstances, Adlai never doubted in 1952 that he would win. He believed in the rightness of what he was saying and drew confidence from his ability to "talk sense to the American people." An incident near the end of the campaign illustrates his conviction that victory would be his. Wilson Wyatt, his campaign manager, and I insisted that on a visit to a certain city he must pay a call on a powerful leader of a minority group who, he thought, was a charlatan. He reacted with annoyance and indignation. "Don't you characters believe," he asked, "that we are going to win with such a big vote that that kind of noxious business isn't necessary?"

As the campaign wore on, neither Wyatt nor I shared Adlai's faith in the outcome. The polls were too consistently running against us. His opponent was a great war hero, who had promised, if elected, to go to Korea and put an end to a war of which the American people had become tired. Besides, it was time for a change.

In the afternoon of Election Day, when the crescendo pace of the campaign had come to a shuddering and unnerving halt, Wilson and I took a long walk along the back streets of Springfield. In the intimacy of the gathering dusk we each confessed to what neither had up to then been willing to admit: that we were not going to win. Wilson was, as usual, clear-headed and honest.

"It hasn't worked. We haven't had time. We haven't been able to turn it around," he said. But we were in accord even at that final hour that Adlai still believed he would win and win roundly.

Yet, though he expected victory, he looked defeat in the eye with a dignity and style few other men could have shown. Adlai in defeat was the gallant champion. His thoughts, as usual, were of others. Those of us who had helped and worked with him were sustained by his grace under that hardest of pressures for a public man. He would have been just as fine in victory.

Late election evening a small group of old friends gathered at the Governor's Mansion. We were, all of us, in a state of shock. Though we had known in our hearts that victory was unlikely, the fact and magnitude of the defeat were bewildering and deeply daunting—especially when we contrasted the magnificent expression of American purpose set forth by our man with what we regarded as the pedestrian and opportunistic performance of his opponent. We were physically and spiritually exhausted— and troubled in our souls about the future of our country.

On that occasion as on others the stiff-upper-lip Stevenson tradition was fully maintained by the Stevenson sons, even by John Fell, who was at that time no more than fifteen. Once only in the evening did he betray his disappointment, wistfully observing to one of the women present that, while for himself he didn't much mind his father's defeat, "It would have been nice to have been the President's son just for a little while."

Adlai was remarkably composed and serene, the only blithe member of a doleful group. He had no taste, he said, for political wakes—"especially when I'm the corpse." He consoled us as though we, not he, were the losers, at one point disappearing into the kitchen for a jeroboam of victory champagne someone had sent him. Always the Scotsman, he insisted on not wasting it. Always the considerate host, he insisted on pouring it himself.

Finally, he announced that since he had lost the election the least he could do was to make the toast. And so, with Adlai, we all raised our glasses while he offered a tribute to "Wilson Wyatt, the best campaign manager any unsuccessful politician ever had."

He described himself wrongly, of course, as we all knew. He was no "unsuccessful politician," but a brave leader who had given a whole generation of Americans a cause for which many could, for the first time, feel deeply proud—a man of prophetic quality who, in Arthur Schlesinger's phrase, "set the tone for a new era in Democratic politics."

Only one person present that evening would have dared to call Adlai Stevenson "unsuccessful"—and we loved him for it. For we had each of us, at different times and in different ways, discovered that sense of decency and proportion, humility and infallible good manners which led him so often to understatement—particularly when he spoke of himself. And we would not have had him otherwise.

Pencils, Pads and Chronic Stamina

ADLAI STEVENSON influenced the lives of just about everybody who was ever associated with him. He certainly did mine. When we first met, some twelve years ago, I was a contented, apolitical magazine writer. Because of him, I became, among other things, a Democrat, a U.S. Ambassador and, I hope, a better American.

I may even have become a better writer, for my association with Stevenson was mainly, if sporadically, one of literary and forensic collaboration. Let me hasten to add that this is not a roundabout way of saying I was his ghost writer or speechwriter. Words I have written have appeared intact under such diverse by-lines as Eleanor Roosevelt, Jackie Robinson and John F. Kennedy; but I doubt if I ever wrote a paragraph for Stevenson that he did not manage to make his own by penciling in some fresh sentence or phrase in his neat but not always legible script.

He had such pride of authorship, such an affection for the

William Attwood, former Foreign Editor of Look *magazine, served on the Stevenson staff at the United Nations in 1963, between assignments as Ambassador to Guinea and Ambassador to Kenya.*

right (for him) sentence, that he inwardly—and sometimes out-
wardly—winced at the mention of anyone being his speechwriter; with those of us so described he could be brusque,
impatient and argumentative during the agony of editing. It was
as if he resented never having the time to do all of his writing
himself. But our friendship—certainly in my case—survived the
collaboration, mainly because Stevenson, no matter how fretful
and harassed, always kept his sense of humor.

We first met in 1953, soon after his presidential campaign.
He was about to take a trip around the world, and *Look* magazine, for which I worked, had secured the rights to eight pieces
he would write en route. I was to go along to make sure the
copy made the fortnightly deadlines—and was what the editors
wanted. It seemed like a wonderful way to see the world, and
I was the envy of all my journalistic colleagues, most of them
Democrats. Little did they, or I, realize that getting the right
words (for *Look*) out of Stevenson on time would be such a
nerve-racking experience (tranquilizers had not yet been invented); or that my duties, in the thirty-odd countries we passed
through, would also include the logistics of moving our five-man
group from one exotic two-night stand to another, handling the
excitable local press, arranging for stenographers and picture
coverage (often with my own battered Rolleiflex) and trying
to keep track of expenses in currencies no one had ever heard of.

The fact that Stevenson suffered from chronic stamina did not
make things easier. Many a morning, after tottering away from
a postmidnight South Asian state banquet, we would be up at
five to prowl around the local waterfronts or markets (he loved
markets) before boarding the next plane. And he was never
able to resist an opportunity to see one more pyramid, temple
or museum.

Our literary—if that is the word—collaboration began in Hong
Kong. After stops in Japan, Korea and Formosa, and four days
before our deadline for his first article, Stevenson finally got out

Stevenson and Attwood sightseeing in Egypt.

one of his big, yellow ruled pads, looked over some of my notes and began writing. As the pages drifted back to me, I soon realized that the graceful travelogue I was reading would neither grip *Look*'s readers nor boost its circulation. With some trepidation—this was after all a *Stevenson* manuscript, the first I'd ever seen—I began editing, cutting and sharpening the copy. Off and on for three days, the yellow pages passed back and forth between us, progressively more illegible, until we grudgingly compromised on a final version that reached the cable office with only hours to spare.

We went through this exercise seven more times in the next few weeks—in steaming Jakarta and Rangoon, where the yellow pads became stained with sweat; on a houseboat in Kashmir, where the staff addressed Stevenson as "Your Majesty"; on a mountaintop in Pakistan, a beach in Cyprus, a small château in Versailles; and on a hotel terrace in Positano, where we fled a gushing July 4 summons from Ambassador Clare Luce ("Good Lord," Stevenson had exclaimed, "we've got to get out of *that!*").

As social and official obligations multiplied (or was it the heat?), Stevenson consented to my producing rough first drafts which he then labored over late at night, usually wearing only shorts and sitting under an electric fan. Four or five drafts later —luckily most embassy typists were Stevenson buffs—I would have four thousand words to take to the nearest cable office, invariably just in the nick of time. Then we would begin sweating, both figuratively and literally, over the next installment.

My wife, who joined us in Cairo and took over the typing chores, said later that getting out one of these articles was like childbirth—except that it took longer and happened more often.

Today, twelve years later, the copy still looks good. Stevenson wrote about the new "revolution of rising expectations" and Asian aspirations ("respect and rice") at a time when U.S. policy was anchored to the concept of military containment. He wrote prophetically about India, Pakistan and Kashmir; and so perceptively and objectively about Israel and the Arabs that neither side could really like the piece. And he ended his last article by listing six realities America must face up to:

First: Our leadership and influence have sagged. Fear is contagious, and if we appear to distrust ourselves and our ideals, we can't expect others to trust us.

Second: Germany is imperative to the West.

Third: Red China is a reality that cannot be wished away; Formosa must be a bastion of peace and security in the Pacific.

Fourth: Trade is life itself for the great industrial nations, and their well-being is our security.

Fifth: Southeast Asia's security hinges on war in Indochina.

Sixth: The crisis of our times is moral as well as material, and the spirit of man is stronger and hungrier than the body.

And he added: "I don't recommend a working trip around the world, to anyone who likes to keep cool, sleep in the mornings or take Sundays off. But I strongly recommend it to anyone who thinks the world's problems are simple and that we can solve them all."

All the way around the world, Stevenson was a wonderfully tactful and disciplined roving ambassador for his country. Although McCarthyism was at its ugliest peak back home, and despite loaded questions at his every press conference, Stevenson never allowed himself to criticize in public what he privately deplored about the performance of the Eisenhower administration. He invariably spoke about what was best in our society and by doing so brightened America's tarnished image in every country we visited.

We parted in England—Stevenson still full of bounce and heading back to law practice in Chicago; I, twenty years his junior, to stagger away for three months' recuperation in Majorca. On the photograph he gave me, he wrote the first words in months that I was not required to edit and that, for me, suddenly transformed our grueling odyssey into a memorable experience:

"Farewell, but not for long, I hope, to a dear and gifted friend and companion in many adventures—from a junior reporter!"

The last phrase and exclamation mark were typically Stevensonian; so was the prophetic "not for long." Within a few months I was in Chicago doing a piece called "Stevenson Is Running Again." And over the next few years our editorial collaboration continued on all the articles he wrote for *Look*—about his trips to South America and Africa, about the need for a nuclear test ban (in 1957), about his 1958 visit with Khrushchev in Moscow. I think he liked writing for *Look* because he could always say

Look Magazine Photo © Cowles Communications, Inc., 1953

William Attwood and Adlai Stevenson with Nehru in 1953.

whatever he wished to a large audience with only my (by now) tolerable editorial interference with how he said it.

My participation in his 1956 campaign was marginal: a post-convention memo urging a hard-hitting campaign focused on three or four key issues—a memo obviously filed and forgotten; a lively but futile effort to stem the Republican landslide in my home town—an effort which merely got my wife elected secretary of the Democratic Town Committee; and one short speech, written in exasperation late one night after watching Stevenson talking on past his television deadline for the sixth time. He liked this speech well enough to use it repeatedly in the last week before the election, and it may have induced him to ask me, in December, 1959, to take a leave of absence and help him prepare speech material for the 1960 campaign—just in case.

With Nixon going after the presidency, 1960 was not a year for anyone who felt strongly about America's role in the world to be on the sidelines. While I was not enthusiastic about another Stevenson nomination (especially when I recalled his chaotic 1956 campaign), there was reason to believe, late in 1959, that the convention would deadlock. To many political pros, Kennedy's religion then seemed too great a handicap in what promised to be a close election, Humphrey would alienate too many conservative Democrats, and Johnson too many liberals and Negroes. Other than Symington, who never seemed to catch fire, Stevenson was widely regarded, before the primaries, as the likeliest candidate to keep the party united against the one man all Democrats were most anxious to defeat.

Thus, if another Stevenson nomination was in the cards, it was important that his campaign, for once, be well prepared, the issues clarified and the speeches on tap. Meanwhile, Stevenson had four or five major speech commitments in the spring of 1960; his chief backers—among them George Ball, Tom Finletter and Senator Monroney—felt that while other candidates contested the primaries, Stevenson should, in these speeches, set the stage for the campaign by committing the party (and hopefully the candidate) to a liberal position on the major issues.

And so, when Stevenson suggested that I take leave of my job to assemble and prepare material for this exercise, I readily agreed. At the time I could not anticipate that this decision to become involved in Stevenson's political activities (taken one winter evening as we flew from Washington to New York) would lead, a year later, to my assuming charge of an embassy in West Africa. But that's what keeps life interesting when you're past forty.

Stevenson's first major speech of 1960 was to be given at Founder's Day at the University of Virginia early in April. His backers hoped he would use the occasion to hit the Republicans (by contrasting their performance with Jefferson's ideals) and thereby kick off the 1960 campaign as the Democrats' chief spokesman. A draft of the speech, written by Professor Julian Boyd, the nation's foremost authority on Jefferson, was a literary and historical gem but lacked any political punch. My revision added plenty of punch, but we didn't know whether Stevenson, then vacationing in the West Indies, would be willing to deliver it before an academic audience.

To find out, I flew to Barbados with my draft. Arthur M. Schlesinger, Jr. was there with Stevenson, and the three of us used up a couple of yellow pads producing a version that would satisfy Stevenson and the scholars without sparing Nixon. When we were through, Stevenson sighed and remarked, "Well, here we go again!"

As it turned out, we didn't. The political portions of the speech got a big hand from the assembled professors and big headlines ("Adlai Lashes Out At GOP") in the next day's papers. But Kennedy had won in Wisconsin and was about to win in West Virginia. Determined to maintain his posture as a noncandidate, Stevenson toned down the political content that I kept cranking into his speeches. And a politician who doesn't talk politics in an election year doesn't get much attention.

Yet his supporters were making him a candidate in spite of himself. "Draft Stevenson" clubs mushroomed around the country, and every so often he seemed to be half-encouraging them.

In May I flew to Libertyville after the U-2 incident and found him angry enough to agree to a speech accusing Eisenhower of handing Khrushchev "a crowbar and sledge hammer" to wreck the Paris conference. And that, of course, got headlines. So did a Chicago speech in early June outlining a five-point "grand strategy for peace."

Kennedy, by then confident he had almost enough convention votes, wanted Stevenson's public backing both as insurance for the convention and because he knew he would need the all-out support of Stevenson's loyal legions in the campaign. In mid-June I met Kennedy for dinner in Georgetown, and he asked me what Stevenson was up to. I tried to explain that Stevenson's chief concern was Nixon's defeat and that he still wanted to remain available for a draft in case the convention should deadlock with no one to unite behind.

Kennedy impatiently insisted that he had the nomination sewed up and that Stevenson would find out he was making a big mistake. As for Walter Lippmann's suggestion for a Stevenson-Kennedy ticket, he said flatly he would never take the second spot, no matter what happened. After adding a few more unflattering remarks about Stevenson's political acumen, he relaxed and discussed the coming campaign. For some months, at Stevenson's request, I had been preparing a paper outlining campaign strategy and tactics against Nixon, and I assured him it would be available to whoever was the candidate.

By the end of the evening, Kennedy was practicing chip shots with a golf club on the rug and asking the three of us present whether he should make Stevenson or Chester Bowles Secretary of State. But when I later reported to Stevenson what Kennedy had said about his preconvention posture, his only comment was, "How could I ever go to work for such an arrogant young man!"

A play-by-play account of all that Stevenson did and did not do at the 1960 convention does not belong in this reminiscence of a collaboration. My only duties in Los Angeles were to concoct an airport arrival statement for Stevenson that managed to evade the question of whether or not he was a candidate, and to prepare some partisan remarks for him to deliver at a preconvention dinner. I was then free to observe the turmoil, which included my niece brandishing a Stevenson banner from a double-decker bus.

The pressures on Stevenson to say something definite were intense. Yet he remained curiously detached. Shortly before he made his tumultuous appearance at the convention hall the day before the nominating speeches, he called me in to suggest that I begin work on an address introducing Kennedy as the nominee at a postconvention rally. I remarked that a lot of his supporters would be downcast if they knew this. "Well," he replied, "that's the way it's going to turn out." Yet he still refused to place in nomination the man he knew would be the candidate.

The same evening, after the California caucus had revealed unexpected pro-Stevenson sentiment, a group of suddenly exhilarated Stevenson delegates held a meeting to plan the next day's stop-Kennedy strategy on the floor. The noncandidate appeared after midnight, thanked them gracefully and excused himself with a quotation from Robert Frost: "I have promises to keep and miles to go before I sleep." All cheered his departure, many of them assuming that he had finally decided to do battle and was preparing to spend the night rallying support for his cause. But when I went up to his suite a few minutes later, he was already in his pajamas.

In the morning I wrote a draft for Senator Eugene McCarthy's nominating speech, some of which he used; then, after Kennedy's first-ballot victory, I started working on Stevenson's introduction of Kennedy. I had no sooner wearily typed the opening sentence ("I have come to say good-bye, but not farewell") than Schlesinger appeared, happy to take over the chore. He knocked out a good speech in record time, interrupting his typing only long enough to dash over to the convention in consternation when he heard the news that Johnson was Kennedy's running mate.

Before leaving Los Angeles, Stevenson told me he had agreed to deliver ten campaign speeches for Kennedy, and could I prepare some outlines during July and August? I managed to get these done before joining Kennedy's speech-writing staff in August. But as I traveled with the Kennedy caravan on his first swing through California, Texas and Missouri to New York, it became obvious that Stevenson was going to have to do more than he had planned. Too many of his supporters were still sulking over the convention; too few were out ringing doorbells for Kennedy. Some I talked to were even planning to sit out the election.

Only Stevenson could fire them up. In the plane on the way to New York I suggested to Kennedy that I could be of more use traveling with Stevenson for the next few weeks. (Ted Sorensen and Dick Goodwin were, in any case, very competently producing most of Kennedy's major speeches.) Kennedy fully agreed, and a week later I turned up in Chicago to find Stevenson poring over a suddenly expanded speaking schedule.

Although campaigning with Stevenson in 1960 was arduous, at least the logistics were simple: we had no retinue to worry about. Bill Blair and I comprised the entourage, later reinforced by Bill Wirtz. We traveled commercial—and light. Besides a plentiful supply of vitamins, sleeping pills, yellow pads and Kennedy buttons, I brought along a basic speech for Stevenson to deliver to gatherings of the still faithful. The speech, which evoked nostalgic memories of 1952 and 1956, ended with a clarion call for victory at last in 1960 behind a candidate who stood for all the same things they had bled for together in the past.

The message seemed to have the desired effect. The faithful just wanted to see and hear Stevenson himself say that he was all for Kennedy and that they should be too. My only problem was making sure that Stevenson always had a Kennedy button pinned on his lapel; they kept dropping off, and he never noticed.

We covered a lot of ground—Minnesota, Washington, California, Utah, Colorado, Pennsylvania, Maryland, New Jersey, New York and North Carolina. And Stevenson wound up making not ten speeches but well over seventy.

I knew from past experience that any travel with Stevenson was strenuous, but this tour might have been less so had he been satisfied just to repeat the basic speech with regional variations. He wasn't. He felt, somehow, that he was short-changing his audience if he didn't have new material at every rally (even though we were only getting local press coverage). Fortunately, I had plenty of old Kennedy drafts on hand for him to tinker with. But when we reached Nixon's home state, Wirtz and I decided to produce something both fresh and appropriate.

With a rally coming up in Sacramento (good Stevenson territory), we dug into the files for every wild and reckless statement Nixon had ever made and came up with a speech that let him have it with all barrels. Stevenson, who detested Nixon as much as any man in public life, liked it well enough to make only a few changes. But later he wondered aloud if it wasn't after all too rough. We resolved his doubts by saying it had already been released to the press.

That night the Sacramento audience, part of it still flaunting Stevenson-for-President buttons, roared with delight as Stevenson began pouring it on. The cheering and applause lasted until he left, obviously exhilarated and enjoying himself. Outside, some reporters stopped him. "Governor," said a voice in the dark, "since when have you become Jack Kennedy's hatchet man?"

And that was the last time he delivered *that* speech.

Looking back, I think Stevenson's September and October barnstorming accomplished its purpose. Even though Nixon carried a good many of the states we visited, the essential margins of victory in Illinois and Minnesota alone may well have been

Adlai Stevenson and his party as guests of Tito at Brijoni; Mr. Attwood at far left, Borden behind AES.

provided by his stirring up what some Kennedy lieutenants called the Stevenson "cultists." And a few more Sacramento-style rallies in California might have carried that state too.

The long campaign over, I returned to my magazine job, intending to stay. Stevenson had asked me to join his U.N. team, but working for the government in New York did not tempt me.

What did was working in Africa, and when I was offered the opportunity to be Ambassador to Guinea, I resigned my job and joined the New Frontier.

Eventually, in 1963, I did put in a few months on Stevenson's staff between African assignments. What I recall most vividly is being in his office on November 22, just after hearing the unbelievable news of the shooting in Dallas. Everyone was standing, stunned and silent, before the television screen and then came the announcement that the President was dead. I remember looking over at Stevenson, who was sitting at his desk. For a moment he held his head in his hands; then he began quietly giving instructions on what had to be done before finally reaching for a pad and slowly writing the statement that had to be made.

Our long collaboration was almost but not quite ended. Just before I left the UN in December, Stevenson called me up to his office, where I found him normally harassed and fidgety behind his normally cluttered desk. He had, he told me, been asked by the President to write an introduction to a collection of Johnson speeches; and, with no free time in sight, he would be grateful if I would try my hand at a few appropriate paragraphs for him to work on.

Not knowing how Stevenson felt about Johnson, I asked for some guidance. He pondered a moment and then said he had known Johnson for thirty years; he admired him both as a politician and as a liberal who cared deeply about the basic issues; and he knew Johnson would be the kind of President who would devote all his tremendous energy to making America a better and stronger country. With that much to go on, I managed to produce a draft that survived Stevenson's editing relatively intact. I remember thinking that perhaps, after twelve years, I was finally getting a feel for his style. But those few paragraphs I gave him turned out to be the last.

On second thought, not quite the last. The last words I really wrote for Stevenson were the ones I composed one morning last summer in Nairobi just a few hours after he died. The newspapers had asked me for a statement, and this is what I gave them when I got to the embassy:

Adlai Stevenson died as he lived—at work. And his life's work was to serve not only his country but all mankind.

Those of us who had the privilege of working with him and for him know how much of himself he gave to this cause—how much of his intelligence, his courage, his kindness, his buoyant spirits and his seemingly inexhaustible vitality. We have lost a wonderful friend as well as a leader whose vision enlarged our own.

In everything he said and did, Adlai Stevenson expressed the deepest aspirations of everyone who believes that we are capable of building a safer and saner world. That is why I think that all men of good will, wherever they are, must feel a sense of personal loss today.

I like to think that the Gov would have approved of these last few words I was able to write for him; and that he would not have penciled in too many changes in that neat, not always legible and, to me, forever nostalgic script.

MARY McGRORY

The Perfectionist and the Press

THE FIRST TIME I heard the name of Adlai Stevenson was on March 27, 1952, a Thursday morning—I remember it well. Newbold Noyes, then the Sunday editor of the *Star,* summoned me from the book review department where I worked, and told me to rush around and get a story on the Governor of Illinois.

"Truman is speaking Saturday night at that banquet," said the editor, "and if he bows out, Stevenson will be the hottest politician in the country Sunday morning."

It was to turn out exactly as he prophesied, but that day in Washington few people knew much more about Adlai Stevenson than that he seemed unaccountably uninterested in following Harry Truman to the White House. Finally, a kind soul at the Democratic National Committee referred me to George W. Ball, a former Stevenson law associate, who later became Undersecretary of State. Mr. Ball smilingly broke out his private stock of superlatives for his old friend, and then, to make it live for me, thrust a sheaf of the Governor's veto messages into my hand.

They were my first taste of Stevenson prose and they were fine fare. He came through an essentially negative, political art

Mary McGrory, syndicated columnist of the Washington Star, *became an admiring friend of AES during the political wars.*

form as a witty and literate man, and plain-spoken on prickly issues. It was the high tide of McCarthyism, which swamped some public men and left others wringing their hands on the shore. The Governor of Illinois was unfashionably and unequivocally opposed to the junior Senator from Wisconsin. I wrote the story and went back to reviewing English novels.

The next stage in my encounter began on a hot July night in the mountains of New Hampshire. My brother and I, at my aunt's country house in Antrim, sat up late to listen to the proceedings of the Democratic National Convention. The mountains interfered grievously with the reception, but suddenly at one in the morning the clipped tones of Stevenson rode out over the static and the majestic cadences of his acceptance speech fell on our unbelieving ears.

Politically speaking, it was the Christmas morning of our lives. Boston-born, we had never known a poet in politics. Our father, mortified by the caliber of the Irish candidates of the Democratic party, always voted Republican. My brother and I wished he had lived to hear Stevenson.

When the last strains of the oratory had died, my brother said, "That's the best speech I ever heard in my life." Out of his childhood, he added, "He's too good for politics."

In the campaign that followed, for the first time in my life I read political speeches for pleasure. Stevenson's speeches seemed beautiful to me. I did not realize until much later how bold they were. I liked everything, right down to the concession speech: "Too old to cry, but it hurt too much to laugh."

The third stage of my graduated meeting did not occur until October, 1954, and the details are hazy in my mind. I had left the quiet precincts of book reviewing for political reporting, and one of my early assignments was to trail Governor Stevenson, who was then toiling through the Middle Atlantic provinces in behalf of his party. Somewhere in Delaware, I overtook him, spoke my name and held out my hand. All I recall is a hurried, bright-blue glance and a polite, preoccupied "How do you do, my dear?"

The most vivid memory of those days is the sight of his back as he vanished into his compartment on the train to work on his speeches. One day, having been instructed to seek an interview, I knocked on the door. The governor, in shirt sleeves, suspenders slipped down, looked up, very startled, and over such a palpable abyss of concentration that I excused myself and went away to renew my contemplation of the Jersey landscape. William McCormick Blair, Jr., his aide and friend (now Ambassador to the Philippines), was much amused.

We three finally fetched up in Brooklyn, where at the Academy of Music I had my first sight of Stevenson among Democratic partisans. It was instructive. The Brooklynites were packed to the eaves and in a state of high excitement. Accustomed to symphony-audience raptness during his addresses, Stevenson was plainly nettled at their restiveness. Midway, an uproar, preceded by a flying wedge of policemen and attended by bearers of television lights, began to move down the center aisle.

Adlai Stevenson was the last man in the hall to realize that at the eye of the commotion was Averell Harriman, candidate for Governor of New York. Bewildered by the cheers, blinded by the lights, the Governor pressed on. When his vision cleared and he recognized his old friend and former rival for the Democratic nomination, he said briskly, "Oh, hello, Averell," and then, to the audience, "Shall I go on?"

It was a moment of pure Stevenson, a perfect illustration of his priorities. Any other politician would have ringingly introduced the candidate and abandoned the speech. But not Stevenson. Throughout his public life he believed that the public shared his obsessive concern for the public business and that a politician's whole duty was to state for the citizenry the great issues of the day.

I tried to describe it. Some months later, at a vast Democratic

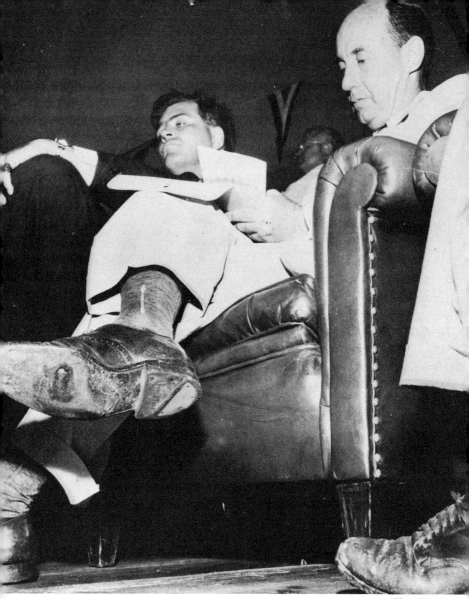

This picture taken during the 1952 campaign won a Pulitzer Prize for William M. Gallagher of the Flint, Michigan, *Journal*. A shoe with a hole in the sole became a campaign symbol.

banquet, I became aware that Stevenson was signaling to me from the dais. Considering the remoteness of our relationship, I was surprised, but went over to the reporters' shelf directly below the dais and was helped up to reach over the centerpiece and greet him.

"My dear," he said, "I read your stories and I found them bewitching."

Our friendship dates from that moment. I had never heard a politician use the word "bewitching" before. I never have since. A precise choice of adjectives was an integral part of the hold that Stevenson had on people.

The next time I saw him, he was caught in the toils of the grim and hopeless second campaign against General Eisenhower. He was seldom visible to his train of reporters. One day he was coaxed from his quarters to move through the press car. ABC commentator Edward P. Morgan reminds me that I told the Governor he had given a line at the previous stop—"that's what Democrats are for: to make dreams come true"—that was close to iambic pentameter.

"I hope it doesn't explode," said Stevenson cheerily.

That was, of course, the year of the great lament from the fourth estate. They wrote volumes about their difficulties in covering a candidate who simply could not get them the speech on time.

My good friend, and Adlai's, Edwin Lahey of the Knight Newspapers, is wont to say when he hears scribblers keen, "Don't forget there are two million people in this country working in steam laundries."

In 1956 we all forgot it. Self-pity is always unattractive, but possibly a word of self-defense is allowable. Part of the problem was the screaming contrast with the butter-smooth Eisenhower press operation. The General's speeches may have been bland; they were always in the reporters' hands well in advance of the earliest deadline.

The running argument in the press bus was that the campaign, like war, reveals the man. It followed as the night the day that a candidate who could not choose between words could not choose between courses of action in the White House. We easily forgot that if the manner was tentative the matter was not. That was the year that Stevenson advocated the end of nuclear testing, a proposal promptly labeled as "catastrophic nonsense" by Vice President Nixon, and later embodied in the test-ban treaty signed by President Kennedy in 1963. But we who were exercising what he called our "friendly but implacable surveillance" were getting the speeches a page at a time in the press room, even as he was speaking them on a nearby podium.

Many of the reporters were despairing admirers. They well understood the search for the right word; they went through it daily themselves. But even his warmest advocates could see that he was paying a great price for perfectionism.

On October 18, to pick a striking instance, in the Cincinnati Hall of Music, the Governor gave the most impassioned speech of the campaign—an eloquent denunciation of Eisenhower's foreign policy as "timid, naïve, sterile" at the height of the Suez crisis.

When it was over, the audience rose to shout its approval. They stormed the stage to hail the orator. Even the wire-service photographers, a professionally impervious breed, joined the stampede that knocked over the potted palms on the platform to shake the candidate's hand.

Against the exultation in the hall there was consternation in the press room. The reporters for the big Eastern dailies, due to the tardiness of the text delivery, had missed their first editions. The last eleven minutes of a stirring peroration had not been seen by the television audience. The purchased time ran out, the technicians had signaled Stevenson in vain.

Incomprehensible as it may seem in an era when "public relations" is reverently regarded as an art or a science, or both, Stevenson had absolutely no sense of it at all. The term itself was alien to him. In the Stevenson scale of values only private relations mattered. He had good friends among the reporters. He treated them with the same warmth, consideration, and confidence he showed all his friends. The press as a whole was, I think, a blur to him. He was aware of their problems—he must have been, since he was lectured and exhorted often on the point—but he never considered them of comparable consequence to his own. He understood intellectually perhaps that they were also engaged in the communication which so absorbed him, but the inescapable conclusion is that he thought—if he ever considered it at all— that they were cheering him on in his endless safari for the ultimate expression. He was so busy carrying on his part of "the dialogue of democracy" he hardly noticed who was following him. To the Washington press corps, which is much petted and spoiled, a candidate who did not know their names was something of an affront.

The Governor was much wounded by harsh criticism. He complained to his friends, but never, so far as I know, to the source. It was not his style.

I have reason to think that the longest and most ambitious analysis of him I ever attempted did not please him, but his feeling was only indirectly conveyed.

In 1959 a publisher's representative asked me to contribute a Stevenson chapter to a book of profiles entitled *Candidates, 1960*. Like my subject a sufferer at the writing table, my first impulse was to refuse. But then it occurred to me that someone who thought him an "indecisive egghead" would write and hurt his feelings, so, with appropriate misgivings and doubts, I agreed.

I spent a whole winter staring at blank paper in the typewriter and talking to the Governor's friends and enemies.

I also talked to him at some length. From one meeting in his New York law office I came away with two overriding impressions. One was that in spite of elaborate public protestations to the contrary he had a good opinion of his own worth, of his knowledge of the world and of his capacity for the presidency. The other was that the failure of his marriage had blighted his life. With troops of friends, legions of admirers, he was a lonely man. He accepted too many speaking engagements, too many dinner engagements, because, as he often said, "I have no life of my own."

He also explained to me his agonies over the speeches. An early abhorrence of public speaking had made him compulsively anxious to be letter-perfect.

During my researches, Eric Sevareid, the editor of the book, pointed out to me that his favorite Stevenson speech was spontaneous. Unexpectedly called upon to say a word at the funeral of his friend, Lloyd Lewis, the editor and historian, Stevenson spoke with the felicity that he thought could only be achieved after sacrificial cogitation.

He said, in part, that day, without notes:

It is April now, and all life is being renewed along the bank of this river that he loved so well. I think we will all be happy that it happened on this day, here by the river with the spring sky so clear and the west wind so warm and fresh. . . . I think it will always be April in our memory of him. It will always be a bright, fresh day, full of infinite variety and promise of new life.

I have before me a twenty-four-line statement the Governor made in 1957 on winding up a three-week tour of State Department duty with Secretary of State John Foster Dulles. He had penciled in thirteen corrections and amendments and a whole new last paragraph. Like all perfectionists, he was subject to second thoughts, and he took as much time as he could to scrounge for just one word more.

The Governor never mentioned the book chapter to me. But once, with a distinct edge to his voice, he said, "Of course, I know nothing about practical politics like those Bostonians you're always writing about."

The subtitle of the profile was "Uneasy Politician." The theme was that Stevenson had carried the hobbling gentility and fatal diffidence taught in the nursery into the political arena. Like all of us, he had his Walter Mitty side. His fancy was that he was a demon politician.

During the 1960 preconvention struggle I ran into him somewhere in the West. He inquired how it was going, and I told him that Humphrey was not catching on while Kennedy was bowling them over. In one of his celebrated, candid asides, he mused, "I guess Hubert doesn't have enough charm and Jack has too much."

I was in his suite in Los Angeles the night he knew for once and for all he would never be President. He watched Senator Eugene McCarthy's memorable plea, "Do not reject this man who has made us all proud to be Democrats," and the convention exploded in its one authentic emotional moment. He murmured, "Magnificent." After Wyoming put Kennedy over, he went off to another room with George Ball to compose a statement.

"Now for some purple prose," he said lightly, whether in resignation or relief I could not tell.

Later that season in California, where he was king, he introduced John Kennedy with a speech of exceptional felicity and generosity. "Do you remember that in classical times when Cicero had finished speaking, the people said, 'How well he spoke,' but when Demosthenes had finished speaking, they said, 'Let us march'?"

Afterward, spotting me in the crowd, he gallantly offered me a ride back to town in the candidate's Cadillac. The conversation between the old and the new heroes of the Democrats was slightly strained.

"You look wonderfully well, Jack," said the Governor. "So tan."

The triumphant young nominee explained it came from riding on the backs of open cars.

"I never would do that," said Stevenson with some feeling.

"It's awful, the sun in your eyes, and dust. You can't see for hours afterward."

It was just one of the differences between them.

With the death of the presidential dream, Stevenson obviously yearned to be Secretary of State.

During the 1960 Republican Convention in Chicago a friend gave a party for Stevenson. A number of his old friends showed up and a surreptitious gaiety informed the evening. The Governor told me that Senator Kennedy had invited him to come to Hyannis Port, supposedly with a thought to asking him to campaign.

Facetiously I suggested the Governor memorize a short sentence in the native idiom: "What's in it for me, Jack?" We both laughed uproariously at the idea of his ever saying it.

On an icy December afternoon I stood outside the Kennedy home in Georgetown and watched the President-elect and the Governor unhappily emerge. The President had offered Stevenson the ambassadorship to the United Nations. Stevenson was withholding his reply pending the appointment of the Secretary of State.

He took Nan McEvoy and me back to the home of his friend Dr. Paul Magnuson, and the comfort of an open fire. We all knew, despite his doubts and disappointments, he would end up saying yes. Professionally and socially, he needed to be needed. He groaned when asked; he inevitably accepted.

Some time after the Bay of Pigs, when, on instruction, he had denied flatly any American complicity, I saw him as he came away from a White House meeting.

"That young man," he said, shaking his head, "he never says 'please' and he never says 'I'm sorry.'"

The United Nations years were not happy. He resented articulating policies he had little hand in making. He disliked dealing with State Department underlings. His vanity was never in self-expression; it was in his grasp of foreign affairs.

He was much sustained by the regard of the other diplomats. Many of them he had met on his travels or were readers of his speeches. He told me with great pride of having called on every representative of the hundred-odd nations at the UN. He described with relish an evening in Greenwich Village, where, as the guest of a new African republic, he had sat on the floor and watched native dances by candlelight.

I was out of the country during the great furor of December, 1962, when, in a magazine account of the missiles crisis in Cuba, Charles Bartlett and Stewart Alsop wrote that he had advocated "another Munich." When I next saw him, he said he was tired and would soon quit to go home to Libertyville to write his memoirs.

With all his frustrations, he was always marvelously merry at social occasions. Once he came to my home in Washington and was immediately enfolded in the attention of the whole room. Among the guests were several matrons who, at the sound of his voice accepting the nomination in 1952, had doffed their aprons and set out for Democratic headquarters. One of them, Elizabeth Acosta, of Falls Church, told him she could remember his words. "You said you looked forward to the day when no man would rattle a saber and no man would drag a chain."

The competition to sit beside him became intense. A self-appointed timekeeper imposed a five-minute limit and was discovered cheating. He seemed to enjoy it all hugely, particularly when a fellow Illinoisan, Mrs. Daniel Cleary, sang two stanzas of "The Illinois Hymn" in his honor. As he left, he said, "Let me know when the club is meeting again. I'd like to become a member."

The last time I saw him was in San Francisco at the home of his son, John Fell. The President had discarded his draft for a twentieth anniversary speech to the United Nations. Accustomed to such setbacks, the Governor was in fine fettle. All around him were old friends of California, where the Stevenson fires had always burned most brightly. He twitted his daughter-in-law about the appointments, warned the guests there would not be seats and food enough to go around. He laughed at his two-year-old grandson, John Fell, Jr., a square-jawed, stern-faced child whom he happily called "Mao Tse-tung."

During a quiet moment I told him about the prospects of a mutual friend, Daniel P. Moynihan, a then Assistant Secretary of Labor who was being mentioned as a candidate for Mayor of New York.

He was instantly and vividly alert. He said he would try to speak to the President on the way from the airport.

On July 14 I was home making peanut butter and jelly sandwiches for a children's picnic when the telephone rang and the national editor told me that Stevenson had died suddenly on the streets of London. Other members of the *Star* staff who were involved in the outing called and asked if we should call it off. I said the last thing we should do would be to call off a children's picnic on Adlai Stevenson's account. We went forward and spent much of the afternoon talking about him. Then we went back to the office to write.

The next night I walked up and down the lines waiting to file past his bier in the crypt of the National Cathedral. The grief was subdued but intensely personal. One woman told me she had brought her children and, trying to explain what Stevenson was and what his life had meant, had finally told them, "He was a failure, but not a failure at all." A number of people spoke of hearing the acceptance speech of 1952 as of the moment of falling in love. One man grumbled that the details in the paper about the hours for the public viewing had been vague. He was, like all true Stevensonians, protective; he suspected that his hero, in death as in life, would somehow be imposed upon, be cheated of the full honor he deserved. In the line were many reporters who had followed him on his campaigns and who had, like me, complained of the lateness of the speeches. They were remembering the man, not the delay.

When I think of him now, it is with gratitude. I am indebted to him for the best moments I have spent at countless political banquets and rallies. I am indebted to him for his ideas, for his language, for his courtliness and his incorruptible good breeding, for the men he brought with him to public life, for the tone he gave to politics and, like everyone who knew him, for the pleasure of his company.

NEWTON N. MINOW

Marching to
the Beat of Mankind

FEBRUARY 5, 1900, was Adlai E. Stevenson's birthday. Fifty years later, while he was Governor of Illinois, some of his close friends began an annual celebration which was to continue for fifteen years. Although the setting shifted from downstate Illinois to the Chicago suburbs, and then, after 1960, detoured East to suit the tight schedule of the newly appointed Ambassador to the United Nations, the festivities always attracted a diverse, eclectic group of the Governor's closest friends. This collection held in common an abiding devotion to Adlai E. Stevenson, a devotion formed at varying stages of his life and career.

In the comfortable environment of those who loved him, the Governor was always at his humorous best, and sometimes at his sentimental best. When we toasted him with our amateurish efforts at wit and wisdom, his incomparable rejoinders quickly

---

Newton N. Minow was a Stevenson assistant in Springfield and later a law partner. He served as Chairman of the Federal Communications Commission from 1961 to 1963, when he became executive vice president of Encyclopaedia Britannica, Inc. He is now a senior partner in the Chicago law firm of Leibman, Williams, Bennett, Baird and Minow.

reminded all of us that he was the undefeated champion of the deflating retort, the complete squelch and the droll epigram.

On his sixty-third birthday he gave the party himself at the United States Embassy in the Waldorf Towers in New York, his home while he served as our United Nations Ambassador.

It was an especially gay evening, for added to the party regulars were some very special guests, including Art Buchwald and Al Capp. Keyed up by the high level of humor, the Governor was in splendid form and responded to our toasts with *élan*.

Suddenly, I was called on—at the least propitious moment. My unenviable assignment was to follow Buchwald, who had just topped Capp. In my desperation, I borrowed a toast made in 1957 by Bill Blair, our former law partner who was then Ambassador to Denmark. Not long after the 1956 election Bill had raised his glass to the Governor and said, "It takes a great man to go through two defeats and not lose heart. But you, Governor, have done something infinitely more remarkable. You have gone through two defeats, and not only haven't lost heart, you also haven't lost weight." Heartened by the group's enthusiastic reaction, I continued on my own, and predicted to the Governor that at sixty-three his troubles were almost over; if things continued their present course, in two years he might play his most significant federal role. "By 1965," I said, "you'll qualify for Medicare!"

With the inevitably twinkling eyes, pursed-as-if-mortally-wounded lips, he turned and responded: "That's one thing about my old friend Newt Minow. He always tells me the truth, even when it hurts . . . me! He told me not to run in 1952. He told me not to run in 1956. He told me not to run in 1960. And now he tells me two more years and I can retire with Medicare."

As I look back over the fourteen years in which the Governor was such an intimate, organic part of my life, I recall most strongly the times I spoke my mind to him. Sometimes my words were blunt and must have hurt. And I marvel, now in retrospect, that the Governor always accepted with grace and patience a young man's impudence. Impudence, yes, and inexperience and shortsightedness—for now, in the light of history, I can look back and see how often wrong I was, and that he, sometimes early and sometimes late, proved to be right.

In 1952 the Governor hired me on the recommendation of Carl McGowan to become one of his assistants in Springfield to help him with his legislative program as Governor of Illinois. At that time I was working as a law clerk to Fred M. Vinson, Chief Justice of the Supreme Court, and was to report to Springfield in the summer of 1952 when the Court term had ended. Knowing that I wanted to go to the Democratic Convention, the Chief Justice kindly let me leave a week early. But as he said good-bye and wished me well, he said, "Newt, I don't want you to be too disappointed. Your man Adlai is not going to be nominated. President Truman has decided to back Alben Barkley for President."

When I arrived in Chicago, I passed this news on to the Governor and his staff. It was, of course, true, but they had not yet heard of President Truman's decision. Being twenty-six and inexperienced, I brashly volunteered my own view that this was good news; with General Eisenhower's nomination there was no chance for any Democratic candidate to win. I thought Governor Stevenson should run for a second term as Governor, for which position his exceptional record gave him an excellent chance of re-election. At his age, a later presidential effort, perhaps against less formidable Republican opposition, was a likely prospect, it seemed to me.

I know that the Governor personally agreed with this assessment of his presidential prospects. But he had a different view of political leadership and political responsibility. He believed that if a great political party chose him to carry its standard, his personal preferences were irrelevant. He believed it his duty to accept the nomination and to fight for that election with all his heart and soul, even in the expectation of defeat. As he said in his acceptance speech:

That my heart has been troubled, that I have not sought this nomination, that I could not seek it in good conscience, that I would not seek it in honest self-appraisal, is not to say that I value it the less. Rather it is that I revere the office of the presidency of the United States.

Although he lost the election, his decision to run was right. In losing the election, he elevated American political discussion, advanced American and international understanding of the issues, and brought his own party new vision and purpose.

In 1956 many of the Gov's friends urged him to try again. This time I felt the chance to win was, if anything, even more hopeless than in 1952. Once again I advanced the arguments against the race. This time, however, there was no reluctance on his part to seek the presidency. He believed so deeply in the need to end the drift and complacency of the fifties that he assumed the burdens and responsibilities of another campaign.

In the course of that campaign he introduced the issue of a ban on nuclear testing, and vigorously advocated the necessity of stopping the amounts of nuclear fallout blowing down from the atmosphere. Many of us in the campaign warned that this issue could only lose votes. The public opinion polls supported our fears, but the Gov was determined. He said one day, "There are worse things that can happen to a man than losing an election. The worst thing is to lose one's convictions and not tell the people the truth."

He was ridiculed by his opponents on this fallout issue, as on others which subsequently became sound national policies. And he lost the election. But his courage and his eloquence helped to educate the nation and to change public opinion and political opinion as well. He lived to see a treaty outlawing nuclear testing. Millions of children, born and unborn, can thank him for being so right, so brave and so faithful to his own convictions.

With his law partners the day Stevenson ended private practice to become Ambassador to the UN, January 12, 1961. Standing, from left, Edward McDougal, William McCormick Blair, Jr., Willard Wirtz, Newton Minow and John Hunt.

There are those, and I confess I was often among them, who believed, more in sorrow than anger, that the Gov did not have acute political instincts. In many of his campaign moves, including the ban on nuclear testing, he did make wrong political decisions. In the narrow sense of politics, in the adding-machine verdict of vote gains and losses, our judgment was often superior to his.

But what we failed to comprehend immediately, and only began to understand later, was that his political instincts were generally keener than ours. He was very much aware of the political repercussions and drawbacks of many of the moves he made on the chessboard of electoral politics. The point is that he knew the political hazards and still rejected these short-term considerations. Even after he correctly assessed the immediate gains and losses, the Gov invariably chose that course, not with the largest vote-getting appeal but with the longer-range values. His guide was the effect, not on the vote next week but on the nation next year, and the next decade.

He was right when he said I always told him the truth—or at least the truth as I saw it. But this was only a small, narrow, thin part of the truth. I was right, many times, in my assessment of the damage he would do to his career by certain decisions. But his was the larger wisdom, the wisdom of a Socrates who pointed out that the difference between a wise man and a fool was simply a sense of measurement: the fool saw a small figure miles away and concluded that the figure was really only an inch tall, but the wise man recognized the distance and measured the figure by the distance and concluded that it was really a hundred feet high. So the Gov looked ahead and noted the small specks and concluded that these specks, the atomic fallouts and the education of the electorate, were really massive in their implications. And he sized them up far better than those of us who concerned ourselves with the here and the now, with political fortunes on Election Day, not judgment day.

The Gov never lectured us about values, but by his own courage, his wisdom, his example of self-sacrifice, he taught millions of his fellow countrymen, and fellow beings, to search out in the quiet of our hearts and minds the paths to peace, integrity, morality and international understanding.

Adlai E. Stevenson was often out of step with some of us near him who tore our hair at his political mistakes. But he was marching to a more distant drummer. He was marching to the beat, not of his personal victory but of mankind's.

With Adlai in Asia

I DON'T KNOW a better way for friends to test a friendship than to take a long, hot, tiring trip together. Next to sharing service in a prisoner-of-war camp, there is nothing that so strips down human beings to the bare essentials of their nature.

I was lucky enough to take such a journey with Adlai Stevenson in 1953. Our friendship survived. In addition, I learned many new things to admire about him under the pressure cooker of travel.

Adlai was eager for a fresh look at things after the rigors of the 1952 campaign. He decided to take a swing around the world with a small party of friends. He and I spoke from the same platform at a service honoring the press martyr, Elijah Lovejoy, in Alton, Illinois, and on the way back to Chicago he asked me to go along.

Our companions were Bill Blair, Walter Johnson and Bill Attwood, then of *Look*. The whole trip took more than five months. I spent the first three months of it with them, moving across twelve countries of Asia from Japan to Pakistan.

Adlai expounded his plans to us on the first lap of the journey

Barry Bingham is editor and publisher of the Louisville Courier-Journal *and the Louisville* Times. *He was national chairman of the Volunteers for Stevenson-Kefauver.*

across the Pacific. He had made it clear in public statements that his purpose was purely "self-education." He saw himself as a private citizen, out to learn what everyday people were doing and thinking in a part of the world, Asia, which he had never before visited.

He told us that he had felt he should follow correct form by reporting his plans to President Eisenhower. He had been asked to come to luncheon at the White House. The conversation had been amiable, but without any clear points of direction from the President.

Adlai on his side was determined to avoid any possible misunderstanding of his mission on the part of people in the countries he planned to visit. He wanted it clear that he was traveling neither as the President's emissary nor as his critical opponent.

He told us, with the little flash of impatience he sometimes showed when bothered by formalities, that the State Department had insisted on "alerting" every embassy along the way of his impending arrival. He was determined not to let this mean an endless series of official receptions and dinners.

His plan, he insisted, was to see all kinds of unofficial people—journalists, educators, labor leaders, writers, students—and avoid the tedious duties of an official visit. He was just a private traveler, eager to listen and learn.

He did talk to all sorts and conditions of men on that journey, because he tirelessly insisted on it. But he also talked to every important political leader in every country along the way, because they insisted on it.

What he did not in the least anticipate was the ardent interest his presence would stir among the peoples of Asia. It did not occur to him that they would show a warm desire to establish through him a contact with the mind and heart of America.

Did the people of Asia see him as a typical American? I am sure they did not. They recognized in him, however, a quality of Americanness that may have been less obvious to his own

Malay aborigines presenting Stevenson with a native blowgun and quiver of arrows.

fellow countrymen. It was a feeling that came from the rich, warm earth of Illinois, the countryside he loved, and the one in which his ancestral roots ran so deep.

I think Asians found in him the sort of American they had always hoped to see. Instead of arrogance, he brought them an utterly natural air of humility. In place of patronage, he gave them the kind of grave courtesy that runs far beyond the range of good manners.

The surprise began the moment we touched down in Tokyo. Almost unmanageable crowds thronged the airfield. Amateur photographers elbowed aside the professionals of the press. Babies were held up on shoulders for a look. Autograph books fluttered like autumn leaves.

Adlai stepped down from the plane into that milling throng with a look of mild perplexity, a slight air of apology for causing all the fuss. It was the same scene at every city in every country we visited. There was a positive longing to see the man who thought of himself as a private citizen from Illinois.

On the day he arrived the English-language Tokyo *Evening News* printed in full the acceptance speech he had given at the Democratic Convention in Chicago nearly a year before. The editor explained in a note that the speech was no longer news, but that it demanded rereading because it contained "one of the most cogent interpretations of the spirit of democracy—humility coupled with a recognition of the obligation to serve the general welfare." That phrase caught Stevenson's attitude with remarkable clarity.

Impatience is a quality Asians expect all Americans to show, and not without reason. Stevenson surprised his audience in that connection in his first and only formal speech of the trip, before the Japan-America Society in Tokyo.

"Wise men," he observed, "do not try to hurry history. The contest against tyranny is not a hundred-yard dash. It is a test of endurance."

Americans often assume an air of omniscience when they travel in far places, possibly because they are secretly unsure of themselves in strange territory. Peripatetic politicians are especially subject to that failing.

Stevenson again surprised Asians by refusing to be categorical on all subjects. To some questions thrown at him at press conferences he simply replied, "I don't know." To some others he said, "I'm sorry, but I don't feel qualified to answer that question." Asians had never heard an American public figure respond in that way.

He managed to be tactful under an extraordinary variety of circumstances. At the same time, he avoided seeming wary, guarded or solemnly noncommittal.

Reporters on Taiwan pressed him for his views on the military effectiveness of Chiang Kai-shek's forces, which we had just seen in a display of training methods. Stevenson met the question with a chuckle. "I am no military expert," he explained. "The highest military rank I ever achieved was as an apprentice seaman in the United States Navy in World War I."

The wonderful rightness of Adlai's manner won a tribute from Ernie Hill of the Chicago *Daily News*. He reported from Tokyo: "Stevenson has evidently made a firm resolve that he will not be the new American pop-off. People are amazed at his firmness in this determination. For that and other reasons, he made a tremendous hit in Japan and Korea. He is regarded here as a statesman with intellect and wit."

In Kuala Lumpur the *Malay Mail* made this comment: "Stevenson's visit is in many ways a unique one. Officially, he has no standing whatever, and is only known to the mass of people here as the man who failed to win a particularly important election. And, generally speaking, people are not very interested in failures, however distinguished. But Mr. Stevenson is in a very different category. He is still a power to be reckoned with in United States and world politics."

An American long resident in the Far East told us that the people of Asia want two things above all others: respect and rice. I was interested that he put them in that order.

Adlai gave respect to every person he encountered, from the venerable Dr. Syngman Rhee in Seoul to a worker bent from labor in a Vietnamese rice paddy. This quality of his nature, so genuine and unforced, paid handsome dividends in his later work at the United Nations. The gift of human respect he so freely offered won respect in turn for him and for his country.

Adlai had to be amazingly nimble at press conferences to avoid the booby traps that were laid for him. The remarkable thing was that he managed to say so much of substance without once crossing the line of propriety on American foreign policy he had drawn in his own mind.

He offered no automatic defense of everything American. He did not respond to criticism with the hot and haughty anger that so often afflicts our spokesmen abroad. All the same, his intense national pride came into play at the moments when it could have the maximum effect on those who heard his words.

He brought his matchless eloquence to the task of making America more understandable to young audiences in particular. He sought occasions to talk to groups of young people. Some of the students showed plainly that they had been swilling the potent brew of Communist propaganda.

At a breakfast meeting in a Japanese university, some students undertook to explain to him the attraction of Communism for many of their fellows, while denying its appeal to themselves. They complained of disorders in Japanese political life since America had "imposed" democracy on their country. "Just what is democracy, anyway?" one student asked in a shrill, provocative voice.

Stevenson's reply may have taken as much as five minutes. The fire of his conviction seemed to warm the unheated classroom in which we met.

Democracy, he explained, is honest disagreement. It is the right to hold the opinion you believe in, and to fight for it with self-respect and determination. The virtue of democracy is not cold order. It is the heat of men's minds rubbing against each other and sending out sparks. It is liberty coupled with responsibility. It is a struggle that never ends and is always worth the fight.

In Jakarta we encountered a group of young intellectuals. One of them informed us that only America has an important stake in fighting Communism, since we have so much to lose.

Stevenson erupted at that point. Every free country, he declared, has the most important of all things to lose if the Communists take over—the liberty of the people. That possession, he noted, should be particularly precious to those nations which have only lately gained their freedom after generations of colonial rule.

He followed with a brief outline of early American history. Our country, he reminded his listeners, has not always been rich and powerful. It won its independence through bloody revolution against what was then the world's dominant power. Its resources were meager, its friends few.

The American people formed their nation with their own hands. Men went out into the trackless forests with axes over their shoulders. Women traveled agonizing and dangerous journeys in covered wagons. The pioneers had to fight the forces of nature and human enemies at the same time.

It was from this struggle that our nation developed its greatest strength, not our national wealth but our national unity and self-respect.

Then Adlai apologized for making a speech. It was a statement, as he phrased it, that I wish could have been recorded and heard in all parts of the world.

Stevenson's humor was justly famous. I have not heard comment on one aspect of its nature, however, which impressed me strongly: he never won a laugh at the expense of another human being. All his best jokes were told on himself.

This point was especially apparent in Asia. It is all too easy there for a visitor to offend local sensibilities without having the slightest intention of doing so. Adlai's humor was always quick and spontaneous. His innate taste was so good, however, that he never once touched an Asian sore spot with one of his fast, rapier-like quips.

Stevenson was a consummately good talker, but in Asia he established his credentials as an excellent listener. His family newspaper in Bloomington, the *Daily Pantagraph,* lost a fine reporter when he went into other fields. He had an instinct for asking the question that brings out the significant reply. His eye for the shape of a situation, his memory for the details of an interview, would have given pride to an experienced foreign correspondent.

These qualities and others were especially apparent in two lengthy conversations with Prime Minister Nehru in New Delhi. I had the advantage of sitting in on both, in the enviable position of the fly on the wall.

The play of intellect between Stevenson and Nehru was fascinating to observe. Adlai was of course noted for his command of English. Nehru, who was said by Gandhi to have dreamed in English, showed the same delicate grasp of the nuances of the language.

Those two men, from opposite ends of the world, talked as though they had enjoyed an intellectual friendship for decades. Each spoke lucidly and with candor. They were not talking at each other for effect, but striving to communicate ideas as though they had been storing up thoughts for years for this particular occasion.

At one point they fell to talking about the rigors of political compaigning in America. To my surprise, Nehru expressed a positive joy in contact with multitudes of people. Whenever he grew stale and restless from the grind of administrative work, he said, he found that the best tonic was to go out among crowds and refresh himself from their inexhaustible enthusiasm.

Stevenson nodded in complete understanding. Here were two men, both considered almost too civilized for the sweaty business of politics, acknowledging the same feeling of satisfaction in communion with swarms of eager people along the highways and in town squares.

After spending the month of May in India with Adlai, I gave up worrying about his ability to endure the physical hardships of political life. The heat was relentless, by night as by day, the pace intensive.

I remember one night we spent in Benares. We were sharing a room in a small hotel. When we went to bed we found ourselves almost smothered under mosquito netting, with no breath of air coming through the staring windows. Each of us tossed and turned in his bed for a while, remembering the burning ghats we had seen that day loaded with corpses, remembering, too, the wrecks of humanity we had seen creeping through the streets, people who had come to die in the holy city by the Ganges.

After a while we gave up and began to talk. We talked all night, until a pale light came to herald another burning day. An hour later Adlai was up, apparently rested and ready to continue the inexorable schedule.

He had a rather low threshold of boredom when it came to conventional sight-seeing, though he did enjoy such contrasting sights as a crowded village square on market day, or an ancient ruin. He did agree to take off part of a day, to visit the ruins of Angkor Wat in Cambodia.

Adlai was dutifully following our guide along the dragon bridge that approaches the main temple, a building like an ornament carved in amber in an emerald setting of jungle growth.

Suddenly the air was rent by a voice raised in purest Americanese. "Ad-lie, Ad-lie!" it called, following the common mispronunciation of his given name. A large, amiable, overheated American lady came steaming up, her camera bumping at her ample bosom. "Ad-lie!" she cried, "I've been saving my last film for a picture of a water buffalo, but I think I'll take you instead!"

Adlai posed, shook her hand warmly and went away chuckling to look at the fantastic wall carvings of the temple. He was still laughing days later at the glory of substituting for a water buffalo.

That humorous, quizzical, uninflated view of himself was one of Stevenson's rarest qualities. He was a completely unstuffed shirt in a profession, politics, where stuffed shirts abound.

His happy quality of self-deflation was one of the things that made him so attractive to his friends. That feature of his character was of a good deal greater importance, however.

Barry Bingham and AES arriving at Louisville.

Courier-Journal and Louisville Times

The honest modesty of Adlai Stevenson was felt by every person who came in contact with him. This aspect of his personality made it easier for him to get on friendly terms with the simplest of people, as well as the most sophisticated. The value of such a human touch was demonstrated on every day of our long march across Asia.

Traveling with Adlai in that part of the world taught me a lasting lesson. It made me understand that people in many lands can feel hostility to the United States Government, yet display warm friendliness to individual Americans if given a chance. Stevenson always gave them that chance.

People listened to Adlai in Asia because he listened to them. He told them his ideas with clear conviction, but he did not shout at them. That voice of reason, of good sense and good will is the tone America needs to use in addressing the people of all countries.

The actual voice of Adlai Stevenson will be heard no more. Some of his statements were recorded for posterity, and it is a happy thing for all of us, though we still cannot hear them without a lump in the throat.

It was not just his voice, or his gift of phrase, that must be preserved, however. It was the way he spoke to all kinds of people, with such warmth and simplicity, and with that slight twinkle of the eye that seemed to signal a private source of amusement between him and each of his listeners—that is what must not be forgotten. His was the tone in human relations that we would like to identify everywhere as the real voice of America.

WILLIAM BENTON

Ambassador of Good Will in Latin America

FOR ANY MAN, and more particularly for any woman, an association with Adlai Stevenson was memorable. My own friendship with the Governor goes back to the late thirties in Chicago. My recollections of him are rich in incident and detail—and in history. I well remember his efforts to buy the Chicago *Daily News* after the death of its publisher, Colonel Knox.

In the spring of 1960, when our friendship was more than twenty years old and had been firmly cemented by our joint interest in the Democratic party and in the *Encyclopaedia Britannica* and its various enterprises, Governor Stevenson and I took a trip together through Latin America. This trip, with its concentrated fourteen-hours-a-day association for more than two months, was a revelation, and my contribution to this book will largely consist of my recollections of it.

William Benton is chairman and publisher of Encyclopaedia Britannica Inc., former Assistant Secretary of State and U.S. Senator from Connecticut, and currently U.S. Ambassador to UNESCO. He and Governor Stevenson were friends for more than twenty-five years and close associates through the Governor's membership on the Board of Directors of the Encyclopaedia Britannica *and Encyclopaedia Britannica Films.*

When news of the Governor's death was brought to me on a plane over the Atlantic last summer, only a few hours after I had lunched with him in London, my reaction was not simply one of grievous personal loss. I knew that the world had lost not merely its best interpreter in the continuing fight for peace; it had lost its "first gentleman." It was in Latin America that I learned, more abundantly than I can say, how much he deserved this title, in small matters as in large. And it was in Latin America that I realized fully the extent, and even more the intensity—the depth and sincerity—of the world's admiration for Adlai Stevenson, as the very conscience of the American people.

Until our trip neither of us had ever visited the great cities of South America. The problems of that continent were not unknown to us. But it is one thing to deal with the affairs of a country or a region as they appear in government documents or in conferences; it is quite a different thing to absorb the temper of a people by being physically among them, and particularly to absorb it in the setting of their capital cities. This Governor Stevenson had been able to do in Africa and Asia during the previous seven years when he crisscrossed much of both continents. I had been able to do so in Asia not long before the war, when I had spent much of a year there. Above all, Governor Stevenson and I had been able to do this in Europe over the preceding thirty years, during which each of us had crossed the Atlantic times without number. I had observed again and again the high esteem in which he was held in France and in England, where we had spent a total of many weeks together.

Belatedly—as Latin America has impinged belatedly on the horizons of so many Americans—in the year both Governor Stevenson and I had reached the age of sixty, we devoted sixty-odd intensive days to twelve Latin-American countries. Counterclockwise facing south, we flew to Mexico, Guatemala, Costa Rica, Panama, Colombia, Ecuador, Peru, Chile, Argentina, Uruguay, Brazil and Venezuela. The entire journey was a personal triumph for Governor Stevenson. He seemed to be known to almost every Latin American. More popular than any motion picture star, he was besieged everywhere by admiring crowds seeking autographs, handshakes, waves and smiles. The Latin Americans adored him. Nelson Rockefeller, who had been a big figure in the Latin-American countries for two decades, was an

John Fell Stevenson—Magnum

William Benton and AES on a balcony in Panama.

"also ran" in comparison to Stevenson. Indeed, I came back from our trip convinced that if these twenty republics had been states of our Union, they would have swept Governor Stevenson into the presidency.

Although we traveled as private citizens, his appearances became a triumph for the United States. President Eisenhower would have been well advised to have asked him to go officially because he did us great good in every country. He was a true ambassador of good will. In his learning, his wisdom and wit, his urbanity, his eloquence and his humane qualities, he symbolized the characteristics the Latin Americans most admire in their intellectuals and their political leaders.

Many Americans find it amusing that many Latin Americans list themselves in their biographical material as "orator," something no American or Anglo-Saxon would dream of claiming. The Latins place high value on elegant articulateness. The Governor gave them continuous cause for admiration. I heard him give at least sixty extemporaneous speeches. And he repeated himself only once. Twice he made the same deft response to a flattering introduction with the comment that he "did not know whether the toastmaster would go to heaven for his charity or to hell for his falsehood." When I asked him why he didn't use a good speech a second time, why he didn't repeat himself, he laughed gently, "Because I can't remember what I said yesterday."

We talked with eleven of the twelve presidents of these countries, and with the Prime Minister of Peru, whose President was in Europe. We met also with cabinet ministers, with leaders of the opposition, with intellectuals, labor leaders and students. Our own embassies, indeed, treated us as if we were on an official mission. We were expected to attend so many formal luncheons and formal dinners that our schedules gave us no time for naps or siestas, and frequently only four or five hours' sleep a night. I would not recommend to the tourist seeking a good time the regime to which the Governor and I were subjected. Our Latin-American hosts and the United States embassies vied with each other in homicidal hospitality. Often this devoured us with ceremony and protocol: the two-and-a-half or three-hour luncheon, the late dinner and reception with toasts and speeches and brandy still being served at 1 A.M., six hours before plane time. All of this was meant to compliment us, and much of it was instructive, but it was not the best way to relax—nor was it always the best way to learn the facts of political life.

The Governor was more patient than I. With generosity of spirit he allowed himself to be put upon and taken advantage of. His energy was unflagging. When I rebelled and refused to accompany him on a couple of side trips, he chided me on missing the experiences that were the most fun (as I'm sure they were), but I was doing my daily dictation of notes and correspondence while the Governor was indulging his instinct for exploring every native market and archaeological ruin he could find.

As an example of the pressures which were ours, and a sample of what was expected from us, let me describe the first day of our journey, in Mexico City—a not untypical day. The city is 7,500 feet above sea level, and my doctor had warned us we should allow a full day to adjust ourselves to the altitude. Our tourist plane from Chicago arrived at night an hour or more late. Dinnerless, we got to the hotel about 10:30 to find the Overseas Press Club waiting for us. We met with them until about one o'clock, gulping scrambled eggs and Coca-Cola.

The next morning we were up at seven. At 9:30 our U.S. Ambassador had assembled his entire staff to greet us in the embassy's gardens—about five or six hundred people. (This is one of our two or three largest embassies.) We gave little speeches. Then we had our "briefing" by the able and energetic Ambassador Hill and his aides, until some time around noon, when we called on the Mexican Foreign Minister. This visit was followed by the Foreign Minister's three-hour formal luncheon of welcome, and this in turn by a visit to the Palacio de Bellas Artes with the famous Mexican artist Rufino Tamayo, to see his murals. Back at the hotel at 5:05 with no time for a siesta, we were picked up at 5:40 for a call on President Adolfo López Mateos.

From the President's mansion we were rushed to the U.S. Embassy at 7:30 to stand in line to shake hands with 750 people. We were still on our feet after ten—with no supper, but with a well-pleased Ambassador and staff.

Some of our days during the next sixty would end with a protocol dinner which would perhaps start at ten after an hour and a half of standing at a reception. After these dinners Governor Stevenson would speak with ease, with wit, with originality —and he would be emotionally moving, with material closely keyed to his audience.

Our trip followed shortly after a visit by President Eisenhower to the Latin-American countries. In the opinion of many observers, one of the most significant events of the President's trip had been an open letter addressed to him by the Federation of Chilean Students. This letter, which was discussed widely throughout Latin America, recited many of the grievances we were to hear time after time. It spoke of the "merciless exploitation" of Latin America by European and North American capital. It emphasized the "need for just prices" for Latin-American commodities. It argued that the United States had failed to provide initiative for a nonmilitary system of security in the hemisphere; that we had supported dictators; that we had not encouraged "the economic integration of Latin America's industrialization." It contended that because 40 percent of Latin America's population is illiterate, and because two-thirds are in a "chronic state of malnutrition," the "policies of the status quo" are inadequate.

Thus one of the most significant and at the same time most typical events of our own trip became the all-morning meeting which Governor Stevenson and I had with the Chilean students. The Chilean Communists took our meeting with these students— and took Stevenson's and my visit to Latin America—seriously enough to cast aspersions on Stevenson's "propaganda" motives. Their story was headlined "Stevenson Comes to Reap Where

Ike and Nixon Failed." Thus they obliquely gave witness to his tremendous popularity in Latin America.

We met the students in a classroom which contained a small library of perhaps five or six hundred volumes. There were about twenty-five student chairs in front of us, each chair labeled with the name of the student who occupied it—the type of protocol one sees at an embassy banquet. Some students were from the Catholic University, some from the National University. All parties were represented, the Communists as well as the Christian Democrats. All the chairs were occupied by young men—there were five girls listening in an adjoining room. The heads of the Student Federations of the two universities delivered long opening addresses, read from handwritten manuscripts. They weren't really talking to Governor Stevenson or to me. They were making campaign speeches to the other students, many of whom looked bored. Then the Governor's conference followed. It was a memorable performance.

Many of the students were of course bursting with hopes and ideals, as well as impatience. Governor Stevenson made the appropriate acknowledgment: "I trust this will always be so, for the idealism of today is the best hope for the practice of tomorrow."

One of the students complained that the high level of armaments in South America diverted funds from education. He was touching upon a theme upon which Governor Stevenson hammered constantly throughout our Latin-American tour. In every country we visited, he asked, "Why doesn't Latin America take world leadership in disarmament?" When political leaders lectured us on the United States' responsibility to bring about Latin America's economic development, the Governor often retorted rather sharply that it was hard for us to justify financial aid to countries which spent such large percentages of their budgets on armaments. "Why should American taxpayers want to give money away for such unproductive purposes?" he would ask.

In the mountains of Peru.

The president of the Students Federation from the Catholic University maintained that "Capitalism is not right for Latin America; we don't have the same conditions as the U.S."

"In our country," he continued, "benefits go to a small number; the great masses do not take part in them. But Communism is not a solution; with its tyranny and its loss of human dignity it operates in a human void."

Governor Stevenson rejoined, "What are the alternatives to Communism? You've said capitalism is not a solution. If you mean that without capital you will have no capitalism, I agree that it isn't a solution. But I am confident that as capital is formed, and above all reinvested in Latin America, capitalism will serve a valuable purpose. Your problem is this: if governments are unstable, if your economies are stagnant, capital will take refuge elsewhere." The Governor went on: "Where there is little private capital available, certainly you must use any available government capital. If some recoil at the thought of government capital, don't include me. I'm one American who is not afraid of the word 'planning'!"

The Governor pointed out that the nationals of many South American countries keep their own capital in Switzerland, in the United States and elsewhere. He asked, "If your own Latin-American nationals won't invest their own money in their own countries, is it likely that foreigners will?" In Mexico City Governor Stevenson had sat next to a rich banker-industrialist who told him he had twelve million dollars in the banks of New York and had asked him if he had any ideas as to how best to invest it!

The Governor agreed emphatically with the students that the masses in Latin America do not benefit sufficiently from the system as it presently exists, and that those with high incomes pay too little in taxes. The latter concentrate too much on what Thorstein Veblen called "conspicuous consumption." Throughout our whole tour Governor Stevenson stressed the "social responsibility of the rich." Unfortunately, Latin America has developed no tradition of philanthropy by the wealthy.

The Governor insisted that the great issue throughout Latin America is whether the goal of democracy will prevail. "Shall we have the triumph of government by the consent of the governed?" (The Governor was thinking of all the voiceless governed —the Indians, the rural poor and those searching the will-o'-the-wisp of a better life in the slums we had visited in the great cities.) The Governor exhorted the students, "As Lincoln said, a nation cannot live half slave and half free; and Franklin D. Roosevelt said, 'We cannot live half bust and half boom'; and I say that the hemisphere cannot continue in peace and prosperity while it is half rich and half poor."

The Governor went on to conclude: "The decade we are

entering is perhaps the most perilous in history. We need moral and practical hemispheric solidarity. History teaches us we can do much for one another, but what our countries do for ourselves is decisive." Governor Stevenson reminded them that the United States had its New Deal in the thirties, and that perhaps Latin America now needed its own New Deal.

A week or so after our visit with the Chilean students we were in Buenos Aires speaking to the then Argentine Minister of the Interior, Alfredo Vítolo. His enthusiasm about our trip was boundless. The Minister told us that no foreign minister who had visited Latin America could possibly be called "disinterested." He emphasized that Governor Stevenson's trip would have "tremendous repercussions" because it "seems disinterested," because it "dramatizes the human element." He told us that "the climate" of our relations was more important over the long pull than financial aid.

I have dwelt in some detail on the imaginative rapport which Stevenson achieved with one group of Chilean students to help explain the high consideration which Latin Americans such as Minister Vítolo accorded him.

My last period of close day-by-day association with Governor Stevenson was brief, and tragically so. I was with him almost continuously for a week before he died. I left him at 3:30 on the afternoon he died, at Claridge's Hotel in London. I left him to catch my plane for New York.

I had given a luncheon for him and Dr. Robert Hutchins, both of them directors of the *Encyclopaedia Britannica,* of which I am publisher, with the three top officers of the London *Britannica* office and their wives. Governor Stevenson asked me to keep my suite open for him, not to check out, to let him use it for some afternoon appointments. I gave him my key.

A couple of hours later he walked to the hotel desk and turned in the key and said to Mrs. Marietta Tree, the ambassador to the UN who worked under him and who was with him, "I don't need the suite. I shall save Bill Benton an extra day's charge." He was always careful about money, including other people's.

This was his last act. As he walked from the hotel with Mrs. Tree, back through Grosvenor Square, he fell to the sidewalk and died. She knelt beside him to breathe into his mouth in an effort to revive him. The London papers called this "the kiss of life."

I had met him in Geneva the previous Wednesday. We were there for State Department meetings. We had dinner together, the two of us, at the Perle du Lac, the beautiful restaurant on the lake front. Thursday I spoke at a closed session in my role as Ambassador to UNESCO. Friday Governor Stevenson spoke at an open session, and the *New York Times* international edition carried his speech on the front page of its Saturday edition. This speech dealt with the world-wide problems of urbanization, growing from the rush of people to the city. It was his last speech.

Saturday we met in London and had lunch at Chequers with Prime Minister Harold Wilson and spent all afternoon with him at his country residence. Sunday we drove to lunch with Governor Stevenson's "Aunt Mary" Borden, his ex-wife's aunt, now Lady Spears, the wife of General Sir Edward Spears, and then on to Oxford for the afternoon and for dinner with Lord Franks, provost of Worcester College, of which Governor Stevenson was a fellow. As Oliver Franks, he had served as British Ambassador in Washington.

Governor Stevenson had asked Ambassador Bruce and me to play tennis with him early Sunday morning, before he and I left for Oxford at eleven. The Ambassador and I laughed at him; we were too tired. He asked Mrs. Bruce each day for tennis during his five days with the Bruces before he died. He promised to spend the next weekend playing tennis with me at my home in Southport, Connecticut. We were to talk about his future after his anticipated resignation as U.S. Ambassador to the United Nations at the end of 1965.

Thus he died in full vigor, in full force and command of his physical capacities.

The Governor's final public confrontation with the grave issues troubling the world came on Monday night on BBC's *Panorama* TV program, which had been recorded on tape after his lunch with his *Britannica* colleagues. He had devoted himself to the world's problems throughout the last week of his life. He died as he had lived, putting all his great talent and energy into the cause of world progress and peace.

BARBARA WARD

"Affection and Always Respect"

I THINK many of Adlai Stevenson's friends must at times have been surprised by the warmth and extent of his popularity round the world. Defeated candidates for the presidency do not normally occupy a very high place on the list of American world figures. Nor was his a meteoric appeal, shooting up in the 1952 election and then fizzling out. The Governor (as he was known to so many of his friends) had a durable quality, and both his reputation and his following survived not only two decisive defeats at home but also four years in the United Nations in a role more mercilessly exposed than any other on the entire international scene. There he was never beyond the reach of public attention or the constant critical appraisal of some of the shrewdest and not necessarily best-disposed minds in world politics. Yet at the end not many would have dissented from the verdict of the President of the Eighteenth General Assembly of

Barbara Ward, the distinguished British economist and author, is the wife of Sir Robert Jackson, a consultant to the UN and adviser to Liberia and Ghana.

211

the United Nations, Dr. Carlos Sosa-Rodriguez, who said, in sad retrospect, that Stevenson "never inspired hatred but only affection and always respect."

There are, of course, a number of perfectly obvious reasons for the Governor's popularity. He had that quality for which the Africans, who know how to appreciate it, have found a special term. *"Nommo"* is the Bantu word for the gift of making life rather larger and more vivid for everyone else. One might say "life enhancement" if it did not sound so dreary. But whatever you call it, the Governor had it. Any group of people would be likely to feel a lift when he appeared, with his energetic bosun's roll of a walk, his quick look of interest, the smile that was never a formality and the whole manner that seemed to say: "Now, I really am delighted to be just here just now." Perhaps this only suggests the practiced bonhomie of a good mixer. It was the opposite. The Governor never had to practice curiosity or zest. If anything, he had to repress them.

Then, of course, he was very funny. People knew from his speeches that he was witty and that a lot of the wit was directed against himself. But again this was not something he strove for, sweating out the epigrams and agonizing over the bons mots. The humor sprang from a deeper, more spontaneous source. (He *did* agonize, but usually, I think, to get exactly the sense he wanted. The graceful, appropriate words did not seem to fail him.) I remember once reading a brilliant piece of literary criticism about Jane Austen's outrageously funny juvenile works, *Lady Susan* and *Love and Freindship* (*sic*). I think the writer was G. K. Chesterton. Anyway, he points out that the extraordinary polish and wit of Jane Austen's great novels, the shimmer of humor which plays like light over her mature writing, spring from an underlying, perfectly controlled but hilarious sense of fun which borders on farce. This in turn runs back to a yet deeper source—zest for life itself.

I think the Governor had something of this. The humor that

appears in his speeches in well-turned aphorisms and witty asides flowed spontaneously and steadily through his private talk. It hardly mattered what the anecdote was about. It became hilariously funny, usually with the Governor as the butt of the joke. One of his favorites, for instance, was of the large, enthusiastic delegation who met him at Chicago in the 1956 campaign headed by a very large pregnant lady carrying a banner, "Stevenson is the man." His gifts as a raconteur often made one feel that, as he sometimes ruefully complained, a remarkable newspaper correspondent had been lost in him.

Yet a lot of men have been charming and gay and witty. The world, however, does not much mourn or even note their disappearance. Stevenson had to have much more than these personal gifts, engaging though they were, to have become a world figure. And although such things are hard to analyze, especially when there has been no time to stand back a little and look from a longer perspective, it seems to me that the Governor's reputation among his thousands of friends abroad, known and unknown, was based above all on two somewhat opposite reactions. He realized one lively hope about America. And he exorcised an equally lively fear.

The United States is the first and oldest state in the world to be run on the ideological basis of equality. Naturally, the hope has been that such a society would produce a new kind of man —a man unspoilt by privilege, pride and pretension, yet able to absorb and make his own the great traditions of education and culture which, in the West, have deep roots in older, highly privileged orders of society. The pessimists, of course, predicted mannerless louts. An egalitarian society, they maintained, could only lead to the degeneration of courtesy, manners and personal culture. At the Revolution, the extraordinary quality of America's Founding Fathers gave the lie to these gloomy premonitions. Benjamin Franklin in Paris became the archetype of the new American man—fresh, unspoilt, deeply rooted in a new free com-

monwealth, but carrying over into the new order of society learning, manners, wit and a courtesy of the heart.

This hope—that a free society could produce a culture and
a style as noble and rewarding as the old aristocratic refinements
—has had, of course, its ebb and flow. The caricature Americans
in the pages of Dickens and Trollope can be set against the good
and innocent Americans—the Strethers, the Minnie Theales—
of Henry James, the Babbitts against the Hemingway heroes.
But not all the flood of back-slapping salesmen, gum-chewing
GIs and Miami-shirted tourists has been able to efface the conviction that the first great popular society in human history
ought to produce its own good manners, its own grace and learning, its own style.

It is not difficult to see how the Governor satisfied this expectation. One part of his character was a remarkable, unspoilt freshness and directness. He went through a degree of adulation and
attention that would have ruined a more complacent character,
simply remarking, "Flattery is great so long as you don't inhale."
His enjoyment of visits, journeys, parties, new places, new people,
was quite undimmed by long experience. When friends sometimes remonstrated about what they took to be almost over-
sociability, he would say with a laugh, "But you forget, I'm only
a country boy from Bloomington."

And there was a lot of truth in it. The Illinois prairie—the rich
farms, the wide skies, the fields "white unto harvest," the flaming
maples in the fall—nourished his imagination. When he went
back to his farm at Libertyville, he grubbed about continuously,
thinning trees, cutting out undergrowth, dragging off fallen
branches; or he took his visitors to walk along the Des Plaines
River and told them of the old portages (in one campaign nothing
in the day's politics pleased him so much as the discovery in a
little downstate town of an aged voter whose great-grandfather
had come down by canoe with the French); or out in the woods
he would carry friends off to see a recently felled tree and count

the rings which showed it to be older than the first European settler. I think he really did draw a lot of his zest and unimpaired capacity for interest and enjoyment from his rooted love for the wide, untrammeled Illinois countryside.

This was his birthright. So there could be no mistaking his Americanism. There was absolutely nothing of the transplanted European about the Governor. The energy, the curiosity, the good spirits all bore an absolutely authentic transatlantic stamp. This gave a special quality to his learning and his manners. Of course, we are all, Europeans and Americans alike, part of a wider tradition of Western scholarship and Western courtesy. This overarching cultural unity is a fact. We do not behave like Mandarins or look at history like Hindus. But the hope that the American version of a common Western tradition would have a special quality—of spontaneity and energy and frank good will —was very happily confirmed in the Governor. His courtesy, though constant, was not formal. It really seemed to spring from a lively interest in others and genuine good will—the frontier tradition, if you like, of seeing the stranger as a friend and possibly in need of help. And though he had received at Princeton a normal "Western" grounding in the humanities and by his own interest continued to read widely, I always felt that it was the transposition of the West's great political traditions into an American key that moved and sustained him most.

It is strange how the archetypal figures of American politics seem to recapitulate the two vast and formative forces of the Western world. The Founding Fathers are bathed in the rational yet heroic light of ancient Greece. One can imagine that Jefferson would have felt profoundly at home in a Greek polis, and Washington, the farmer turned general, general turned political leader, is the ideal of Attic adaptability. Then in Lincoln the picture darkens. The tragedy and ambiguity of history, the overriding imperatives of moral judgment, the wages of sin, the necessity of fortitude—all these bear a Biblical stamp.

I think, perhaps, Stevenson, by temperament and perhaps family tradition, drew more heavily on the eighteenth-century aspects of Western thought. He had the Enlightenment's cool, Deist religion, its belief in reason and the possibility of progress, its fundamental optimism and intellectual curiosity—he would certainly have subscribed to the first Encyclopedia—its sense of natural law and of the community of all mankind. A correspondent once called him a "modern Benjamin Franklin"—a comparison which could also include his love of fun, his delight in conversation, his ease and pleasure in the company of pretty, clever women, his zest for entertainment, in short, his "urbanity" in the broadest sense, however deep his country roots.

Yet Lincoln was his profoundest inspiration in politics. All Lincoln's works, every book written about Lincoln, lay within arm's reach of his desk at Libertyville. In any case, no responsible statesman could confront the second half of the twentieth century without tempering hope with fortitude and underpinning optimism with stern faith. The golden light has faded from the hopeful dawn of the Founding Fathers. By temperament, the Governor may have belonged to that world. By daunting experience, public and private, he became a man of tragic faith, and again and again, he found its deepest expression in Lincoln's own words. How often, for instance, in the middle of the appalling pressures, dilemmas and compromises of an election campaign would he guard his own and his supporters' integrity with Lincoln's touching phrase: "I must keep some consciousness of being somewhere near right. I must keep some standards of principle fixed within myself."

I think I can best give a sense of his particular appeal to people outside America by giving a couple of personal experiences of its dual character—the zest and spontaneity on the one hand, the courtesy and culture on the other, and both deeply, unmistakably American.

The Governor came to stay with my husband and myself in Ghana in 1955. I think it was his first African journey and the place fascinated him. We took him to the markets where the market women—who have their own network of political intelligence—gave him a hero's welcome, and he wandered in absorbed interest from stall to stall, questioning, comparing prices, wondering which brilliant "mammy cloth" would do for the girls back home in his office, studying with special care the stands for selling magic and love potions. Dried monkey's heads, ground roots, strings of seeds, wicked little amulets—he exclaimed over them all, asking about their potency and making up a list of friends and acquaintances who could, in his view, use them with advantage. The "mammy traders" entered into the game, adding song, handclapping, a shuffling dance and ecstasies of laughter as one or other of them commended some particularly potent love charm for the Governor's own use. The visit ended in a nice mixture of political parade and near-riot. The Africans recognized at once the man with their own special gift—"*Nommo*"—the man who, simply passing by, could make the day ten times more fun.

We went down several times to swim in the surf on Labadi Beach. The Governor's insatiable curiosity soon took him wandering off from the beach huts and the bathers to the fishing village beyond. He watched fascinated as the rough fishing smacks, hollowed out from tree trunks, were dragged up the sand and the inevitable mammies arrived to barter for the silver catch, still alive and slapping up and down in the nets.

One evening when the last of the canoes had been drawn up above the tide line, he came back, his face alive with satisfaction. "You know," he said, "I've been watching those fellows for half an hour pulling up those boats. What a time they have —there's singing and dragging all together and, I suspect, a good deal of good-natured cussing and swearing and such a sense of life and vigor and working together. I think I know why they've never invented winches for winding up their boats. It would simply spoil the fun."

On the last night of the visit, Dr. Nkrumah, who was by then Prime Minister of the nearly independent colony, came to dine, bringing a magnificent Kente cloth as a gift from the government. The African Cabinet had, incidentally, given a private dinner in Stevenson's honor, a gesture never made before and possibly not since for an unofficial American visitor. These Kente cloths are woven in long strips in brilliant threads with a thread of gold and then sewn together to make a coat of many colors about the size and shape of a Roman toga and worn in the same way. Dr. Nkrumah showed the Governor the swing and the shake which settle the Kente over the shoulder and then hopefully keep it there. But his swings and shakes invariably brought the toga to the ground, and the Prime Minister was reduced to helpless laughter before the Governor at last secured the garment and did an elegant demonstration strut along the stoep. Then both men settled down to a serious and down-to-earth exchange on the rights and risks of political opposition in new states and the values and limits of moderation. Neither the earlier gaiety nor the later seriousness had anything forced about it. There was, above all, not the slightest trace of the condescension with which even Europeans of immense good will sometimes treat— and irritate—their African acquaintances. Stevenson entered with wholehearted participation into both the fun and the sobriety.

That was a large part of the secret. He could communicate interest and enjoyment because they were exactly what he felt. He always found people interesting, and since so many go through life with the depressing feeling that perhaps they have really not got very much to offer, nothing was more beguiling than the Governor's ability to make anyone feel the object of genuine interest and attention. There is no courtesy to equal this.

For the other aspect of Stevenson's attraction for the outside world—his learning, his style, his sense of belonging to a great tradition—I choose an example from his visit to a place which is, in effect, one of the great sources of that tradition. In 1957 I was at Oxford when the university, in a special convocation,

Lloyd Garrison (law partner of AES), Barbara Ward and Adlai Stevenson on their way to dine with Kwame Nkrumah.

conferred upon the Governor the honorary degree of Doctor of Laws. Since words written at the time can be more vivid than later memories, I have taken some sentences from a letter I wrote to Mrs. Edison Dick just after the ceremony:

We waited in the Sheldonian Theatre perched on our high benches.
. . . There were confused sounds outside, a certain amount of cheering
and, to the trained eye, the unmistakable flash of light-bulbs in the
gray afternoon light. The great doors at the end of the arena—facing
the tiers—opened once and a cautious face looked in. Through the
crack, we could see the distant figure of the Governor, gorgeous in
scarlet, standing beside the Public Orator and surrounded by a bedlam
of press photographers. This only added to the hush and decorum
within. The face that peered in must have been satisfied, for, a moment
later . . . the great doors swung open, the Proctors . . . stamped slowly
back followed by the Governor, looking pale and moved, and the
Public Orator. There was absolute silence until the procession reached
the open space before the throne. There, in clear Latin, the Public
Orator read out the citation, very gracefully, savoring every phrase
(and why not, for he wrote it?), and then the Governor advanced and
climbed the execessively abrupt steps to the throne. The Vice-Chancellor raised his mortarboard, then grasped the Governor's hand and declared him a Doctor Honoris Causa.

Thereafter a really very surprising thing happened—for Oxford at
least. The assembled audience raised the roof. They clapped, they
stamped, they banged the benches and the hurricane went on for a
least two minutes. Many of the dons were visibly surprised—and as
visibly delighted. I am told that all over the upper tier, where the
undergraduates were thickest, there appeared a rash of Stevenson
buttons. The four conspicuous gentlemen perched in their pulpits almost fell to the arena in their excitement. It was a wonderful demonstration of affection and respect and, I believe, unique in Oxford, at
least in these last cynical unemotional decades.

The Governor then lectured for nearly an hour and was listened to
with deep attention. I doubt if the acoustics of the Sheldonian are any
too good, certainly not for the benches where we sat, since the lectern
was immediately to the right of the Vice-Chancellor's throne and
slightly below it. But in spite of the fact that perhaps half the audience
had to strain to hear, there was none of that coughing and restlessness
which comes when people lose interest or lose heart. At times, there
was that hush of complete communication when an audience is literally
conscious of nothing but the speaker's words. And—since it was the
Governor speaking—there were some enchanting moments of humor
and impromptu reaction, too. He won all hearts at the beginning by
referring to the saying that Oxford is reputed the home of Lost Causes.

Whom, then, could they more fitly distinguish than the man who was probably the world's greated living exponent of the Lost Cause? . . .

At the end, the ovation was as warm as at the start—a test, indeed, after fifty-five minutes of oratory—and when the Governor left in procession with the Vice-Chancellor a small army of students followed him until he was finally retrieved and bundled into a university car. Only, I think, those who know the normal temperature of Oxford's academic occasions will realize how warmly and decisively the faculty and the students demonstrated their appreciation of the Governor's role in domestic and international politics.

Looking back, nearly ten years after the convocation, I think the point I remember most vividly was the naturalness and rightness with which he fitted into that ancient ceremonial Oxford scene. Here was the great tradition. And he was part of it, refreshing it, renewing it, translating it into a new idiom. Whether he was talking over the teacups at the Vice-Chancellor's lodgings or clad in the Tudor splendor of scarlet gown and velvet cap or, in the evening, laughing and making toasts among the shining glasses and candles of the All Souls dining room, he belonged to that tradition with the ease and dignity of a birthright citizen. This sense of a great and common heritage informed the oration with which the Public Orator announced the degree—one of the warmest ever given, I imagine, by a cool, experienced and skeptical university not overgiven to enthusiasm. The citation is worth recalling:

. . . The eminent American citizen, whom we are happy to see with us today, is particularly welcome to a university audience. We all know his distinguished record in his own political arena and among the dissensions of the United Nations, and we see in him one who has never failed to exemplify just those virtues which it is the duty of a university to foster, the passion of truth, sound learning spiced with charm, wit without rancor, eloquence without self-advertisement. Small wonder that with such endowments he was twice chosen as candidate for the supreme office of President; he "failed in the high emprise, yet greatly failed." Through the campaigns he preserved his rectitude, his courtesy, his charm and, at the very height of the election, his equanimity. We could tell from his courage in defeat what a great President he would have been, had the victory fallen to him. Our admiration might find expression in Addison's famous lines:

> 'Tis not in mortals to command success,
> But we'll do more, Sempronius; we'll deserve it. . . .

I present to you, for the degree of Honorary Doctor of Civil Law, Adlai Stevenson, amid the strains and stresses of national and international politics, the champion of humanism in word and deed, and himself the source.

And this citation takes us, I think, from the more personal and private reasons for Adlai Stevenson's world-wide reputation to the vastly more important public reasons for his stature. We can turn at this point from the hope he realized to the fear he was able in some measure to dispel.

It is perhaps hard for Americans to realize even now the overwhelming superiority of their military and economic strength. No state in history has ever commanded such power. Few states in history have acquired such preponderance. No matter that the Americans neither sought it nor wanted it—they have it and the neighborhood of a giant state is always a little disconcerting to the pygmies. In Shakespeare's well-known phrase: "O, it is excellent to have a giant's strength; but it is tyrannous to use it like a giant." Can any state, suddenly aware of such strength and such disparity, resist the temptation of arrogance and aggression? Given the fact that nothing is more agreeable to many human psyches than giving orders and seeing them enforced, can anyone be sure that all American leaders are immune to such temptation and that the very scale and disproportion of power will not bring out the Hyde of some latter-day Napoleon behind the Jekyll of Woodrow Wilson or Franklin Roosevelt?

There is, after all, a non-Wilsonian side to American tradition —the tradition of Manifest Destiny and "Send in the Marines." There have been a few alarming postwar manifestations of hysterical nationalism. There has been some talk of "holy wars" against Communism. Above all, Americans themselves have commented on America's impatience with imperfect, partial solutions and its itch to settle the issue once and for all by the short cut of war. But short cuts today take the world over the brink of atomic annihilation. Could the world's fate be to plunge to an unchosen doom because of American might and American impatience?

This, I think, is part of the context which explains why the

Adlai Stevenson being escorted to receive an honorary degree at Oxford University, May 24, 1957.

Wide World

Governor became and remained so popular and reassuring a figure abroad. He was an American leader who always contrived to suggest that American power would be used generously, reasonably and with a scrupulous concern for peace. There was, we should add, no suggestion that it would never be used, that America's posture would be retreat, that the Governor himself did not coolly and realistically understand the politics of power. In the great debates in the United Nations, particularly at the time of the Cuban crisis in 1962, there could be no doubt about the stern vigor of Stevenson's interventions. One remembers his tough confrontation of Zorin with the evidence of Soviet missiles and his stated readiness to wait for an answer until "Hell freezes over." Only those who had mistakenly pictured him as an amiable man and little more were surprised. In fact, he always had an inner core of indestructible strength, and indeed could not have survived his grueling political destiny without it.

But of course the strength was part of the reassurance. It is not reassuring to know that the greatest nation on earth does not intend or know how to use its power. The reassurance lies in the belief that the strength will be used wisely and with due respect for the human community. This the Governor's whole public career helped to demonstrate.

It began for the outside world in his work with the Preparatory Commission for the United Nations. He brought to it the sustained convictions and ardent faith of a true citizen of man's wider commonwealth. He was not doing a perfunctory or routine job. He really felt himself to be engaged in building a safer order for the survival of humanity. Nor was there ever any deviation from this fundamental, Wilsonian dedication to the vision of an ordered, rational world society as the only means of lasting peace. In two presidential campaigns—the second including his proposal for the abolition of nuclear testing—he attracted the fire of all the forces in America who most frighten the rest of the human race, the superpatriots, the Cold War warriors, the believers, conscious or bemused, in the possibility of unfettered power.

His last years were entirely dedicated to the task of convincing the world that America, the superstate of all history, would nevertheless be ready for some mediation of its power through the institutions of the United Nations. The giant's power would not, if he could help it, be used tyrannously. There would be a "decent respect for the opinions of mankind." When, at the beginning of the world's nearest brush with nuclear disaster, he brought the case of the Cuban missiles before the Security Council, his speech, firm and controlled, ended not with threats and but with a generous and eloquent plea: "Let [this day] be remembered not as the day when the world came to the edge of nuclear war but as the day when men resolved to let nothing thereafter stop them in their quest for peace."

This is not, of course, to say that America, any more than any other state, was or is ready for the abrogation of sovereignty. But Stevenson's presence at the United Nations and his participation in the American Cabinet's decision-making were taken by vast numbers of people abroad as a guarantee that the overwhelming, irresistible power of the United States would not be used arrogantly or unthinkingly to override the interests and susceptibilities of other, smaller communities. There were of course doubts—strongly nourished by the Bay of Pigs disaster—that the Governor was really at the center of decision-making. But the feeling was pretty general that he stood near enough to the center of power for his voice—of reason and restraint—to be heard and weighed. The subsequent revelations of the sane and steady part he played in the Cuban confrontation have only reinforced the feeling. People may not have known how much influence he had. But they went on believing that whatever influence he did have gave them a strong sense of reassurance.

The survival of this confidence through four years and more

of tough international infighting has its roots in the Governor's known conviction, expressed in a hundred different speeches, that the world has to find its way to a rule of law and neighborly responsibility or perish. I doubt if it has ever been more movingly expressed than in his speech on patriotism given to the students of Notre Dame, in which he urged them to enlarge their love of country by a larger loyalty—to the whole human experiment:

> I can, therefore, wish no more for your profound patriotism as Americans than that you will add to it a new dedication to the world-wide brotherhood of which you are a part and that, together with your love of America, there will grow a wider love which seeks to transform our earthly city, with all its races and peoples, all its creeds and aspirations, into Saint Augustine's Heavenly city where truth reigns, love is the law, and whose extent is eternity.

Such convictions, of course, reassured people abroad. But perhaps a deeper source of their confidence must be looked for in the kind of man the Governor was. He found any form of militarism, national arrogance or bullyboy pretensions profoundly antipathetic. False rhetoric, above all the false rhetoric of superpatriotism, set his teeth on edge. He loved his country precisely because it was "dedicated to the proposition" of liberty and equality, because it had first proposed the extension of ordered liberty to all mankind, because it could still be "the last best hope" for a decent society for the whole human experiment. He found the opposite America—of proud claims and national boasting, of saber-rattling and chest-thumping—personally nauseating. Such behavior seemed to him nothing but a profound betrayal of the true meaning of patriotism in the American context.

This deep, unshakable dedication to America's authentic vision of greatness informed even his smallest acts of policy and diplomacy—the courtesy of his language, the warmth of his interest, the modesty of his bearing. After his death, Chief Adebo, Nigeria's immensely able and influential delegate to the United Nations, told a visitor of the effect on himself and on other ambassadors of Stevenson's unfailing courtesy. During the long discussions over the UN's financial difficulties, Stevenson always came to see the chairman of the working committee, Chief Adebo, in his own office. "He would insist on coming to my office. He would come to me. The representative from the United States would not have it that somebody should come to see him. . . . You know, African countries do not, ah, always agree with your government and your spokesmen. But we admired him so much as a man. He gave. But it was the way in which he gave. So charmingly. Oh, I saw him in San Francisco. I just cannot believe that I will not see that man any more."

Opponents in the United Nations could and did berate American policy; they could never make a case of arrogance or bad manners or contemptuous assertiveness against America's chief representative. Thus he remained, even when policies and interests diverged violently, a symbol of America's readiness to live within the limits of civilized and responsible power. And he died regretted above all, perhaps, as a citizen of a world-wide community in which respect, courtesy, attention and the search for understanding are themselves symbols of a wider will to live at peace.

HARRY S. ASHMORE

Too Old to Cry

THEY WILL, of course, remember Adlai Stevenson's wit. It became his trade-mark, and there are those who say it cost him the presidency.

I suppose it is true that his humor was out of phase with his times. It had substance, and relevance, and he had to direct it to audiences conditioned on one side by the banalities of television and on the other by mordant sophisticates who demand blood as the price of laughter.

Adlai was without cruelty, and so, more often than not, the joke was on himself. Somehow even his gaiety was touched by the melancholy that often darkened his serious passages; he could never divorce his delight in the antic quality of the human condition from his abiding compassion. The anecdote most frequently employed in his obituaries was one he used in defeat, when he reached into his endless store of Lincoln apocrypha to quote a little boy with a stubbed toe who said he was too old to cry, and couldn't laugh because it hurt too much.

Harry S. Ashmore, chairman of the Executive Committee, Fund for the Republic, and director of editorial research and development, Encyclopaedia Britannica, *was personal assistant to Adlai Stevenson in 1955-1956. As executive editor of the* Arkansas Gazette *he won a Pulitzer Prize in 1958.*

228

His critics embroidered his natural self-deprecation into a Hamlet legend, and said the American people could never trust a man so beset by indecision. The contrast was marked, certainly, when he went forth to campaign against a confidently smiling symbol of certitude and pedestrian virtue. I remember riding behind his open campaign car with James Reston of the *New York Times,* who compared Adlai's diffident wave to Ike's spread arms flung overhead in V for victory. "The difference can beat him," Reston said, and maybe it did.

There was, God knows, a mighty effort to change the image. Professionals from Madison Avenue and volunteers from Hollywood and Broadway and the upper reaches of television flocked in to plead with him to watch his timing, take his laughs, project for the cameras. City ward heelers and county seat bosses gave him instruction in handshaking, bagel-eating and the proper tilt of a cowboy's Stetson.

He tolerated such advice, and he may even have listened to it. Once when we were whistle-stopping down the spine of Florida in the 1956 primary he turned to me as we drove out of a little town and asked how he had done. "Well," I said, "it wasn't bad. But when you are shaking hands in a supermarket and a little girl in a starched dress steps out of the crowd and hands you a stuffed alligator, what you say is, 'Thanks very much, I've always wanted one of these for the mantelpiece at Libertyville.' What you don't say is what you did say: 'For Christ's sake, what's this?'" He was delighted, and recounted our conversation at the next stop, and probably lost another hundred votes to Estes Kefauver, who was born knowing what to do with an outthrust alligator.

Yes, we all tried, but the image endured, about as I first saw it in Springfield, when the brilliant young Chicago lawyer came out of nowhere to the governor's office. He never did learn to put a hat on right, not even when his diplomatic duties required him to escort the Dowager Queen of England.

I think it was this amused appreciation of the preposterous quality of presidential campaigning that sustained him through those two interminable ordeals, when physical exhaustion was compounded by the unspoken certainty that we were losing. Yet he took his obligations with dead seriousness, and he kept his pledge to talk sense to the American people. If I had to cite a summary reason for his defeat, I would say that it was because he insisted on giving voice to hard truths his opponent pretended did not exist and his listeners did not want to hear.

Still, my sharpest memories are of things he did not do—of times when those bright, blue eyes grew hard as he glared stubbornly across that marvelously twisted nose.

I think of him up in Minnesota, at bay before a circle of corn-belt politicians led by Hubert Humphrey. He was through, they argued, unless he came out without qualification for farm price supports at 100 percent of parity. He wouldn't do it, Adlai said—he grew corn himself on his farm in Illinois and he knew the price support program wasn't working and he'd be damned if he would endorse something that simply didn't make any sense. And he didn't. And Estes Kefauver took Minnesota in the first, critical primary of the second campaign.

I remember him in Oregon, refusing to support the demand for punitive action against the Southern states in the mounting segregation crisis, and in San Francisco and Los Angeles standing by his moderate statement in the face of hysterical pressure from Negro and liberal white supporters. And then, of course, going to Little Rock in his first Southern campaign appearance to warn bluntly that there could be no compromise on full and immediate civil rights for the Negro citizens of the Old Confederacy.

I remember quiet moods of introspection, when he talked out loud about his inner doubts and fears. One of these came at the time when the political writers were speculating on his backing and filling over his appointment by President Kennedy as Ambassador to the United Nations.

"The point is that Jack Kennedy is going to make his own foreign policy, as he should, and there simply isn't enough in his record to indicate how much of it I might agree with," he said.

Arkansas Gazette

With Harry Ashmore at the Little Rock airport, December, 1955.

"And yet if I accept this appointment, I am committed to support him this side of treason or madness. There is no way for a man as prominent as I am to quietly step down. If I were to resign, no

Ed Wergeles

At Libertyville, January, 1960.

matter the excuse, it would signal a major political break over
United States policy."

The time came, at the Bay of Pigs, when he had to measure his
loyalty in terms of the deepest personal humiliation. He did not

fare much better in his last days under President Johnson, when it was his duty to go forth to the United Nations and defend American policy in Vietnam and the Dominican Republic.

I last saw him a little over a month before his death, at breakfast in the elegant Waldorf ambassadorial quarters his presence somehow reduced to old-shoe comfort. It was, he said, the roughest season he had known at the United Nations. His daily duels with the Russians over Vietnam were compounded by the onslaught of former allies who had been shocked by the return of U.S. Marines to the Caribbean.

"The issues are hard and sharp enough," he said. "But now there is an added emotional dimension. We're playing the game of symbols, and we're cast as the big bully wearing a Texas hat. It's all forensic, without real substance, like an endless courtroom argument. Well, anyway, I'm turning out to be a pretty good lawyer."

Then the famous, wry grin.

"But I'd better not say that or somebody will suggest that I go back to private practice!"

If it was rough inside the UN, it may have been rougher outside. In the Assembly and the Council he faced old, familiar adversaries. Outside the halls he was caught up in bitter, unreasoning criticism directed at policy he did not make but was bound in conscience to support.

Now it was the more passionate of his old admirers from the intellectual community who turned on him with the special fury reserved for the presumed apostate. I am sure this drumfire of simplistic moralism wounded him, but he had endured it before when he had matched his gift for soaring words with his politician's genius for compromise.

I left him deeply concerned but not unhopeful. The main thing, he said, was somehow to find a channel for negotiation. He was on duty when he died in London, a city that became him.

The verdict may be that it was not only his wit but his psyche that was out of phase with the times. He remained a gentleman in the face of a declining political market for civility. He considered courage a virtue to be practiced, not talked about; loyalty a matter of course, not of complaint.

Patriotism, he once told the American Legion, can be the last refuge of scoundrels. It also can be, as it was for Adlai Stevenson, a shining mantle.

WILLIAM McC. BLAIR, JR.

A Dazzling Decade

As I sit here in Manila, my mind is flooded with memories of ten years' association with Adlai Stevenson, ten years working with him and accompanying him on trips through all fifty states and sixty-four countries:

The day in 1950 when I reported for work in Springfield, Illinois, and, reminding him that I was still a registered Republican, was told, "That's all right. I believe in the forgiveness of sin."

"The most rewarding years of my life," he used to say of his governorship, a time when urgent needs were met vigorously and brilliantly and changes were wrought in the quality of state government which stand today among his proudest memorials. Those eighteen-hour-day, seven-day weeks! His preoccupation particularly with the care and treatment of the mentally ill; weekends spent in state prisons and welfare institutions; that wonderful afternoon at one of the giant mental hospitals when during a social hour one of the patients who was under the impression she was the widow of Abraham Lincoln asked the Governor to dance, and, as

William McCormick Blair, Jr. was an early supporter of Governor Stevenson, an assistant at Springfield and during the 1952 and 1956 campaigns, and later a law partner. He was U.S. Ambassador to Denmark from 1961 to 1964 and since then has been Ambassador to the Republic of the Philippines.

235

they waltzed away, I heard the old lady say, "My husband spoke of you so often."

Memories of the wonderfully able men and women he enlisted in his relentless campaign to restore integrity to the state services in Springfield, imbuing them with his own sense of dedication, his incredible energy and virtually unlimited endurance. I recall trying to persuade him to take more rest, to leave his office occasionally at night and walk down the street from the Executive Mansion to take in a movie. He was always too busy working—so busy that when once I succeeded he came back and asked, "Who is this fellow Gary Cooper?"

The early months of 1952 when the Governor found himself swept up in speculation about his possible candidacy for the presidency. The pleas of some friends to withdraw unequivocally from the race and seek re-election as Governor, and the insistence of others that he must run—that his party had an obligation to put up its best and strongest candidate.

The impossibility of declining all invitations and his first foray into California, where in Hollywood he was asked to say a few words at a party and so completely captivated the audience that one of the guests was heard to say, "How can anyone be so charming and not be Jewish?"

The trip a month later to New York on state business, where he found time to attend a dinner honoring Fred Allen and revealed, not for the first time, his abysmal ignorance in those days of show business and show people. Seated next to Jack Benny, inquiring several times, "Who is this Mary people keep talking about?" and finally making so many *faux pas* that Jack Benny was constrained to say to him, "Governor, where in the hell have you been all your life?"

The grueling 1952 presidential campaign, the impossibly demanding but necessary schedules for one who was relatively new to politics and virtually unknown in many parts of the country. As usual, he expressed it best himself: "You must write at every chance, think if possible, read mail and newspapers, talk on the telephone, talk to everybody, and ride through city after city on the back of an open car smiling until your mouth is dehydrated by the wind, waving until the blood runs out of your arms . . . bounce gaily, confidently, masterfully, into great howling halls, shaved and made up for television with the right color shirt and tie—I always forgot that—and a manuscript so defaced with chicken tracks and last-minute jottings that you couldn't follow it even if the spotlights weren't blinding and even if still photographers didn't shoot you in the eye every time you looked at them."

The repeated chants of "I like Ike," and the Governor's cheerful rejoinder, "So do I."

That marvelous Garment District rally in New York in late October when 300,000 people roared their approval and visibly moved a man whose innate modesty was sometimes mistaken for aloofness.

The time in California, which he loved to refer to, when a woman who had lost a diamond ring reported to the police that she had last seen it when she had shaken hands with Adlai Stevenson.

That day in Baltimore where in a parade the Governor was seated on top of a convertible between two local candidates, pinned in by them, finding it impossible to wave to the crowds lining the streets. I ran back to urge the two candidates to sit down and leave the Governor alone on the top. He whispered to me, "*Fat* chance of their doing that!"—and he was right.

Sixteen speeches a day and then more work far into the night preparing for the next day, worried all the time about his responsibilities as Governor. Racing back to Illinois at midnight from a rally in Pittsburgh to direct the quelling of a prison riot.

The exhausting whistle-stopping train, with the first speech at 6:30 A.M. and the last one late at night and in between tens of thousands of people; those trips off the train to the city squares ("Sheer physical exhaustion was for me a continuous and disquiet-

ing menace to equilibrium, judgment and creative concentration"). All the time the train packed with party leaders wanting
to see him, finding it impossible because of the Governor's insistence that every crowd deserved a different speech. His growing optimism and hope for victory. The disappointment at the end
but great satisfaction with the kind of campaign waged.

Then four years of incessant travel in all parts of the world.

That six-month trip around the world in 1953 to thirty countries—a triumphal journey ("The sights I have seen—moving
and beautiful, sordid and sickening"). Tea with Emperor Hirohito;
visits with American troops in Korea after being greeted by a
quarter of a million people in Seoul; a day with the French
Foreign Legion in Hanoi; thousands upon thousands of refugees
everywhere ("huddled in squalid camps and hovels stretching
from Korea across Asia to Western Europe"); two hours at Angkor
Wat; an evening with the Royal Cambodian Ballet in Phnompenh;
a meeting with a British Jungle Patrol in Malaysia; house guest
of the Presidents of Burma and India; several meetings with
Nehru (the Governor, a few years before in Chicago, had reduced
a crowd, including himself and Nehru, to helpless laughter by
asking the crowd to remain seated "until the Prime Minister passes
out"); two days as guest of the King of Saudi Arabia (I shall always remember the Governor saying to the King in the middle of
the state banquet just as His Majesty was about to put a piece of
roast sheep into his mouth, "President Truman asked to be remembered to you," at which the King practically choked); a first
meeting with a Colonel Nasser on his way up; crisscrossing Israel
in a plane piloted by an eighteen-year-old girl; well-earned rest
and writing periods in Hong Kong and Baguio, the Philippines
(when the Governor arrived at Baguio, he saw a large crowd at
the airport. Visibly pleased, he stepped out of the plane, waving
his hat, only to see the crowd rush by to greet "Miss Universe"
arriving on another plane); blissful rests at Nathia Gali in the
Himalayas, Cyprus, Positano; a visit to Marshal Tito on the island

Queen Elizabeth and Stevenson watch the races at Goodwood in 1953.

of Brijoni, luncheon with Winston Churchill, tea with Queen Elizabeth. (When Her Majesty, seeing the Governor's young son John Fell with camera, asked him if he would like to take her picture, and, if so, where, he replied, "Would you please move over by Dad?")

And, of course, markets, markets, markets. The Governor loved them, never passed one by, feeling it was the best place to see and meet the people. And his great curiosity and determination to sample every kind and variety of food and his complaints, particularly in Africa, that I would eat nothing but hamburgers— and he was right.

Another Congressional election in 1954, preceded by months of travel and speeches around the country to erase an $830,000 deficit from the previous campaign; his renewed and courageous attack, against the advice of party leaders, on McCarthyism for "staining the vision of democracy for us and for the world we seek to lead."

More travel, some law and then in 1956 another presidential campaign, more whistle stops, more twenty-hour days, more exhaustion and fatigue, but also the great satisfaction once again of articulating brilliantly his party's faith in America and in the future.

The disheartening landslide for President Eisenhower and the strong feeling that had it not been for the Israeli invasion of Egypt he might still have lost but the results would have been closer than in 1952—and perhaps there would have been another chance.

More trips abroad to Africa, Scandinavia, the Soviet Union. (His complaints that I used to put him up at luxury hotels and his insistence on one trip to Paris that he make his own reservations and found himself in a small hotel where the concierge operated the switchboard, the elevator and everything else. And that first night, with no soap, no service, no messages delivered, but plenty of water descending on him from an overflowing bathtub above and my reappointment the next morning as reservation manager.)

In 1957 a new law firm and four favorite clients who made possible more travel and more opportunities to serve his country.

And long trips to Central and South America. One of the high points was Bogotá, where after a bull fight the Governor was carried out of the arena on the shoulders of cheering young Colombians. One of the low points, and it made him miserable: a tour in Lima of a giant, steaming garbage dump on which lived thousands of people and pigs.

Three or four trips to Africa. The Governor's quiet fury one day in Johannesburg when the concierge of the hotel refused to permit a young African who had an appointment with the Governor to enter the hotel. The Governor descending to the hotel entrance and then walking around the block with the young man, who wanted nothing more than some help in persuading his government to let him accept a medical scholarship in the United States. The African's desperation equaled only by that of the Governor, who was unable to help him.

Two wonderful days with Albert Schweitzer in Lambaréné and the Governor's impatience with people critical of the aged Doctor. "How presumptuous," he used to say, "for people to come into this jungle for forty-eight hours and criticize a man who has spent almost forty-eight years here healing the sick." His humiliation when he arrived at the hospital to be greeted by Schweitzer and, forgetting a moment about his reverence-for-life theory, crushed a mosquito which had lit on Schweitzer's shirt, and the Doctor looking at him, wagging his finger, saying, "He belonged to me."

The 1960 presidential primary campaign, with the Governor unwilling to discourage his supporters, wishing, as was only natural for one who had lost twice, for another chance. The convention, then more crisscrossing of the country, more eighteen-hour days, doing his best for a candidate whom he admired greatly. His disappointment at not becoming Secretary of State, but once again his overriding sense of duty and then four magnificent years at the UN.

Our paths went different ways in 1960. He did visit me and my wife in Denmark on two occasions and we always stayed with him when we were in New York. When my son was born, he cabled: "Bravo. One William down here is better than two astronauts up there. Loving Cheers." And there were more letters and notes from time to time, always thoughtful, always amusing.

Crowded years they were, but exhilarating ones, and unforgettable, too, for those who had the great good fortune to know and work with one who had in such abundance moral courage, superb

AES, arriving in Copenhagen, is greeted by Ambassador William McCormick Blair, Jr. and his son William III.

J. Stahnke Hansen, Copenhagen

intellect, irrepressible humor, inexhaustible energy, insatiable curiosity about places and people and always, always genuine compassion and concern for his fellow man.

"Acting with enthusiasm and faith is the condition of acting greatly," Adlai Stevenson once said. Few in our time have matched his greatness.

A. S. MIKE MONRONEY

The Plot Against Adlai

Humility is a rare quality among politicians. So rare, in fact, that when we encounter it, we are apt to call it by another name, either guile or indecisiveness. The politician who is humble without lacking self-confidence is rarer still and even more likely to confuse those who record and participate in American politics. Loyalty to one's friends is assumed to be a necessary characteristic of the successful politician, but we expect it to be tempered by self-interest and grow impatient with those who jeopardize their own political careers for the sake of their supporters. As I look back on Stevenson's public career, I am struck by the irony that even his most devoted friends consistently underestimated the sincerity of his humility and the strength of his personal loyalties. This was one of the ingredients of the plot by his friends against Adlai Stevenson in 1960.

His failure at the impossible political tasks which his party

The nationwide migration of thousands of Stevenson followers to the 1960 Democratic Convention was a spontaneous, unorganized affair. Senator A. S. Mike Monroney, Democrat, of Oklahoma, and Tom Finney, Jr., whose assistance in the preparation of this article is gratefully acknowledged by the Senator, were two or three coordinators of the effort. Others were the Honorable James Doyle of Madison, Wisconsin, now a Federal Judge in that state, and John Sharon of Washington, D.C.

imposed on him in 1952 and which his sense of public duty imposed on him in 1956 made Stevenson vulnerable to his critics, and he had many. He offended the pompous because he found humor in our mistakes. He offended the fanatics of both right and left because he rejected pat answers to our problems. But most of all, he offended the ambitious in his own party because he insisted on playing the game by different rules.

His defeats and his detractors combined to obscure even from Stevenson himself the depth of the affection and respect in which he was held by the American people. He was considered a figure more beloved by foreigners than by his fellow citizens—a prophet not without honor save in his own country. This, too, was to compound the difficulties and finally confound the conspirators against him in 1960.

During the years between 1956 and 1960 Stevenson had consistently told his friends that he would not again seek the presidency. He did not relish the physical and emotional ordeal of another campaign, nor did he believe that after two defeats the nomination would be offered by the convention. He had spoken of the need for new and younger leadership in the party. A number of his most devoted advisers and aides in past campaigns had sought his advice and had been encouraged to work for the nomination of other candidates. However, in the early months of 1960 the emerging contenders for the nomination seemed either untried or unlikely to succeed. The opportunities and challenges which were to plumb the greatness of other leaders were yet to come. As the failure to deal with the world's crises grew more alarming in the closing months of the Eisenhower administration, it seemed to many of us that the task of restoring American leadership and giving it purpose and direction could safely be entrusted only to our best. We had no doubts that our best was Adlai Stevenson.

While Stevenson's decision not to seek the nomination was an honest one, his commitment to public service was too complete to permit him to speak in Sherman's terms. It was unthinkable to him that a party leader would refuse his party's banner or that a patriot would withhold his service from his country. More than this, he was devoted to the principles that be believed should guide America's conduct and never doubted his own capacity to translate them into public policy as President of the United States. While he had a realistic view of his own limitations, he was equally perceptive of the limitations of others. In the months ahead he would be alternately irritated and amused by those who expected a simple answer to the question, "Does he want it?" To him, of all the questions which could be asked, this was the most totally irrelevant.

Early in 1960 Adlai had used the excuse of a number of legal matters for private clients for a two-month trip to South America. He returned in time to keep a long-standing commitment to deliver the Founder's Day address at the University of Virginia on April 12, 1960. He made it the occasion for a sweeping examination of our moral flabbiness at home and declining influence abroad. The speech was to set the tone of the subsequent Democratic assault on the Republican administration. He identified Jefferson's great hope "not to extend our national power but to spread the dominion of our national ideals." He reminded us that "Americans of today . . . can no longer indulge in the comfortable illusion . . . that 'history does not happen to us.'" He called on his countrymen to "rise up to the altitude of man's peril" and condemned "concealment of the true nature of the crisis" through "an effort to suspend political debate, a drift away from government through discussion and toward a curbing of criticism." Then, in an amazing prologue to all that has happened since, he capsuled the essential issues of public policy.

In the months ahead, I hope . . . the Democratic party will open up the avenues to many truths, avenues that have been obscured too long. The people have a right to know why we have lost our once unquestioned military superiority; why we have repeatedly allowed the Soviets to seize the diplomatic initiative; why we have faltered in the fight for disarmament; why we are not providing our children with education to which they are entitled; why—nearly a century after the Fourteenth and Fifteenth Amendments—all of our citizens have still not been guaranteed the right to vote; why we spend billions of dollars storing surplus food when one-third of humanity goes to bed hungry; why we have not formulated an economic development program geared to the world-wide passion for economic growth; why we have failed to win the confidence and respect of the billions of impatient people in Asia, Africa and Latin America; why millions of Americans lead blighted lives in our spreading urban slums; why we have fewer doctors per capita than we did fifty years ago and pay more for our medical care than ever before; why we spent more money last year on tranquilizers than on space exploration, and more on leisure than on learning; why the richest nation in the history of the world cannot support the public services and facilities we must have not only for world power but for national growth and opportunity.

And he attributed to Jefferson the essence of his own political conviction, his belief in "the capacity of the people to rise to greatness once they know, once they are told, once they are summoned."

By this time a small band had determined that an effort must be made to secure the Democratic nomination for Stevenson. I still remember vividly our sense of elation at the Charlottesville speech. Adlai had given us a marvelous weapon to use in his behalf. More important, he had given us a weapon against his own reluctance. True, the people would rise to greatness once they were summoned. But, we challenged him, who else can summon them?

Then in May of 1960 an unbelievable series of blunders served as awful confirmation of the Stevenson indictment. On the eve of the summit meeting between Eisenhower and Khrushchev, an American U-2 airplane was shot down over the Soviet Union and its pilot captured. There followed Soviet accusations, American denials, the pilot's confession and finally our government's admission of all that we had solemnly denied. Ever the responsible leader, Stevenson calmly urged that these events not be the subject of partisan censure on the eve of the summit meeting. America waited in confusion and apprehension for the final act of the tragedy.

It was sheer coincidence that in this interval Americans were exposed to a totally different dimension of Adlai Stevenson's insight: his capacity to translate his intrinsic confidence in the democratic process into practical means of improving its effectiveness. *This Week* magazine had carried a provocative article by Stevenson calling for a series of televised debates between the two major candidates for President.

From his own experience in campaigning for the presidency, he described the obstacles and frustrations encountered by the candidate, who is forced to travel and speak incessantly, often to small, unrepresentative groups, on issues ranging from global to local. The traditions and demands of the campaign made it impossible to discuss major national problems coherently and to reach any substantial portion of the electorate with a thoughtful presentation of his program.

> I do not mean to criticize these candidates for succumbing to the inevitable. I have been in similar predicaments. I've worn silly hats and eaten indigestible food; I've bitterly denounced the Japanese beetle and fearlessly attacked the Mediterranean fruit fly.

Stevenson believed that the democratic process would be better served by turning to television. He proposed that "we transform our circus-atmosphere presidential campaign into a great debate conducted in full view of all the people."

> It would end the tendency to reduce everything to assertions and slogans. It would diminish the temptation of politicians to entertain, to please and to evade the unpleasant realities. It might even help to restore what we seem to have lost—our sense of national purpose.

On May 16 Stevenson appeared before a Senate committee in support of legislation to make such debates possible. At that meeting he reviewed the faults of traditional campaigns and presented his ideas on the creative possibilities of televised political debates. He struck a responsive chord with the committee when he referred to the risks of buying time to be taken from regular commercial programs. In 1956 a five-minute speech had been rewarded with a telegram saying, "I like Ike, and I love Lucy; drop dead."

Urging Congress and the networks to cooperate in resolving the practical obstacles, Stevenson suggested prophetically, "For in the long run it may turn out that the direction we give to political television is one of the great decisions of the decisive decade of the 1960's."

This was to be a fateful day. In Paris the summit conference met and exploded in a barrage of angry accusations, while in Washington Adlai Stevenson spoke in a room packed to capacity. These were no visionary intellectuals, but political pros—Senators and Congressmen, members of their staffs, White House and Capitol reporters—and they had come to hail and to hear the man to whom they naturally turned for leadership in time of crisis.

Most of the crowd followed Stevenson from the hearing room, and as he entered the hall outside, he confronted a mob of hundreds more pressing forward to ask a question or shake his hand. Slowly he made his way down the hall toward my office. As he reached the door his faithful favorite, Mary McGrory, caught him for a final question. "Governor, are you going to the convention?" Stevenson answered with a couplet, "I am growing too old for the kind of affairs where the people outnumber the comfortable chairs." He finally escaped into my office, visibly shaken by his experience.

When the crowd finally drifted away, we guided him to a private room where he met with Lyndon Johnson and received a stern warning that he might yet be the nominee of the Democratic party. It was a sober Adlai Stevenson who returned to meet with some of his advocates, understanding, I think for the first time, the extent of his responsibility. And in this atmosphere we levied our demands: that he provide the voice of leadership for the Democratic party, that he do nothing to handicap our effort to secure his nomination. We asked more, but to these two he agreed.

As I look back on the events of that year, I realize that we had placed Stevenson in an impossible dilemma. He felt a deep

Stevenson and Senator Monroney at a 1954 Democratic meeting.

responsibility to his friends and to others in the party whom he admired and respected who were seeking the Democratic nomination on the strength of his earlier statements that he would not be a candidate. He felt an equal or greater responsibility to those of us who demanded that he be the nominee because of the desperate nature of the times. The first commitment prevented an active candidacy. The second commitment prevented a graceful withdrawal. Our cause was to founder solely on this dilemma.

The collapse of the summit conference was used by Republican spokesmen as an excuse to call for national unity and to demand that the critics be silent and all support our insulted President. It was a matter, they said, of our national honor. Stevenson was deeply offended by this latest effort to suppress dissent and forestall discussion. He accepted an invitation to appear before a Democratic party meeting in Illinois a few days later in order to answer the demands for silence.

Reviewing the U-2 incident and the collapse of the summit conference, Stevenson reminded the audience that while Khrushchev was responsible for wrecking the conference, "the crowbar and sledge hammer" were handed to him by the United States.

He placed responsible discussion in proper perspective in these words:

Republican leaders are now saying that in this grave crisis we must all rally round the President in the name of national unity. Our respect for the presidency will find us joined in salute to President Eisenhower upon his return. We resent deeply and bitterly the gross affront to the President and his office.

There is no question about national unity in a time of crisis. But errors must be corrected, and we must not forget that the opposition party also has an obligation to our country and to our allies whose security is also involved. It is the duty of responsible opposition in a democracy to expose and criticize carelessness and mistakes, especially in a case of such national and world importance as this. We must see to it that we profit from such grave mistakes and misfortunes. . . .

It will be our duty, it will be the duty of all thoughtful, concerned citizens, to help the situation and to face the hard inescapable facts; that this administration played into Khrushchev's hands; that if Khrushchev wanted to wreck the conference our government made it possible; that the administration has acutely embarrassed our allies and endangered our bases; that they have helped make successful negotiations with the Russians—negotiations that are vital to our survival—impossible so long as they are in power.

As the pace of the preconvention campaign quickened in the weeks that followed, the nature of the final confrontation coming at Los Angeles became increasingly clear. The Symington campaign made little progress. The Humphrey campaign ended with failure in Wisconsin and disaster in West Virginia. The Johnson strength grew to encompass most of the South and Southwest and a scattering of delegates from other sections, then grew no more. But the delegate commitments to Jack Kennedy grew steadily week by week.

While it was obvious that Kennedy would have the greatest number of convention delegates, it became equally obvious that Stevenson had by far the greatest popular support. In almost every state a "Draft Stevenson" movement sprang spontaneously from the people's concern for their country and their confidence in Adlai Stevenson. His small band of organized supporters established a beachhead at Los Angeles and sought to create the opportunity for the delegates to follow their hearts and the country's clamor.

Throughout this period every public appearance, every statement to the press, every conversation with party leaders by Stevenson became for us a crisis. On each occasion we pressed him to declare his candidacy or, if not his candidacy, his availability. On each occasion other friends pressed him to withdraw his name from consideration. Constantly pulled in opposite directions, admonished, harangued, he never lost his patience or his good humor—and he never budged. When on the eve of the convention he said in a television interview that if nominated he would campaign "with vigor and a sense of real purpose," we hailed it as a move toward a more active candidacy. But, in truth, it was what he had felt from the beginning.

The story of the rendezvous of the Democratic party in Los Angeles has been well told by others. Our effort to create the opportunity for Stevenson's nomination did not fail, for the opportunity was created on three different occasions. When Stevenson addressed the Minnesota delegation on Tuesday before the balloting on Wednesday, when the same day his appearance on the convention floor produced a near-riot of enthusiasm, when late Tuesday night he met with more than two hundred delegates —each time he had but to say, "I seek your nomination, I need your help." He did not say it. And so they "thrice presented him a kingly crown, which he did thrice refuse."

We told him that he alone could lead his party and his nation, but he knew this was not so. His faith in the free processes of a democracy was greater than ours. We told him that his word given to trusted friends was unimportant when measured against the public need. He understood better than we that ambition finds excuses that conscience cannot accept. Others told him to disavow our efforts and thus save himself from the indignity of defeat and win the promise of public honor. He understood better than they the motives that impelled us to seek a broader range for his leadership.

After the furor of the convention was over and its decision made, a few of us gathered at his hotel to say our farewell. As we came out to walk with him to his car, we saw parked across the street a dilapidated automobile which had brought a few of the hundreds of Stevenson volunteers to Los Angeles. It carried an enormous banner on which was crudely lettered the lesson of 1960: "'Tis better to have loved and lost than never to have loved at all." Adlai Stevenson laughed and waved and went on to greater service.

FRANCIS T. P. PLIMPTON

They Sent You Our Best

THE UNITED NATIONS CHARTER contemplates that each member state shall have a "permanent representative" at the headquarters district.

Adlai Stevenson filled that always exacting, often exasperating, sometimes exciting, inevitably exhausting and occasionally exhilarating post on behalf of the United States, with the rank of Ambassador Extraordinary and Plenipotentiary, from January 23, 1961, until his sudden death on the streets of London on July 14, 1965.

He was an old hand at the UN. He was at San Francisco at its birth as an Assistant to Secretary of State Stettinius and as an adviser to the U.S. delegation, and he was chief of the U.S. delegation to the UN Preparatory Commission in London in 1946, and a member of the U.S. delegation to the First and Second UN General Assemblies in 1946 and 1947.

So, when he came back to the UN in January, 1961, it was a homecoming. But it was more than that; there was in him no sense of a relaxing return to a familiar resting place, rather the stimulus

Francis T. P. Plimpton of the New York law firm of Debevoise, Plimpton, Lyons and Gates was a Harvard Law School classmate of Adlai Stevenson. He served as deputy to him on the U.S. delegation to the United Nations.

of a known but challenging platform as a launching base for the hopes of the future.

His first press conference on January 27, 1961, was unforgettable. Committee Room 4 in the UN basement is, oddly, the biggest: low-ceilinged but wide and broad, crammed, that afternoon, with the UN press corps—the largest in the world—Europeans, Asians, Communists, Africans, Latin Americans, professionals, amateurs, dilettantes, stringers, hangers-on, delegates. There was an electric quality of anticipation, of curiosity, of friendliness.

In he came with that quick, preoccupied walk, the slightly baggy, gray tweed coat, the almost shy side glances, along behind the long blond writing desk and blond fixed chairs, until he came toward the center chair and the microphones and stood silent, erect, as the standing crowd exploded in applause. And then that sudden, delighted smile that transformed thoughtfulness into pleased awareness, into glowing acceptance of the warmth of welcome.

First, an off-the-cuff, lighthearted reference to his own newspaper past, and then his prepared statement, eloquent in its evocation of the UN's past and of what might and should be its future, and of the United States' determination to strengthen and expand its influence and authority.

"Eloquent" never seems quite the right word for Stevenson—it sounds too much like elocution. It is true that his words had a soaring quality; but it was not the words themselves that lifted us up, it was the soaring mind and spirit behind those words.

Being an ambassador to—or, rather, at—the UN is like no other post in the diplomatic—or any other—world. An ordinary ambassador deals with only one government; at the UN one is dealing with the representatives and delegates of 116 (with more to come), plus a Secretary General and the Secretariat. At the usual post the other ambassadors are colleagues in the merely social sense; at the UN they represent votes, and the day has long since passed when the United States did not need votes and need to work hard to get them.

So a U.S. Ambassador at the UN needs the flexibility to negotiate successfully with Latin Americans, Communists, Arabs, Israelis, Pakistanis, Indians, Africans (French- or English-speaking)—the whole gamut of the diverse peoples of our turbulent world. He needs broad and deep background knowledge of these countries and problems; he should know their leaders and like them. He should be able to understand conflicting and contradictory positions and devise acceptable compromises, without sacrificing principle.

As Secretary of State Dean Rusk said at the UN memorial ceremony for Adlai Stevenson on July 19, 1965, the United Nations "calls out for the best that can be produced by the societies of man. Three Presidents of the United States sent Adlai Stevenson to the United Nations. They sent you our best."

He was our best. It was not only that he had been an adviser at San Francisco and an experienced Assembly delegate in the past; it was that he came to the world organization as a true man of the world—not in terms of sophistication (although he was sophisticated in the best sense of the word) but in terms of knowledge of the whole world and understanding of the whole world.

If the name of an obscure airport in the Congo came up in debate, he had been there; the prime minister of the newly admitted member state he had stayed with; his first trip to the Soviet Union was in 1926; there could not be more than six or so of the 116 UN members whose capitals he had not visited and with whose leaders he had not talked.

He was a master of words, and words matter at the UN. Its councils, assemblies and committees act by resolution, and resolutions are words, words fought over, dissected, shaded, sharpened, blunted, fused or defused. Which shall it be: "Recalling," "mindful of" or "reaffirming"? "Requests," "urges," "calls upon" or "demands"? "Regrets," "deplores," "condemns" or "denounces"? Many times his would be the phrase that would reconcile the apparently irreconcilable.

But, above all, he came to the UN equipped with moderation and reason. These are not prevalent qualities in that glass house where people do throw stones, where emotion too often does run rampant and where vituperation too often does supplant debate. His low, calm, measured voice was all the more effective in contrast to the invective which he so often had to listen and reply to.

One cannot be what is in effect an ambassador to 116 govern-

The U.S. Delegation to the UN in 1947. Seated, Eleanor Roosevelt, Secretary of State Marshall and Warren Austin; standing, Herschel V. Johnson, John Foster Dulles, Adlai E. Stevenson, Francis B. Sayre and Charles Fahy.

United Press International

ments without knowing their representatives and delegates—whence that activity known in the State Department budget as "representation"—i.e., entertainment.

Whatever a diplomatic reception—i.e., cocktail party—may be like in Washington or in other capitals, the UN variety is work. You are after votes, after information; you want someone to sponsor a resolution; you want someone else to agree to an amendment; and everyone else wants something from you. The result is a constant series of minor (or major) negotiations and fencing matches, with almost always a grist of meaningful news or surmise for the nightly information telegrams to the Department in Washington (and for the repeats to interested capitals).

The Governor did not enjoy these functions—particularly when there were four or five an evening (he defined UN social life as "protocol, alcohol and Geritol"). He preferred, and rightly, to talk and listen in quiet and not in an alcoholic din. The result was that his staff sometimes had to prod him, virtually with a cattle goad, to get him to go to a particular reception. Once at it, he would display an unerring eye for some side exit he could slip quietly out of without being seen by the receiving line—indeed, his knowledge of New York hotel ballroom kitchen exits was extensive and notorious.

His own entertainments were something else again. The top floor (twelfth) of the United States Mission building, across UN Plaza (First Avenue) from the UN, is virtually all one glass-enclosed room, with a curious, slightly concave ceiling. There are striking night views to the west and north of the brilliantly lit wall of skyscrapers and to the east of the black river and Long Island City, beyond the top of the General Assembly building and the gleaming slab of the Secretariat.

There he produced some memorable evenings: his own Second City (i.e., Chicago) satirists, some of whose savage barbs would have sent them to Siberia if they had been playing in Moscow and had dealt with Soviet policy as they did on the twelfth floor with American; American folk singers redolent of the American past—and they, too, bluntly frank about some of the American present; and good dance music that kept the last Latin Americans dancing until the small-houred lights figuratively winked good night.

He liked better the quieter entertaining at the U.S. Embassy —for so reads the shield over Apartment 42-A, forty-two floors up at the Waldorf Astoria Towers at Park Avenue and Fiftieth Street. It is one of the most attractive places to live in New York: a lovely white Louis XV living room with spectacular views of the East River and the Grand Central towers (alas, the latter are blotting out the faraway Wall Street pinnacles), a gracious smaller living room and a charming dining room, all beautifully furnished (credit the Henry Cabot Lodges) and adorned with paintings he borrowed from museums and friends—Sargent, Thomas Hart Benton, Childe Hassam, Corot, Monet, Goya— and his own things—original Lincoln letters, a Valentine from and drawn by Jacqueline Kennedy, the medaled freedom of the City of New York, books galore.

Here he entertained steady kaleidoscopic streams of UN people and friends—breakfast with a foreign minister (an old friend), lunch for Latin Americans in honor of a new ambassador (gracefully amusing and warm words of welcome), working drinks with the top British, dinner for a Middle Eastern head of state, music by a gifted young American pianist and supper—not, of course, a daily schedule, but not far from it.

In a sense a U.S. Ambassador to the UN is a UN Ambassador to the U.S. Stevenson certainly was. Of the literally thousands of invitations to speak that poured in on him from all around the country, he accepted almost more than he should have—out of conviction that it was part of his mission to talk sense to the American people (shades of 1952) about the UN and the position of the United States in the UN and in the world. And talk sense he did, at conventions and conferences and dinners from Boston to New Orleans to Chicago to Dallas (where a Birch lady smote him with an anti-UN sign) to San Francisco.

How he worried and worked over those speeches. Usually he would outline some ideas to someone on the staff, who would come up with a draft; then he would start redrafting (often completely), revising, polishing until the last hectic deadline, never satisfied, but satisfying the listeners, for he *did* talk sense, uncommon common sense, about the UN, the U.S. and the world.

Speeches at the UN itself in a way went through the same process but in a way were something else again. USUN (namely, U.S. Mission to the UN) is on the other end of several leased telephone lines to the State Department—a situation which has its advantages and disadvantages. Actually, they are in theory all advantages, since the closer any embassy is to its principal the better, but it depends on the point of view.

There is probably not a single U.S. mission (a word which embraces embassies, legations, etc.) anywhere that is not profoundly convinced that it knows much more about what U.S. policy in its area should be than does the State Department. USUN is not immune to this conviction as to its area (the whole world, if you please), and it is certainly true that USUN is in a unique close-up position, as observer and as participant, to analyze the international problems and crises that crowd the UN's agenda and to evaluate the shifting currents of world opinion that swirl through the UN's halls.

But the fact (and it is a fact) remains that U.S. policy at the UN is—and should be—finally determined in the State Department. Only there can reports from all the world's capitals (not only the sounding board of the UN) be correlated, and only there can the views and interests of Congress and the country at large and of other governmental departments and agencies be taken fully into account in the formulation of final foreign policy decisions.

What actually happens over those leased telephone lines is a constant USUN–State Department dialogue—indeed negotiation —as to exactly what instructions USUN should get (a sometimes heard USUN saying is that it's easier to deal with the Soviets than with the department).

Stevenson was an active and vigorous participant in those dialogues, and usually carried the day—and it must not be forgotten that he was a member of the Cabinet (and the New York–Washington airline shuttle's most constant patron) and thus intimately involved in the working out of fundamental American foreign policy.

All of this means that Stevenson's speeches in the UN (locally called statements or interventions) were conglomerates of State Department drafts, USUN and AES objections (sometimes substantive and always stylistic) and redrafts, occasional White House arbitrations of those objections, and eventual hard-fought cease-fires and compromises.

No matter how confused the exact parentage of Stevenson's UN speeches may have been, they invariably bore his stamp of clarity and vividness (often added in the last postdepartment clearance minute), and they most certainly reached what was for the UN unprecedented heights of reasoned intelligence—just as did his 1952 and 1956 presidential campaign speeches for the United States.

Speeches do not make the UN go around; negotiations do, and they are endless. One remembers the interminable Stevensonian palavers after Dag Hammarskjöld's tragic death, fighting off repeated Soviet attempts to hamstring the UN with a three-headed troika, and finally working out the election of an unfettered U Thant; constant conferences with the Secretary General and Secretariat officials and with other delegations as to UN peacekeeping efforts in the Congo, along Israeli-Arab borders, in West Irian, Kashmir, Yemen and Cyprus; repeated (and repetitive) negotiations with the Soviets on virtually all the UN's thorny problems and crises.

Soviet negotiating technique is almost invariable: to restate at each meeting in wearisome detail each and every Soviet argument on the point in issue, no matter how many times previously made and previously answered or refuted. It is as though the negotiator were afraid (maybe he is) that a verbatim record of the session might not show, on Kremlin examination, proper 100 percent zeal for each and every Communist contention. (When negotiating in the Soviet Mission one was always tempted to poke the sofa to try to locate the machine that *was* making the verbatim record.)

Stevenson's patience during these ordeals was proverbial. He would listen as attentively as though he had never heard the arguments before, and would then calmly go ahead with his quiet attempts to find solutions rather than debating triumphs. He always sought success, not victory.

He showed much the same patience in enduring the floods of public oratory that engulf UN councils, assemblies and committees (one sometimes forgets that our Senators and Congressmen also are known to talk interminably for home consumption).

Sometimes his patience wore thin. After listening in the Security Council to hours of wild African outbursts misrepresenting and denouncing the Stanleyville rescue operation (when American planes dropped Belgian paratroopers to save hundreds of hostages —European and other—held ready for murder by rebel savages), he said:

I have served in the United Nations from the day of its inception off and on for seventeen years. But never before have I heard such irrational, irresponsible, insulting and repugnant language in these chambers—and language used, if you please, contemptuously to impugn and slander a gallant and successful effort to save human lives of many nationalities and colors.

The Cuba episodes, Bay of Pigs and missiles, deserve separate mention by themselves.

In April, 1961, a young CIA representative came into the then USUN gloomy offices at 2 Park Avenue and guardedly indicated to Stevenson and top USUN personnel that something was likely to happen on the shores of the erstwhile republic. The financing was to be by Cuban *émigrés;* no U.S. facilities were to be involved (perhaps an abandoned U.S. Army post for preliminary training, which, at USUN urging, would again be abandoned); the impression of one listener, at least, was that there would be a succession of clandestine night landings until a real Oriente force was built up—no hint of any overt frontal assault.

When what did happen happened, USUN was as surprised as anyone else. Stevenson accepted as true the CIA story of defecting Castro pilots bombing Castro airfields, and the CIA photography of the supposed Castro planes that had done it—which in good faith he showed to the UN General Assembly's First Committee. The disclosure that these were fakes caused him wounds over which the scar tissue never completely healed.

Easier to deal with was the claim that in some unexplained way Stevenson, who knew nothing about the true nature of the Bay of Pigs exercise, had some part in President Kennedy's decision not to permit U.S. direct air power to be involved. Suffice it to quote the November 1, 1961, telegram of apology to Stevenson from General Van Fleet (emphatically not an admirer of the Governor), who had said in a speech that U.S. air cover for the Cuban invasion had been called off at Stevenson's insistence:

My information from several sources regarding Cuba was evidently erroneous in view of your telegram, which I am glad to have. I stand corrected and am sorry for press statement which was, in fact, not accurate and completely out of context.

Stevenson was involved in the Cuban missile crisis almost from the start, in Washington first and then at the UN. Leaving aside the question of exactly where he stood as between administration hawks and doves (he was very near the JFK middle), it is clear that his advice was of crucial importance in the wise decision to take the matter to the UN Security Council—wise because it made it much easier for Khrushchev to accept (i.e., back down

United Nations

Francis T. P. Plimpton and Adlai E. Stevenson at a Security Council meeting in December, 1964.

before) a UN appeal than would have been the case if only the United States had been involved.

The Security Council meeting of October 25, 1962, was unforgettable. Stevenson opened with a sober and restrained defense of the declaration by the United States of its naval and air quarantine (read "blockade") against the introduction into Cuba of nuclear weapons and equipment, and pointed out that the united action of the Western Hemisphere nations was in necessary defense against the threat of offensive nuclear weapons clandestinely installed in Cuba by the Soviet Union.

The Cuban representative followed, saying that Stevenson had not produced any serious evidence that Cuba constituted a nuclear threat to the Western Hemisphere.

Then came Zorin, the Soviet President (for the month) of the Security Council. A heavy, tough Communist hatchet man, with a face like a battle-ax, he was the engineer of the armed Soviet coup that overthrew the democratic government of Czechoslovakia and turned that unhappy country into one of the most abject of the Soviet satellites.

In his high Russian voice, savage with scornful sarcasm, Zorin attacked the United States as an aggressive bandit threatening international peace by an illegal blockade, and tauntingly claimed that the United States had no evidence of any Soviet nuclear build-up in Cuba except fake evidence produced by the CIA.

STEVENSON (who had been busily scribbling during the translations of Zorin's diatribe—in the Security Council every speech is consecutively translated into English and French even though it has already been simultaneously translated in the earphones): I want to say to you, Mr. Zorin, that I do not have your talent for obfuscation, for distortion, for confusing language and for double-talk—and I must confess to you that I am glad I do not. . . .

All right, sir, let me ask you one simple question: Do you, Ambassador Zorin, deny that the U.S.S.R. has placed and is placing medium and intermediate range missiles and sites in Cuba? Yes or no? Do not wait for the interpretation. Yes or no?

ZORIN: I am not in an American court of law, and therefore do not wish to answer a question put to me in the manner of a prosecuting counsel. You will receive the answer in due course in my capacity as representative of the Soviet Union.

STEVENSON: You are in the courtroom of world opinion right now, and you can answer "yes" or "no." . . . I am prepared to wait for my answer until Hell freezes over, if that is your decision. I am also prepared to present the evidence in this room.

In point of fact USUN had received, two days before, the U-2 photographs showing the missile installations, but had been instructed not to show them—although they had just been inadvertently published in London. (One reason given was that they had to be kept for Press Secretary Salinger's Sunday night TV broadcast!) Also, Stevenson was all against showing them, since he had never forgotten his traumatic experience in 1961 of showing in the UN fake CIA photographs of defecting Castro bombers that were supposed to have bombed Cuban airfields before the Bay of Pigs—and knew that the Russians had never forgotten it.

But Zorin's taunts and USUN insistence had brought Stevenson around, and an urgent USUN telephone call to Secretary Rusk at the White House got permission to use the photographs —with the result that Stevenson, in that never-to-be-forgotten scene, spread before the Security Council, and the world, the convincing visual proof of the Soviet clandestine nuclear threat to the United States and to the Western Hemisphere.

It is an interesting footnote, and sidelight on the impression Stevenson made on others at the UN, that on the day after Stevenson's death, Zorin, who had long since left the UN, had been a Deputy Soviet Foreign Minister and was then Soviet Ambassador to France, made a personal call on U.S. Ambassador Bohlen in Paris to express his personal sympathy at Stevenson's death.

As Ambassador Sosa-Rodriguez, the Venezuelan President of the UN's Eighteenth General Assembly, said at the memorial ceremony for Stevenson held in the Assembly Hall on July 19, 1965:

Adlai Stevenson, like all public men, has been known to have devoted admirers and formidable adversaries, but he has never been known to have enemies. And it is because the goodness and sincerity that flowed from his personality could not allow for feelings of enmity to be forged against him.

The ceremony itself was memorable. The great hall and the balconies and the corridors were filled with the UN and with the great of New York. A minute of complete and poignant silence; tributes of moving sincerity by U Thant and Ambassador Sosa-Rodriguez; perceptive and deeply felt words from poet and friend Archibald MacLeish:

What we have lost, as he said of his friend Mrs. Roosevelt, is not his life. He lived that out, if not to the full, at least more fully than almost any other man. What we have lost is himself. And who can name the warmth and richness of it?

And from Secretary of State Rusk, his colleague, with moving affection:

. . . it has been said, over and over again, that Adlai Stevenson was a universal man. And so he was. But not merely because he was informed, well traveled, urbane, sophisticated, eloquent and gifted; he was all of these. But his universality did not rest upon his being a prince among plain man, but upon his being a plain man even among princes. His was the simplicity of fundamental human values—with what is permanent in the midst of change: the love of peace; the instinct of tolerance; the feeling of compassion; the devotion to human rights; the urge to act for human welfare.

And then the final words of the presider:

This ceremony has ended. The memory and influence of Adlai Stevenson have not ended.

Forty Years of Friendship

I FIRST MET Adlai Stevenson in the mid-1920's when I was making my debut into Chicago's civic and social life. He was then a young lawyer, also making his start in that city.

But while I had grown up in Chicago and its suburbs, he was a new arrival from Bloomington in downstate Illinois. In those heedless days most of us didn't know where Bloomington was or care who Adlai's distinguished ancestors were. We soon discovered, however, that this nice, friendly young man with the funny name and wry sense of humor was attractive, bright, a fascinating talker and good listener who attracted an ever-wider circle of friends. He was enormously interested in the views of others, particularly those that differed from his, and told wonderful stories of his travels—in Russia and other remote places which few of us knew much about in those distant days. More serious-

---

Jane Dick (Mrs. Edison Dick), one of the Governor's oldest and closest friends, took a leading part in his campaign for Governor of Illinois and in his two presidential campaigns. She served under him as a member of the U.S. delegation to the United Nations. Mrs. Dick's article, in its first draft, actually was approved as to all facts by Governor Stevenson himself shortly before his death. She originally wrote it for a magazine but decided to withhold it for use in this volume.

minded than he appeared, and much more aware than most of us of what was going on in the world, he was soon involved in a variety of activities.

These continued to enlarge after he married and moved from Chicago to a lovely tract of farm land on the edge of the Des Plaines River near Libertyville. The first house which the young Stevensons built was burned to the ground shortly after they moved in, and many family treasures were lost in this disaster. They immediately set about building a simpler version, to which Adlai grew almost passionately attached, and it remained his dearly loved home until his death.

The depth of this attachment was often impressed on me, as when my husband and I met him at the airport on his return from a trip around the world after the 1952 presidential campaign. He had been in the Vale of Kashmir, on top of the Khyber Pass, had "leaned against the Bamboo Curtain," and had talked with Nehru, Churchill, Adenauer, Emperor Hirohito, Sukarno, Tito, Queen Elizabeth and other world leaders. But as we approached his farm in the blazing prairie sun, he sighed contentedly and asked, "Is there anything in the world as beautiful as an Illinois cornfield?" Only the spring before he died he characteristically ended a note to me as he left on the country's business: "I hope you can get out to the farm while the jonquils and magnolia are still in glorious bloom."

His farm, which eventually totaled seventy-two acres, was one of the wellsprings of his deep inner resources. When he wanted to inform or distract himself, he went traveling. When he wanted to replenish himself, he came home to his farm and grandchildren.

We lived only seven miles from the Stevensons in these early years. Our children were schoolmates. We had a mutual circle of friends, and my husband and I became increasingly active in the life of Chicago and in organizations and groups devoted to world affairs. All this kept us in close contact.

When I think back to those early days in Libertyville, I remember Adlai stepping off the commuters' train in the evening, carrying a bulging briefcase such as later became a familiar sight at the United Nations. Even more vividly I remember family scenes: picnics, canoe trips and skating parties on the little river that wanders by his farm. Adlai loved to ride and on snowy Sundays he would hitch up one of the horses and take his family sleighriding. In the spring there were long walks through the woods to see the wildflowers and the big blue heron colony nearby. He showed the little boys how to trap and fish along the river bank. They hunted arrowheads in the meadow, and he enlivened canoe trips with tall tales about the Indians. Then there were all the farm chores to learn, and I think his favorite picture, to the last, was one of himself on a tractor with his youngest son, John Fell, perched precariously behind him. The chores done, he would organize his willing "slave labor" to tote the tools and clean up as he pruned bushes and slashed deadwood from his maple trees—a compulsive occupation whenever he got to Libertyville.

Because Adlai deeply loved his young family and his home, it must have been hard indeed for him always to answer that inner voice which spoke to him—as it did to his ancestors—so insistently of duty, obligation and opportunity.

His response to civic duties and later to national responsibilities in the early days of the New Deal and subsequently in wartime was characterized by extreme conscientiousness and industry. This took time away from his home life, but whenever and wherever possible, he took his family with him, to Washington during the war and to London just after.

Adlai worried about these enforced absences. I remember once telling him that his children were far richer than the many "golf orphans" that I knew, for he gave so much of himself when he was with them, and they could take pride in the causes of his absences. The development of his sons into the fine young men they are, their love for him, and the eagerness they always had to

This picture with John Fell was one of Stevenson's favorites.

be with him would seem to prove that they early understood and admired the inner forces which drove him.

Adlai regarded marriage, home and family with old-fashioned reverence. The break-up of his marriage after twenty years and just after his election as Governor was a staggering shock. Only his close friends ever knew the scars it left. His dignity throughout this ordeal, his reticence about discussing personal problems, and his solicitous endeavors to preserve the affection and loyalty of his sons to both parents revealed as much as anything the quality of this man.

A remarkable aspect of Adlai's career was that—to the best of my knowledge—he never sought a job. Jobs sought him, and they were many and diverse—in government, business, law, journalism and education. Frequently he took those that he didn't want because they had to be done, but he worked at them with the same enthusiasm and creativity that he gave to all things. Unlike so many people in public life, he lacked power hunger or driving personal ambition; his accomplishments stemmed rather from the force of his personality and his basic convictions and strength of character. His long-time friends knew how much fortitude it had required to prevail so magnificently over his political and personal misfortunes.

A prime example of the job seeking him occurred in late 1947 while he was serving in New York as a member of the United States delegation to the United Nations. A small "boom" started in Illinois for his nomination as Democratic candidate for the U.S. Senate. Because of his background in national and international affairs, Adlai was receptive but he did nothing to further the movement. When at Christmas the Democratic party leaders urged him, instead, to run for Governor, his decision was a difficult one. He had been away from Illinois for most of seven years, in the Navy Department during the war and the State Department afterward, and he felt ill-prepared for the governorship. But, on New Year's Eve, word reached us that he had agreed to run. When I telephoned to congratulate him, he was still at his office. He was alone, and the voice that came over the wire was one of the loneliest in the world. He accepted, I believe, because of his deep personal commitment to public service and his "desire to participate actively in the life of his generation."

In 1952, after a spectacularly successful first term as Governor, the party wanted him to run again; so did most of the press and most of the people, and so did he. As vice-chairman of the committee for his re-election, I watched him struggle doggedly to discourage the mounting Stevenson-for-President movement. But he was drafted by the Chicago convention—the only genuine draft in three-quarters of a century. Anyone closely associated

AES after a pheasant hunt with (from left) Adlai III, Borden and John Fell.

with him during these months knows the depths of sincerity and humility with which he used the Lord's words in his great acceptance speech—"Let this cup pass from me"—to express his wish to have avoided the nomination. When the cup did not pass, he reacted just as he had in 1948 in Illinois. He plunged with all his vigor, enthusiasm and intelligence into planning and carrying out a hard-fought campaign of "reasoned and precise debate." He talked "sense to the American people" just as he had promised he would.

In 1956 he said, "I'm not going to run again just for the exercise—I've had all that kind of exercise I need." He knew in his heart that another defeat by President Eisenhower was more than likely, but his sense of duty again prevailed. He ran because his party wanted and needed him.

After the election of 1956 he issued a statement later forgotten by his admirers, that he would not seek the nomination again. He didn't. He meant just what he said. For four years he avoided party gatherings and concentrated on the Democratic Advisory Council, which he had conceived to lead an informed "loyal opposition" to the Eisenhower administration.

As the 1960 campaign approached, with victory for a Democratic candidate now a probability and with the old warm Stevenson enthusiasm welling up all over the country, he no doubt did have some yearnings for a third chance, but he did nothing to encourage the growing draft movement or enlist a single delegate. He stuck to his word in spite of ceaseless pressure from many quarters, including his great friend, Mrs. Roosevelt, to say that he was a candidate for the nomination. He even went to South America on a long journey during the spring primaries, and he meticulously avoided expressing any preference among the candidates—all his friends.

In my view the reason he did not make a Sherman-like statement in 1960 was his reluctance to dash the hopes of all those who had been so passionately loyal and who mounted the most amazing demonstration of support for a noncandidate in our political history. This loyalty, I know, touched Adlai deeply; it was one of his major resources in coping with disappointments, frustrations and personal loneliness.

The loyalty, indeed devotion, of the "Stevenson followers" never subsided. In 1964 he was repeatedly mentioned for the vice presidency; and in the two or three years before his death the Democratic leaders of both Illinois and New York asked him to run for the Senate in their states. Each time, though, his answer was the same—that at this critical moment in history the great issues of war and peace must take precedence, and that he could best serve in helping with the conduct of our foreign policy.

As a young man Adlai fought, bled and died for the New Deal. The moment he was asked, he left his law practice and went to work. He had always been passionate about the abuses, injustices and stupidities of the past, and saw in the social reforms of the New Deal an opportunity to correct many of them. This is probably why he was accused by some of his friends of radicalism in the thirties. I was interested to hear one of those early critics say not long ago, "The things Adlai worked for then don't seem so damned radical any more."

It was characteristic of Adlai that on the rare occasions that we saw him during the long war years he frequently leavened his moving accounts of the sacrifice and human suffering he had seen with funny little human-interest stories, such as his encounter with the infuriated Russian officer who stormed into the Navy Department one day complaining about delays in the delivery of certain strategic materials. When reminded that his country was itself behind schedule in performing its part of the bargain, the irate officer shouted: "But I came here to complain not about *my* behind but about *your* behind."

This ability of Adlai's to relieve tension and to sharpen seriousness with humor was one of his great inborn gifts, which he used effectively both in national and international politics. He was often criticized for this and for his irrepressible habit of telling jokes on himself. But I have yet to hear this criticism from anyone with the wit and courage to do likewise.

It was the four challenging years when he served as Governor of Illinois that brought Adlai to national attention, and my recollections of that period are especially vivid.

I was co-chairman of the Women's Division of the first Stevenson for Governor Committee. Despite the man-killing job of whistle-stopping by jalopy for the better part of a year, Adlai occasionally took time to share his experiences with us. One letter sheds light on his character and hints of his later great statement on the stark reality of responsibility:

It has been an amazing experience, and I've come to wonder how anyone can presume to talk about "America" until he has done some political campaigning. Perhaps it's the secret, perhaps the curse, of American political success—the illusive business of finding your way to the heart of the average man, when there is no such thing, and when, unhappily, the human heart is often an organ encased in a pocketbook, and not a textbook, let alone a Bible.

I've seen Illinois in a capsule—the beauty of the south, the fruit belt, the coal fields, the oil fields, the great industrial area around East St. Louis—and everywhere the rich, black, fecund earth stretching away and away. It gives you a great feeling of pride and power. Shut your eyes for a moment and let the fetid, hot places, the scorched islands, the arid, the cold, the small—all the places of the world where men struggle to live and love and breed—dance through your head. Then open your eyes and look at Illinois, and murmur "thrice blessed land." Exult in the power, majesty, wealth, might of it—and then come back to life with a start when a political pal with a cigar says, "Pardon me, Governor, but . . ." I quake a little as the visions die and the responsibility engulfs me—and the long road and endless days and weeks and months stretch out ahead.

But I'm getting a little lyrical for a practical politician!

After Adlai's election my husband and I were frequent visitors to the Executive Mansion. For the most part, my memories of these trips are gay and happy ones, such as Adlai's birthday parties and the Christmas parties he gave for his sons. One year sleep overcame my thirteen-year-old son before the party was over, and he went off to bed.

"Jane, have you never taught your children that they shouldn't waste electricity?" the Governor lectured me later. "When I finally found Eddie, he was sound asleep and every light in his room was ablaze."

In his four years as Governor, Adlai turned out the Mansion lights as zealously as President Johnson in the White House!

In addition, my work as a member of the State Board of Public Welfare Commissioners gave me many opportunities to sit behind the scenes and watch the leading character off stage, struggling with the problems of government and political morality.

I happened to be in Springfield when Adlai had to act on bills passed by the legislature requiring state employees to take a loyalty oath and establishing a legislative commission to investigate subversive activities. Their proponents described these bills simply as "a means to combat the menace of world Communism," but the Governor saw in them a serious danger to traditional American freedoms. He knew that to veto them would open him to the then popular charge of being "soft on Communism" and might well spell political disaster. He was urged by many advisers to let them become law without his signature. But Adlai was never a coward, and I remember him saying to me half humorously, half ruefully the day he vetoed them, "Well, there goes a short but promising political career." The chorus of admiration and praise for his courage and statesmanship, however, effectively drowned out the voices of his critics.

But one act of Adlai's that commands my greatest admiration was his decision to give a deposition in the perjury trial of Alger Hiss. He didn't have to do it, and no one would have criticized him had he taken the easy way out and declined to say under oath what Hiss' reputation had been in the years Adlai had known him in Washington.

Once again I saw him face a decision of overriding importance with no doubt about what he must do—even though he foresaw the resultant political abuse later heaped upon him. When I expressed my respect for his courage in answering the questions put to him by Hiss' counsel, he simply shrugged his shoulders and said he did nothing more than fulfill his responsibility as a citizen and as a lawyer. It would be, he told me that day, and subsequently repeated publicly, "an unhappy day for . . . justice . . . and the ultimate timidity" when a man in public life refused to give testimony in a criminal case because he feared the defendant might later be convicted.

I remember thinking at the time that this was the same brand of moral courage—of boldness, if you will—that had prompted Adlai as far back as 1942 to call for the integration of the armed services. Later it was to become evident to all, when in the 1956 presidential campaign he became the first world statesman to advocate a nuclear test ban treaty. He knew the proposal might cost him votes—and it did—and the opposition exploited it mercilessly. But he also knew a treaty was essential in a world armed with nuclear weapons, and so he spoke without equivocation. It took America and the world seven years to catch up with him!

An earlier time of difficult decision for Adlai was in 1946. That year I had taken my teen-aged daughter to visit the United Nations General Assembly, then meeting at Lake Success, New York. Adlai was a delegate and we found him doing some soul-searching on the partition of Palestine and the setting up of the new state of Israel.

He patiently explained the intricate question to my daughter, presenting each point of view with lucid impartiality. He told us, too, of fascinating talks he had had with the great Dr. Chaim Weizmann in London during the war and also of his meetings with various Arab leaders.

Finally, he said: "I've studied the whole problem a long time and I've concluded that the Zionist case is very convincing. But I constantly remind myself of the preponderant pro-Jewish sentiment in America, while the Arabs have few spokesmen, and I lie awake nights trying to be absolutely certain that I haven't let that fact influence the advice I must give about how the United States should vote."

The President, of course, would decide, but Adlai knew that his recommendation that the United States should vote affirmatively would be one factor in the decision, and he was just as conscientious about making it as if the responsibility were his alone.

I think of these episodes whenever I hear the myth about Adlai being indecisive, for they are illustrative of the way he arrived at recommendations and hard decisions, and then resolutely carried them out. Any doubts or hesitations he might have had on occasion stemmed not from any inability to make up his mind but from judicial weighing of all the evidence.

After Adlai's defeat in 1952, he took a six-month trip around the world and then returned to Libertyville and the establishment of his own law firm in Chicago. Once again we saw the familiar figure hurrying down the commuters' platform, a bulging briefcase in one hand and often a suitcase in the other. He never tended to regard himself as a man apart, a national and world figure. In fact, he seemed to be mildly surprised by the immense popularity of a fellow called Adlai Stevenson whose fortunes he followed with keen interest in the morning paper. After his 1956 defeat he returned again to private life, the law and world travel, but between 1952, when he came to world attention, and 1961, when he moved to New York as Ambassador to the United Nations, the great and humble of the world never ceased to beat a track to his door.

Adlai had a great capacity for friendship. He was not only a gay and stimulating companion, but his keen interest in other human beings and his habit of discussing, even with strangers, a problem that might happen at that moment to be uppermost in his mind combined to establish almost instantaneous personal communication between Adlai and those he met. He would take infinite pains, too, with the problems that members of his family, friends or young people brought to him. He especially enjoyed the young, and they loved and confided in him in return. How many godchildren he had I don't know; he probably lost count, too. In fact, with children he freely displayed a rare tenderness, known to few, over which in the world of adults he set a guard to protect his vulnerability.

There were great depths of reserve in Adlai. He had many very close friends, few intimate ones. One of his long-time friends and colleagues told me that Adlai had never discussed with him any problem which had any emotional content. He felt that Adlai found it less difficult to reveal his inner self in conversation with women than with men.

Yet two or three months after his death a woman who had been a close friend for years said, "I thought I knew him well, but I'm beginning to realize that it was because of his warm personality and his interest in me and my ideas.

"We had few very personal conversations. In retrospect I don't think that I really knew him."

Yet all who were close to him knew that behind the debonair exterior and the friendly smile and the twinkling blue eyes were deep wells of emotion which he revealed rarely and to few people, but which made him the truly warm and sensitive person he was.

Wherever Adlai lived he made it a home. His house in Liberty-ville, simple, charming, filled with books, pictures, campaign and travel trophies, was one of the coziest in the world, whether he was there alone poking up the logs on the living room fire, or whether his grandchildren were playing hopscotch outside his study door as they were during his last visit, ten days before his death. I saw the embassy apartment on the forty-second floor at the Waldorf Towers in New York when he took over in 1961. My heart sank as I looked at those empty, sterile hotel rooms, and I thought of the bleak prospect confronting this man of the woods and prairies. Soon, though, the apartment was filled with a fine collection of the paintings, china, historical documents, photographs of family and friends or of moments he treasured, stacks of books and mementos from all over the world. Moreover, it was usually filled with guests, too, either those who were staying there or whom he had asked in for a drink or a meal.

A guest staying overnight, incidentally, never knew who might be in the other guest room—a State Department official, a foreign dignitary, an old friend or relative, or one of his sons. Breakfast was an adventure, too. One might arrive to find him deep in conversation with a newspaperman, a famous foreigner, a member of his staff, a businessman or a well-known politician. And those breakfasts, prepared by his long-time and devoted housekeeper, were not calculated to diminish his waistline or drive guests away.

Whether at breakfast, lunch or dinner, Adlai was a wonderful host—gay, informal and seeing that everyone was brought into the conversation. The intimate, relaxed atmosphere which he created, even when a formal party was top-heavy with foreign diplomats, was a reflection of his own warm, unaffected approach to people.

Most people who didn't know him well pictured Adlai as a man buried in his books. He wasn't; he was buried in memoranda, documents and the daily papers and complained that he had little time for "reading." Almost all of his vast knowledge came by osmosis. He absorbed from life and people what most people absorb from books. Though he was not reluctant to answer questions, he would rather ask them, as many a well-informed newspaper reporter discovered to his dismay. And his remarkably sensitive and perceptive antennae were accurately attuned not only to people but to places and situations.

This was true from his earliest boyhood. During his years of formal education he showed none of the earmarks of a scholar. He was, rather, an activist, but he applied himself to his studies with the conscientiousness that was so characteristic of all that he ever did.

His informal education at home began almost at birth. His mother believed strongly in the old-fashioned system of "training" children. Whatever they did, whether it was reading, writing, sports or manual dexterity, they must be taught to do it well and thoroughly. Furthermore, Mrs. Stevenson exposed her two children to nothing but the best in literature. She started very early reading mythology and history aloud to them, and as these formed the basis of the library in their Bloomington home, Adlai and his sister naturally gravitated toward them when they could read themselves. Buffie Ives, Adlai's sister, recalls an incident when their father brought the *Cosmopolitan* magazine home one evening, and Mrs. Stevenson hustled him off to his bedroom with it, saying that he could keep it there, but the children must not be exposed to "such trash."

It was Adlai's good fortune that he inherited not only the lively wit but the extraordinarily retentive memory of his grandfather, Adlai, together with a remarkable ability not just to recall facts but to relate them to each other. And as far back as I knew him, apt quotations, felicitous allusions and spontaneous humor bubbled through his conversation as naturally as they peppered his writing.

In his dedication to work and in his passion for perfection, Adlai, perhaps, went to an extreme. Compared with most men in similar circumstances, he took few vacations, and I am sure a prolonged rest would have made him highly nervous. He not only liked to work but developed a sense of guilt when he was not busy.

He was occasionally criticized for the rather frenetic pace of his social activities in New York. This criticism is hard to understand in view of the fact that his diplomatic duties required him to give or attend a staggering number of luncheons, dinners and receptions. As he once said: "I regret I have but one stomach to give to my country!"

New York and Washington hostesses competed for the presence of this attractive, amusing, distinguished single man. Not only they, but sponsors of charity balls, concerts, theater and art show openings insisted on his presence. As for him, he enjoyed the company of women with a dash of glamour, intellect or humor. They were naturally tremendously flattered and he was rather proud of his conquests! This was all heady wine for a man who, despite his world fame, still kept some of the endearing freshness of the small-town boy who came to Chicago from Bloomington to make a name for himself.

Adlai, incidentally, early foresaw many of the dangers of public adulation to the human soul. I remember a walk we took in Springfield when some distant presidential rumblings first were heard. Adlai was deeply disturbed by them. "I can't do it," he said. "I can't face the possibility of never really being alone again—of never, as long as I live, being unidentified, of never again being a private person. One tends to think entirely of oneself under these circumstances. It can't help but happen."

"But you aren't that way," I objected.

"I'll get that way," he said with gloomy finality.

To a certain extent his fears were justified and his forebodings correct. But Adlai was affected less than most, in part, I imagine, because of his own understanding of these dangers and in part because of his remarkable objectivity about himself as a public figure, and his uncanny habit of regarding his public and his private selves as two separate entities. I remember shortly after his first campaign we were stopped by a street light when driving in Chicago. A truck driver next to us leaned out of his cab and said, "Hi, Adlai."

"Where did you know him?" I asked.

"Oh," said the Governor, "he wasn't speaking to *me*, he was speaking to Adlai."

He was unusually objective and candid, too, about himself as a private individual. He recognized that he had a disconcerting quality of sometimes being curt in his dealings with those to whom he felt the closest. One day after he had spoken quite brusquely to one of his sons, he said to me, "I don't understand it; I am always most sharp with those I love the best." Perhaps this

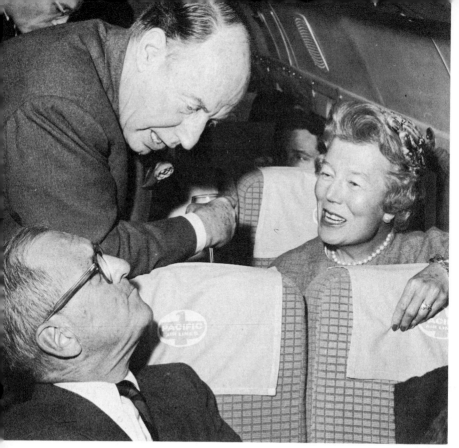

With Mr. and Mrs. Edison Dick en route to California for the wedding of John Fell in February, 1962.

was the result of his own perfectionism. He could not tolerate anything less than his own high standards in those of whom he was fondest.

Another contradiction was that while he gave generously of himself to help his friends or to repay real or fancied debts of gratitude to those who worked for him, he also found it difficult to bestow praise directly upon his colleagues. I cite a personal instance only because I believe it was a typical experience of others.

After I had served for three years at the United Nations I had no idea whether my old friend thought I had conducted myself well or not. When I finally asked him point-blank, his only answer was: "I wouldn't have recommended your appointment if I hadn't had confidence in you."

Yet this response wasn't because of any lack of generosity on his part, for a few days later I received a Christmas card from a California acquaintance which said: "I saw Adlai in Los Angeles for a short time. He tells me you are busy as a beaver and doing a wonderful job at the UN."

On the other hand, my files are full of gay little notes of gratitude, appreciation and affection—some dictated, more dashed off by hand, and occasionally attached to a relevant clipping or letter. And then there were those unexpected delayed personal compliments that women find most flattering: "I've never seen you look lovelier than you did Friday night," or "That was a very pretty dress you wore to the Smiths' party last week."

In any case, one measure of Adlai is that his frailties never diminished the loyalty and devotion of his friends. They knew that these were merely the temperamental quirks of a good and great man who was also their good and loyal friend.

His job at the UN was a round-the-clock affair. He might groan and complain to his friends about its heavy demands, but he enjoyed it. He was by far the most eminent statesman to take a permanent seat at the UN, and while he never seemed to take the high regard in which he was held too seriously, he made friends and influenced people there from the start. More important was his decisive contribution to changing attitudes about United States policy and purpose, especially among the newer nations.

Now I don't mean to imply that all was sweetness and light at the UN, or that every diplomat was ready to do just as Adlai asked. But even our adversaries respected him personally. When Adlai attended his first Security Council meeting, he was greeted with unprecedented enthusiasm. Several ambassadors came over to say that in their countries he had been the favorite for President.

This brought from Adlai the tongue-in-cheek retort: "Thank you, gentlemen. Evidently I ran for President in the wrong country!"—a comment in keeping with his oft-expressed view that "flattery is all right if you don't inhale."

And a member of the Cuban delegation to the United Nations, on hearing of his death, said, "Politically, he was the enemy, but he was an honorable enemy, a human being and a great gentleman."

There was only one time I'm sure that he regretted taking the United Nations job; that was in 1961 on the day of the abortive Bay of Pigs invasion of Cuba. It was a bitter day for Adlai for he had not been fully briefed by Washington when he was suddenly called upon to make a spirited and eloquent speech in the Security Council defending the United States against charges of aggression following the first news of the landings. Shortly after his speech, in which he denied any U.S. involvement, he entered an elevator in the Waldorf just as I emerged. I was shocked by his appearance. He looked dazedly right through me, apparently not seeing me. I was sure that either he was desperately ill or that something frightful had happened. So I followed him to the embassy residence in the Towers.

When I asked him what was wrong, he said quietly, "You heard my speech today? Well, I did not tell the whole truth; I did not know the whole truth. I took this job at the President's request on the understanding that I would be consulted and kept fully informed on everything. I spoke in the United Nations in good faith on that understanding. Now, my credibility has been compromised, and therefore my usefulness. Yet how can I resign at this moment and make things still worse for the President?"

Adlai's loyalty to the country and to the President prevailed. His colleagues were sympathetic, and President Kennedy, moreover, promptly sent him to ten capitals of Latin America, where he was well known and highly respected, to talk about the Alliance for

Progress and to pick up the pieces from the Bay of Pigs fiasco. As things turned out, he emerged unscathed from this shattering episode—a measure of the respect and confidence of his colleagues.

At the time of the Cuban missile crisis in October, 1962, Adlai was among the first to be informed and consulted by President Kennedy, and as that historic week of decision wore on, he found the President in complete agreement that this crisis must be met in accordance with our obligations under the United Nations Charter and the Rio pact. Rarely was he more effective than in the presentation of the United States' case against Russia in the Security Council.

The confrontation with Ambassador Zorin of the U.S.S.R. is now history.

After skillfully leading the Russian representative into repeated denials of Russian perfidy, he demanded that Zorin answer "yes or no" to his charge that the Russians had placed long-distance missiles in Cuba, adding with a sharp edge of sarcasm that he would wait for Zorin's answer "until Hell freezes over." Then after further outraged denials he suddenly produced in "open court" aerial photographs of the missiles.

One of his aides told me, incidentally, that he had not presented the photographic evidence until he himself had been convinced of its authenticity. When he did, it was a fitting finale to the most dramatic day the United Nations had known.

To illustrate the scale and variety of the response to life of this man for all seasons, I recall that the same evening, with friends, he was in high spirits and very funny in recounting the day's events. At one point he said, "Do you think perhaps I went too far? I'm reminded of my grandfather's story of the country lawyer who was cross-questioning a witness who claimed that the lawyer's client had bitten off a man's ear. The lawyer repeatedly asked, 'Did you see the defendant bite off the ear?' and the witness kept answering, 'No.' Finally, to clinch his case, the lawyer asked,

'When did you first see the ear?' The witness hesitated and replied, 'Not until he spat it out.' "

On July 14, 1965, Adlai died in London. A few weeks before, on learning of the sudden death of a friend, he had said, "He was lucky—he died with his boots on." Adlai went as he would have wanted to go, and the English press called it symbolic that this world citizen died in a country where he was as greatly beloved as in his own.

Let me be honest. I pretend to no objectivity in trying to find an answer to the question, "Who can name what he was?" My views are colored by heart-warming recollections of forty years of close association and devoted friendship. But I believe they may provide an insight into his hold on the imagination and affection of a world that will miss him for many tomorrows.

NO